READING IN THE DARK

READING IN THE DARK

Horror in Children's Literature and Culture

Edited by Jessica R. McCort

UNIVERSITY PRESS OF MISSISSIPPI † JACKSON

CHILDREN'S LITERATURE ASSOCIATION SERIES

www.upress.state.ms.us

Designed by Peter D. Halverson

The University Press of Mississippi is a member of the Association of
American University Presses.

First printing 2016

∞

Library of Congress Cataloging-in-Publication Data

Names: McCort, Jessica R., editor of compilation.
Title: Reading in the dark : horror in children's literature and culture /
edited by Jessica R. McCort.
Description: Jackson : University Press of Mississippi, 2016. | Series:
Children's Literature Association series
Identifiers: LCCN 2015042507 | ISBN 9781496806444 (hardback)
Subjects: LCSH: Children's literature—History and criticism. |
Children—Books and reading—History. | Children's films—History and
criticism. | Horror films—History and criticism. | Children's mass
media—History. | BISAC: LITERARY CRITICISM / Children's Literature.
Classification: LCC PN1009.A1 R413 2016 | DDC 809/.89282—dc23 LC
record available at http://lccn.loc.gov/2015042507

British Library Cataloging-in-Publication Data available

For, in life, it is in the darkest zones one finds the brightest beauty and the most luminous wisdom.

And, of course, the most blood.

—ADAM GIDWITZ, *A TALE DARK AND GRIMM*

CONTENTS

READING IN THE DARK

Introduction

Why Horror? (Or, The Importance of Being Frightened)

JESSICA R. McCORT

On one level it's like a ghost-train ride or a furious rollercoaster dash. There's an exhilaration to feeling scared, to feeling the inevitable threat of our mortality, without any actual danger. We can shrug it off, mock the specter of death with impunity, get an adrenaline rush without the need to face real danger. In this context, children can realize, at least implicitly, that looking at the scary side of life—loss, bereavement, fear, the monster under the bed—is possible. They can examine these emotions, even play with them, and by so doing gain some power over them. After all, aren't we told by behavioral scientists that that's how the more intelligent animal species (including the human species) learn—by playing? Horror fiction isn't going to make everyone stable and save society from the ills that horror fiction often depicts, but it can offer a safe forum for examining, and maybe lightening, the dark. Horror stories provide a playground in which children (and adults) can play at fear. And in the end they'll be safe and, hopefully, reassured. Overall, it seems better than repression.

—ROBERT HOOD,

"A PLAYGROUND FOR FEAR: HORROR FICTION FOR CHILDREN"

WHEN I WAS A YOUNG GIRL, I WAS FASCINATED BY MY MOTHER'S PRIZED set of Poe, a centenary collection of his works that came in five compact volumes. Wrapped in stately gray covers that belied their nature, they were housed behind the glass doors of the bookshelves that buttressed the fireplace in our living room. These books, purchased as a set at an auction, were completely forbidden. I could look, but I couldn't touch.

On my seventh birthday, my mother selected one of the books, had my friends and I corral our sleeping bags around her favorite chair, and read to us from "The Tell-Tale Heart." My earliest memories are of my mother's voice, changing shape and texture as it wove stories for me, her voice so intertwined with the tales that even now, as I read them to my own children, I can hear her intonations, the distinct sound of *her*. This, however, was a new story, filled with images that unsettled as they settled. *I had my head in, and was about to open the lantern, when my thumb slipped upon the tin fastening, and the old man sprang up in the bed, crying out—"Who's there?"* (Poe 354).

"The Tell-Tale Heart," a terrifying story if there ever was one, left black trails on my thoughts. My child's mind fixated on the old man's filmed-over eye and the young man's murderous hatred (along with his inability to keep his mouth shut). As I grew, the old man and his nemesis stayed with me, and other frightening figures began to line up behind them: the Headless Horseman, Bloody Fingers, Maleficent and the Evil Queen, Dracula, Princess Mombi and the Wheelers, Sauron, It, and Leland Palmer. That birthday, however, stands out in my memory as my initiation into a grim world marked by a dark aesthetic and the rhythm of a good ghost story.

As this little anecdote suggests, I initially came to horror through my mother's voice. This implies that some of us who love frightening stories have inherited the desire to interact with them, that we have been taught to appreciate the frightening by those who have appreciated it before us. One of the lessons I learned that night was that the Poe volumes were not off limits because my mother thought they were inappropriate for an impressionable and voracious young reader like me. They were off limits because she valued them so highly. When I turned seven, she knew that I was old enough to treat them with a careful hand and a curious mind. My love for the genre, however, can only be partly chalked up to my childish desire to snuggle down near my mother and feel the strings of my nerves rise and fall as her voice led dramatically to each story's crescendo. I realized fairly early on that there must be something more, some deeper switch that got flipped only when my imagination was ignited by fear.

Not every child likes horror. In fact, some run from it as fast as their legs will carry them. But for certain children, horror holds a powerful allure: the more frightening a book or film, the better. Friends and family members who don't share my appreciation for the genre are often puzzled by my affinity for frightening things, on countless occasions posing questions like "Why are you so enthralled by *that stuff*? What appeal does it hold *for people like you*?" The underlying implication to such questions is always that there is something wrong with people like me. The impetus for this book, in fact, initially derived from my attempts to respond to such queries, especially when people began to ask them about my eldest daughter.

So, then, why are some children drawn to tales dark and grim? The essays in this book seek to grapple with this question by extending the critical conversation about the gothic in children's and young adult literature and culture to focus more on the genre of gothic horror and the appropriation and application of motifs, characters, themes, and tropes from horror texts designed for adults in children's and young adult texts.[1] In the pages that follow, the work collected here examines different strains of children's and young adult horror, but it does not pretend to be exhaustive (some of the texts considered are not, in fact, easily classifiable as horror, per the traditional definition of the term). The goal, instead, is to examine a variety of texts that engage, both overtly and subtly, with constructs of gothic horror in order to begin to demonstrate the pervasiveness and the appeal of horror in children's and young adult literature, film, and television. The essays included consider an array of texts—monstrous picturebooks, cautionary tales, Edward Gorey's illustrations of childhood death, contemporary frightening fairy-tale novels, "monster" movies and vampiric TV shows, and the *Hunger Games* series[2]—and look for patterns in the narratives' rules of engagement with the horror genre, as well as with their audiences. In some of these essays, the authors consider the dangers of such texts, examining, for instance, the socializing influences therein that intend to distort children's abilities to empathize with a monstrous Other. In others, they concentrate on horror's pleasurable appeal for young readers and viewers, seeking to come to terms with why the popularity of texts specifically branded as horror for children have flourished since the late 1980s. Still others consider how horror has been appropriated in recent years by authors and filmmakers who seek to domesticate terror, riffing on the motifs of horror while simultaneously stripping them of their power to frighten. Overall, the collection seeks to investigate both the constructive and the troublesome aspects of scary books, movies, and television shows targeted toward children and young adults, considering the complex mechanisms by which they communicate their overt messages and their hidden agendas, as well as the readers' experiences of such mechanisms.

Before turning to these essays, however, what "horror" as a critical term means in terms of the confines of this book, especially when applied to children's and young adult cultures and texts, must be established. First of all, the term "horror" as a genre classification proves rather unwieldy, as it can be applied to a variety of narrative types, including, to name a few, "faux horror" (a brand of horror targeted toward younger children that tends to domesticate terror and make the frightening funny), literary horror (which draws on, participates with, and often critiques landmark texts and traditions, such as fairy tales, cautionary tales, and canonized monster novels such as *Dracula* and *Frankenstein*), serialized tween/teen horror books (which encompass the horror-fiction serials of the *Goosebumps* variety), and young adult horror (of the *Twilight* brand, which is arguably actually a blend of romance, action/adventure, and fantasy infused with horrific elements).[3] Further complicating the issue is that, prior to the late 1980s and early 1990s, horror was not openly considered a distinct, significant vein within children's literature or culture, and texts were not specifically categorized as "horror stories for children" (Shryock-Hood 2). This is not to say that horror hasn't been lurking in the children's library for a long, long time. Consider the fairy tales written by Charles Perrault and the Brothers Grimm, for instance, in which horrific elements are central to many of the stories: Little Snow White's evil stepmother wants to consume the heart of her innocent stepdaughter for dinner (or her lungs and liver, depending on the version you've read); Little Red Riding Hood is devoured by a wolf for straying from the path and, in the Grimm's rendition, is cut from his stomach by the huntsman; Bluebeard's slaughtered wives are ranged along the walls of his secret chamber, their blood congealing on the floor at the curious heroine's feet.[4] Leaping ahead to the 1950s monster craze, the blood-curdling magazines, comics, and other paraphernalia targeted toward young readers and viewers, as Rebecca Brown notes in her essay collected here, also demonstrate that the horror genre had been both popular among and coopted by the young for many years preceding the enthusiastic publication of horror for children that emerged in the late 1980s to early 1990s. Nonetheless, among the first books to be explicitly packaged and heavily marketed as "horror literature for young readers" were horror serials that relied heavily on fright for fright's sake, including the likes of the *Point Horror* novels (written by various authors, including R. L. Stine, Richie Tankersley Cusick, Carol Ellis, and Caroline B. Cooney) and Stine's *Goosebumps* series, both of which, like their monster-magazine predecessors, were partially inspired by the popularity and profitability of the horror films wreaking havoc on the silver screen at that time (Wilson 2; Loer 324).[5]

Not surprisingly, as Michael Wilson has pointed out, the popular and critical response to books explicitly marketed to young readers under the umbrella of horror was sometimes unfavorable, the books regarded by some adults as dangerous influences on the imaginations of young readers: "the very use of the word 'horror' in what was ostensibly children's literature was a very bold step and one that sent shockwaves through the adult world, which often manifested itself as moral outrage" (2). It makes sense, after all, that some adults have objected to other adults profiting heavily off of children's fears; the use of fear as a marketing strategy can seem just as distasteful as the "pedagogy of fear" Maria Tatar has described in relation to the Brothers Grimm's repackaging of fairy tales as morality machines during the nineteenth century.[6] Stine's books in particular have come under fire since their inception, viewed with skepticism by some for capitalizing on children's terror while simultaneously rotting the brains of young readers. As Perry Nodelman describes, "When R. L. Stine's *Goosebumps* books first appeared [. . .], many parents, teachers, and librarians viewed the mere existence of the new series as a monstrous intrusion into the well-intentioned world of children's publishing, and the content of the novels themselves as an equally monstrous intrusion into the ordinarily innocent minds of young readers" (118). Though Nodelman claims adults today are merely dismayed by the books, *Goosebumps* remains one of the most banned/challenged series/books for young American readers. The American Library Association ranked the books #94 in its list of the Top 100 Banned/Challenged Books between 2000 and 2009. Many of the other titles listed can also either be categorized as gothic horror for children and young adults or as books often picked up by young readers that contain gothic or horror elements, including the *Harry Potter* series (#1), Alvin Schwartz's *Scary Stories* (#7), Lois Duncan's *Killing Mr. Griffen* (#25), Alice Sebold's *The Lovely Bones* (#74), Harry Allard's *Bumps in the Night* (#93), and Garth Nix's *Shade's Children* (#95) ("Top 100 Banned/Challenged Books: 2000–2009"). From 1990 to 1999, the *Goosebumps* books were ranked fifteenth on the list (*Scary Stories* claiming the top prize during that decade) ("100 Most Frequently Challenged Books: 1990–1999"). The titles of editorials and newspaper articles that belabored the placement of *Goosebumps* on the banned list capture the spirit of the debate surrounding the books: "Parents Want to Get Rid of *Goosebumps*" (*Columbian* 19 January 1997); "*Goosebumps* against the Law? Kind of Makes You Shiver" (*Orange County Register* 2 February 1997); "Kids' Author Gives Parents Goosebumps" (*Gazette* 4 March 1997); "Horror on the Shelves? Take *Goosebumps* out of School Libraries? Most Fourth and Fifth Graders Say the Books Aren't Scary, Let Alone Harmful" (*The Plain Dealer* 30 March 1997). More recently, *The Hunger Games* has come under fire for its "unsuited to age group" content, largely due to the books' use of horrific child-on-child violence and their "religious viewpoint"; in 2013, *The Hunger Games* ranked fifth among the books reported to the Office for Intellectual Freedom as a result of acts of censorship ("Top Ten Challenged Books List By Year: 2001–2013").

As these listings make clear, the debate over horror fiction for the young, especially in relation to genre serials or texts that explicitly engage gothic/horror themes, rages on; parents, educators, and librarians today continue to express reservations about being the ones to put scary books into the hands of young readers. In her entry on "Horror Fiction" in *Children's Books and Their Creators*, Stephanie Loer notes that many, even if they are opposed to withholding books from young readers, still tend to come to the conclusion that such books are acceptable only as a gateway to better literature. In turn, she describes the reception of children's and young adult horror fiction in much the same fashion as people tend to describe gateway drugs, echoing the critical pigeonholing of horror as a substandard genre: "these books are not good literature, but they are not harmful. Enticing, recreational reading, they can be a hook to get reluctant readers into libraries where they will find books of more substance" (324). For others, however, reading books of the *Goosebumps* ilk just for the sake of reading is simply not good enough. They argue, instead, that readers should be exposed to "quality" literature, claiming that horror books for children, especially Stine's, are inferior and second rate—campy, pulpy, or trite.[7] In short, some deem it inappropriate to present such books to children because the benefits do not outweigh the perceived costs. The costs are not just rooted in the stylistic quality of the books, either. The content of the books is often a major factor in adults' resistance to promoting them to child readers. As the authors of *Frightening Fiction* describe, "Concern about the effects of reading 'horror' stems from the fact that, as a genre, it tends to be associated with kinds of knowledge and forms of experience regarded by many as unsuitable for children, notably those involving the occult or provoking high levels of fear or anxiety" (2). From this point of view, the subject matter of horror in general, whether in a Stine *Goosebumps* serial or in Suzanne Collins's critically acclaimed *Hunger Games* trilogy, is outside the confines of what children should have access to; restricting such access is viewed as a protective gesture.[8] Not surprisingly, many of the books of the gothic or horror in nature that appear on the frequently challenged lists are cited for the following offenses: "insensitivity," "occult/Satanism," "religious viewpoint," and "violence," all compiled under the umbrella "unsuited to age group" ("Top Ten Challenged Books List By Year: 2001–2013").

Despite all of the reservations expressed by adults, the "monstrous intrusions" viewed as unwelcome trespassers by some in positions of authority are welcomed by many young readers as invited guests. Some adults' distaste for horror has done little to hinder the sale and consumption of frightening books and films for the young. In fact, the popularity of horror among children and young adults only continues to grow, and grow rapidly, in the new millennia.[9] The bookshelves of the children's and young adult sections in any major bookstore reveal that the gothic, and more particularly gothic horror, is alive and thriving in today's most popular children's and young adult books and series. Stine has sold more than 350 million books at this point in his career, the majority of them serialized horror novels for tween readers, and he is currently working on new *Fear Street* books ("About R. L.," "Brand New Fear Street Books"). At the time of this publication, the best-selling young adult series include the Harry Potter books, *The Hunger Games* novels, the *Divergent* trilogy, the *Maze Runner* books ("If you aint scared, you aint human"), *The Mortal Instruments* books, and the *Miss Peregrine's Home for Peculiar Children* novels, all of which participate in the horror tradition through their use of stock horror characters, body horror, the monstrous, and a variety of other tropes and themes drawn from the genre ("Best Sellers"). Series such as the *Twilight* saga, *Vampire Academy*, *Beautiful Creatures*, *The Vampire Diaries*, *Pretty Little Liars*, and *Fallen* have also experienced recent success in children's and young adult publishing. Over the last decade especially, the top best sellers have trafficked heavily in gothic horror. In 2009, Meyer's neo-gothic *Twilight* was the best-selling book series, with 26.5 million copies purchased. In 2011 and 2012, Collins's *Hunger Games* books claimed over 30 million copies sold (Roback 39). In 2013, the postapocalyptic series *Divergent*, largely about conquering one's fears, sold a "combined 6.7 million copies [. . .] (three million hardcovers, 1.7 million paperbacks, and just under two million e-books)" (Roback 39). The popularity of these books demonstrates that frightening fictions for children and young adults have been holding center court for the last few decades in American publishing houses, suggesting that the turmoil our society has experienced in recent years—war, school shootings, political back-biting, rampant consumerism, economic collapse, and ever-increasing debt and the mortgage crisis—has trickled down to feed our country's youths' obsessions with horror fantasies.[10] As Robert Latham aptly points out in his examination of the prevalence of the vampire and cyborg in contemporary youth culture, for example, the vampire and the cyborg together "provide fruitful models for apprehending the forms of cultural activity—of labor and of leisure—that contemporary capitalist society has staked out for American youth, offering a potent meditation on the promises and perils inherent in youth consumption" (1). Our cultures' monsters tend to represent our obsessions and anxieties, even in what seem to be the most innocuous of texts.

What, then, should readers and viewers expect to encounter when they enter the wonderland of children's and young adult horror? To use the basic definition of the term "horror," a text has traditionally been classified as of the horror genre if it elicits the following emotional, psychological, and physical responses: "A painful emotion compounded of loathing and fear; a shuddering with terror and repugnance; strong aversion mingled with dread; [and] feeling excited by something shocking or frightful" (*Oxford English Dictionary*). To explicate the term further in relation to literary, filmic, and televisual horror, the reader or viewer must be emotionally invested in the situation at hand, must experience a physical response to the text that is rooted in fear, disgust, and repulsion, must reject the terrifying thing while also fearing that he or she might become its next victim, and, perhaps most important, must feel *excited* by the horrifying experience that he or she has willingly engaged in as the reader or viewer of the text. This last part of the definition is typically what pulls some adults up short: that young readers and viewers, like many adults, find delight and pleasure in that which makes them frightened. The physical thrill of the horror experience is responsible here, to a degree. As many theorists have shown, the appeal of horror, for those young and old, is deeply rooted in the rush of excitement that comes from the physical responses experienced by the human body while readers or viewers interact with the terrifying book, film, or show.[11] As John Morreall notes, this bodily thrill includes "an increase in alertness and muscle tension, a faster and stronger heartbeat, a redistribution of the blood from the skin and internal organs to the voluntary muscles and brain, and a release of stored sugar from the liver into the bloodstream" (96).[12] This feeling of excitement is arguably one of the main reasons that some readers and viewers become so enthralled with horror at a young age. Randi Dickson has demonstrated, in her examination of children's pleasurable experiences of horror, that young readers often cite such bodily responses when describing their affinity for the genre—young readers in her study reported feeling "surprised," "scared," and "nervous" and getting "goosebumps," all while thinking that "what's happening could happen to me" (117–18).

This last statement is important. Drawing on Noël Carroll's definition of "art-horror," Dickson argues that, for a horror text targeted toward young readers to be received pleasurably, it must fulfill certain requirements: first, it must include a threatening monster that both attracts and repulses the reader, and second, it must evoke an empathetic response from the reader in relation to the book's protagonists (117–19).[13] For Dickson, young readers' pleasurable interaction with horror texts depends on their feelings of emotional connection to the text's protagonists, who are typically under assault by some monstrous threat. According to Dickson's research, young readers in her study regularly reported "experienc[ing] emotions and feelings similar to those described by the fictional characters" (117). Dickson also argues that there must be some satisfying resolution to the horrific events, usually revolving around the discovery of the monster's true nature by the protagonist (118). In such iterations of horror, the monster/villain is usually not permitted to remain at large, and the conflict is somehow resolved. The old terrifying tale "Hansel and Gretel," for instance, demonstrates this paradigm. The reader anticipates the dangers the children may experience in the forest, confronts an unpredictable and violent witch who wants to consume the children's flesh (the tale uses, like many fairy tales and children's horror novels, the threat of cannibalistic consumption to generate fear), and is relieved when Gretel pushes the witch into the oven and good fortune ensues (both the evil witch and the evil stepmother wind up dead, while the children have figured out a way to earn their keep).[14]

In the vein of "Hansel and Gretel," many popular children's and young adult texts that engage horrific themes emphasize closure; they are typically not open-ended, unless there is an intended sequel. Though the child reading a scary picturebook or a tween horror novel may report feeling many of the same physical and emotional responses as adults watching a contemporary horror film, the closure achieved by children's and young adult horror is more often than not markedly different, mainly because the true nature of the monster is discovered and its power is usually dissipated. Horror texts for adults, especially recent horror films, often allow the door to remain ajar at their conclusion, leaving their readers and viewers devoid of full comprehension of the monstrous being and fearful that such nightmares might actually be milling around in their own closets or attics (as in the *Insidious* or the *Paranormal Activity* films, for example). Children's horror novels and films tend to shut down the possibility of terror as the story ends, even if the ones riding off into the sunset are the monsters themselves, as in a picturebook like Kelly DiPucchio's *Zombies in Love* (2011). Children's and young adult horror novels, films, and television shows, in general, rarely leave the reader feeling utterly insecure, terrified that the world will never return to some semblance of normality. Even a series as shocking and radical as *The Hunger Games* ends with a gesture toward the traditional happy ending, with Katniss Everdeen watching her children play in the meadow, much as Jo March watches her sons tumble around on the grass at the conclusion of the children's classic *Little Women*.[15] Furthermore, this happy ending is expected by young readers and viewers. The trajectory of many a children's and young adult horror tale, as quick summaries of any number of the classics can attest, falls squarely within the typical narrative pattern described above. They tend to be formulaic, suggesting that readers who enjoy the genre enjoy the predictability of it. What we're often left with, as the authors of *Frightening Fiction* so aptly point out, is really "a hybrid genre, which masquerades under the label 'horror,' but which in reality combines characteristics of what literary critics have traditionally termed the fantastic, the marvelous, the grotesque, the Gothic, the uncanny, literature of terror, and literature of the occult" (3–4). Perhaps Neil Gaiman described this formula best when he noted in an NPR interview that he uses "horror as a condiment [. . .] in the way that you might add salt or ketchup to a meal. You just want to add a little to make it taste a little bit better, but you definitely don't want a meal that's all salt and ketchup" ("Kids' Book Club: A Graveyard Tour with Neil Gaiman").[16]

It should be noted at this point that some children's and young adult texts that appropriate horror, especially those designed for the very young, transform the monster into the protagonist, as in the monstrous picturebooks Rebecca Brown discusses here and the monster movies examined by Peter Kunze. These texts depend on the child's appreciation of and identification with the monster (Brown and Kunze theorize this appropriation extensively in their essays; I have therefore refrained from doing so here). Under Dickson's definition, such texts should not be classified as horror. I argue, however, that they represent an important and popular subset of horror texts for children. They have been included here as examples of how horror has been coopted by children's literature and film and made comfortable for young readers and viewers, especially those ages ten and under. Not every horror text for children intends to horrify. Many, in fact, playfully engage the themes and tropes of horror to encourage children to release their darker emotions within the safe space of the book and to produce laughter. The classic picturebook *Where the Wild Things Are* (1963) is a good example of what might be termed "faux horror," which adopts what has traditionally been found terrifying and adapts it into something to be befriended and desired. The films that Peter Kunze considers in his chapter on the postmodern monster movie likewise transform the frightening monster under the bed and the child-devouring ogre into lovable, comical creatures that become the companions of the children or creatures they initially sought to scare out of their wits. These monsters tend to suffer from self-esteem issues because of their appearance and their monstrosity, coping with it by constructing meaningful relationships with those they initially sought to repulse. Furthermore, much faux horror targeted toward the young is either overtly or covertly funny, especially in the texts targeted toward young readers/viewers in which the monsters are the protagonists.[17] Children's "monster movies," such as *Monsters, Inc.* or the *Shrek* films, are sound examples of this application of humor to horror in the children's text. In *Monsters, Inc.*, the monsters children imagine lurking in their closets or under their beds are transformed from scream machines into congenial buddies who learn that producing laughter is more rewarding than producing fear.[18] These creatures are not really unpleasant at all; they are, in fact, shown in many cases to be just like the viewers experiencing the text. As Rebecca Brown argues in her examination of contemporary monstrous picturebooks collected here, such texts often make the monsters therein veiled representations of their readers, with both experiencing such childhood/adolescent problems as resisting bedtime, figuring out a social identity that feels true to oneself, and finding love. In doing so, these books and films allow young readers and viewers to express deep-rooted feelings that aren't always pretty.

The desire to make the monstrous either appealing or something to be befriended rather than feared echoes the turn toward what Victoria Nelson describes as the "bright Gothick" in contemporary popular iterations of the monster. Nelson defines a key characteristic of the bright "Gothick," drawing on Rene Girard, as "'the metamorphosis of the maleficent into the beneficent,' in which antagonist-villains (vampires, werewolves, assorted demons and imps of hell) have become protagonist-heroes who struggle with their darkness even as they incarnate on earth as gods" (8). The Disney film *Maleficent*, released on 30 May 2014, perfectly demonstrates this trend. While in her original incarnation in the film *Sleeping Beauty*, she was the Mistress of All Evil with no remorse and no back-story, the 2014 film seeks to rehabilitate her image, making her a loving, doting fairy godmother that the audience can identify with and feel empathy for. The vampires that

Janani Subramanian and Jorie Lagerwey examine in their chapter collected here on *The Vampire Diaries* also demonstrate this trend, as do Alan Ball's vampiric creatures on *True Blood* or the glittery vamps in Stephenie Meyer's *Twilight*, in which the antagonists become romantic and sexually desirable, and at least some of the protagonists want to give up their human lives in order to join the ranks of the undead. The "bright gothick" only represents one thread of gothic horror for the young, however. A character like Katniss Everdeen, for example, does not desire the monsters with which she is confronted; she is instead repulsed by their hybridity and their constructedness, as Emily Hiltz points out in her essay collected here on the abject in relation to the muttations created by the Capitol. What makes *The Hunger Games* different from the brand of gothic to be found in *Twilight* is that the series forces Katniss to question her own monstrosity as a creation of the state. Though Katniss has thrown in her weight with humanity, she has, nonetheless, been herself redesigned by the Capitol into something Other—after her body is beaten and battered in the arena, the Capitol performs all sorts of plastic surgery and medicinal therapies that make Katniss appear almost superhuman. By the time the Capitol is done with her, her skin is smoother than it has ever been, her hair more lustrous—her breasts even seem larger. Katniss, in choosing to retain the scars she receives in the battles that ensue, demonstrates that she chooses to remain human, to reject the monstrous, self-preserving warrior that the Capitol wanted her to become. Riffing on the character of the "last girl," Katniss is the final one standing at the end of the horrifying reality show she cast herself in the moment she chose to take her sister's place in the Capitol's lottery. In either scenario, the portrayal of monstrosity in these texts typically emphasizes what Jeffrey Jerome Cohen describes as a "cultural fascination with monsters" that is "born of the twin desire to name that which is difficult to apprehend and to domesticate (and therefore disempower) that which threatens" (viii). To again use *The Hunger Games* as an example, Katniss's bodily monstrosity echoes our culture's obsession with transforming the human body through plastic surgery and modern medicine, procedures that are both desired and feared in the millennial social imagination. Katniss's rejection of her reformation proposes that morally, at least, readers should be opposed to treatments that distort one's sense of self and bodily integrity.

To return to the notion of happy endings in what are supposedly scary contexts, many texts of this sort can function to help young readers and viewers cope with frightening things in reality, translating those things into a fantasy world where fear is rendered manageable. When I think of horror's functionality thus, I think of Ofelia's fantasy world in Guillermo del Toro's critically acclaimed film *Pan's Labyrinth* (2006). Though this film (based on its R-rating and its level of graphic violence) is obviously not meant for children, *Pan's Labyrinth* does concentrate on the imaginative life of a young girl and exaggerates and amplifies the horrific undertones that can be found in many traditional fairy tales and classic children's books.[19] Ofelia operates in a real world that is so filled with brutality that she escapes into a fantasy world that is equally as dark. Some might argue that a child's imaginative world, in order to function as a true form of escape, should be filled only with things that elicit contentment and comfort. But Ofelia's fantasy world is horrific for a reason; it allows her to manage the fear she experiences in the Captain's mill. The Underworld is a space where she can overcome the worst that she can possibly imagine. In the external real world, she has no control whatsoever. She must abide by the Captain's orders or be severely punished. In her fantasy world, however, she can outwit or vanquish monsters that are veiled symbols of some limb of the Captain's power. In this scenario, the fantasy of horror offers the young girl a dreamscape that parallels her reality, making it easier to cope with the monsters she must face in the real world. In del Toro's film, the success of Ofelia's fantasy as a coping mechanism is called into question by the film's conclusion.[20] Nonetheless, the horrific fantasy therein does function as a proving ground, as it also does in much of the children's and young adult literature and film that seeks to elicit a visceral and psychological experience of terror through an encounter with the monstrous, be it real or imagined.

Under this theoretical framework, the appeal of horror in many children's and young adult horror texts lies in what I have come to call the defeat of the Jabberwock, the triumph over a fearsome monster that is achieved by both the child within the text and the child without (sometimes, importantly, this monster is no monster at all, but a human being, like the Captain in *Pan's Labyrinth*, whom we quickly learn is the true source of terror in Ofelia's world; even the Jabberwock, with his buckteeth, waistcoat, and whiskers, is disturbingly familiar).[21] Here it helps to think back to the image of the "boy" battling the Jabberwock in Lewis Carroll's *Through the Looking-Glass*, remembering that Alice experiences the Jabberwock through the pages of a book she finds in the Looking-Glass house.

The poem "Jabberwocky" focuses on a young boy defeating, with his sword, the terrorizing Jabberwock, of whom he is warned thus: "Beware the Jabberwock, my son! / The jaws that bite, the claws that catch!" After reading the poem, Alice thinks out loud: "Somehow it seems to fill my head with

0.1. John Tenniel, "Alice Battling the Jabberwock"

ideas—only I don't exactly know what they are! However, *somebody* killed *something*: that's clear, at any rate" (Carroll 118). If we look at the image accompanying the poem, however, we can get a sense of just what ideas have filled Alice's head, as it is *Alice* drawn in the position of the young crusader (if we compare the hair and tights of the figure in the image to the other images of Alice in the book).

Here, Alice has leapt into the book to behead the monster; she is the one holding the vorpal blade. She vicariously experiences the defeat of the monster through her reading because, in her imagination at least, she slays the beast. Many children's and young adult books, films, and shows that engage horrific themes turn on this paradigm. One of the more widely read horror-fantasy novels among young readers in recent years, Neil Gaiman's *Coraline*, foregrounds the defeat of the metaphorical "dragon," for example. In the epigraph to *Coraline*, drawn from G. K. Chesterton, Gaiman asks his readers to go into the book seeing the terrifying as something that, with a lot of pluck and a little luck, can be soundly defeated: "Fairy tales are more than true: not because they tell us that dragons exist, but because they tell us that dragons can be beaten" (*Coraline* Epigraph). Using the epigraph as a guide, readers enter Coraline's world expecting to confront some petrifying things, but they are assured that by the end of the novel, she (and they) will defeat them.[22] As a result, as Thomas Fahy notes in his comparison of the experience of horror to the thrill of skydiving, horror texts tend to produce "the feeling of relief and regained control" following the confrontation with the "unpredictable and dangerous" (1–2). The bigger and scarier the monster, the greater the sense of satisfaction.

In this capacity, children's and young adult books, movies, and shows that trade in horror can be viewed as a space of symbolic release.[23] As Maria Tatar aptly notes, much of "Children's literature traffics in sensory bliss and horror, offering a secure place for children to go and face down the twin seductions of good and evil. Where else can you safely become the deranged visionary who beholds Oz? And where else can you meet Lord Voldemort and find that you are not in any real danger?" (*Enchanted Hunters* 12). M. P. Dunleavy and Sally Lodge concur, arguing that scary texts typically allow children to tackle, from "the safety of their armchairs," the dangers they may find lurking in the shadowed corners of their very own worlds (28). Such texts might push their protagonists to the brink of destruction, but the conclusions of the stories typically restore equilibrium, even if only tenuously. Furthermore, as Geraldine Brennan, Kevin McCarron, and Kimberly Reynolds argue in their study of frightening fiction for young adults, the monster is sometimes revealed to be no monster at all:

> Instead of ambiguous endings, the closure of these novels is typically a disclosure in which what was thought to be inexplicable is explained, and what seemed dangerous and menacing is made safe and often even comfortable. [...] Though such texts imitate the narrative voice associated with traditional horror—strong on suspense, intimating impending crisis, trying to create a sense that something dreadful is about to happen—they are in fact primarily concerned with showing many childish fears to be unfounded. (2–3)

Such imitations of horror in children's and young adult texts, especially those targeted toward the very young, generally appropriate the horror genre to teach a lesson. Newer versions of children's horror, in fact, can be viewed as an answer to what Vigen Guroian bemoans as the movement toward a societal embrasure of "an antihuman trinity of pragmatism, subjectivism, and cultural relativism that denies the existence of a moral sense or a moral law" (4). Rather than denying the existence of moral law, many children's and young adult gothic horror texts ask young readers and viewers to consider, through horror fantasy, the moral codes by which their societies operate (Guroian himself notes that all of the books he discusses in his treatise on children's moral education through classic children's literature are either fairy tales or children's fantasy stories) (8).[24]

This time, however, the emphasis is not always on a pedagogy of fear that uses violence to warn children away from bad behavior, but a pedagogy of bravery and choice that operates on the cultural belief that fear is a weakness to be overcome, or at the very least handled with intelligence. During the earlier years of children's publishing, the "intentional elicitation of dread, visceral disgust, fear, or startlement" in children's literature and culture tended to be directly linked to the adult desire to encourage self-containment and sanctioned behavior among children (Nickel 15). As Jackie Stallcup notes, "from at least the mid-eighteenth century through today, adults have used children's literature as a means of transmitting ideology, repressing children, and assuring adult mastery—often through inducing fear" (129). Earlier invocations of horror tend to demonstrate an "unusually cruel and coercive streak" that "relie[s] on brutal intimidation to frighten children into complying with parental demands" (Tatar *Off with Their Heads!* 8). As Tatar notes in *The Hard Facts of Grimm's Fairy Tales*, the stories collected by the Grimm Brothers, for example, are filled with "graphic descriptions of murder, mutilation, cannibalism, infanticide, and incest," each linked to some sort of moral (3). Heinrich Hoffman's *Struwwelpeter*, published in 1845, also demonstrates (at least on the surface) the use of textual violence to encourage children to adhere to a repressive moral code. There are still indeed some books, shows, and films that deploy the pedagogy of fear, as Stallcup rightly suggests in the quotation above; the slasher films aimed at teens during the 1980s and 1990s, for example, are arguably deeply conservative as moral texts—while the virgins were often the last girls standing, for instance, those who enjoyed sex were the first to be attacked, the camera lingering over their punishing deaths.[25] Horror for children and adolescents today, however, tends to exercise its scares in order to teach readers and viewers how to weigh and determine the best possible course of action, asking them to ponder the motivations for and correctness of their behaviors instead of just accepting the moral code as law.

The perennial childhood favorite *The Monster at the End of This Book*, published by Little Golden Books in 1971 and voted one of the top 100 picturebooks of all time in 2012 by *School Library Journal*, models the innocuous use of the monster in service of the pedagogy of bravery and choice, for example (Bird). In the book, the main character, Grover, is afraid to turn the page because he believes there will be a terrorizing monster on the very last one; as a result, he repeatedly tries to get the reader to collude with him in closing the book, and eventually resorts to constructing various barriers to keep the reader from moving forward (all of which are torn down by the child as he or she progresses in his or her reading). Grover discovers, however, along with the reader, that the monster at the end of the book is really himself, learning that he, all along, has been afraid of his own shadow. As they turn the pages of *The Monster at the End of This Book*, the children reading internalize the desire to get to the end of the story, savoring the suspense that builds each time they turn the page, while also learning that their worst fears are actually sometimes entirely in their own imaginations. *The Monster at the End of This Book* also explicitly asks for participation on the part of the reader. In *The Monster*, the reader is literally pitted against Grover, the act of reading a defiance of the monster's authority that is rooted in a willful desire to confront the Big Bad Wolf supposedly lurking at the book's conclusion. Part of the pleasure of reading the book comes from defying the authority of its narrator. This represents the inverse of the deeply authoritarian use of horror in a story like "Hansel and Gretel," which makes young readers complicit in the tale's violence against the children (they are asked, after all, to accept the reunion between the children and their abandoning, good-for-nothing father as desirable).

In this, *The Monster at the End of This Book* echoes the wickedly rebellious streak that is also present in many of the books under consideration here, a characteristic that is nonetheless a vital part of their appeal. As Wilson notes in his study of horror's popularity among teen readers, "horror serves a subversive function. Stories of horror and the supernatural subvert the rationality of the adult world. They create worlds where adult-imposed order is undermined and chaos reigns" (3). Much as Lewis Carroll ridiculed, through figures like Humpty Dumpty, the Mad Hatter, and the Red and White Queens (and perhaps the Jabberwock), the lessons and behaviors that Victorian children had been taught to emulate, many horrific children's books, movies, and shows also traffic in the subversion of certain moral platitudes, especially those that children tend to find problematic or difficult to obey. Take, for instance, a book like Edward Gorey's *The Wuggly-Ump*, which derisively mocks the supposedly desirable goal of growing up by imagining it as a galumphing monster hungry for tasty child morsels, or *Where the Wild Things Are*, which allows the protagonist to revel in his wolf-like, animalistic misbehavior at the Wild Rumpus, the very behavior for which he has been punished by his mother. Even a book that is seemingly as authoritarian as *Struwwelpeter*, as Justine Gieni demonstrates in her essay collected here, can be viewed as a deeply subversive "satire of violent pedagogy," with the young readers who enjoy the text being in on the joke. It is no mistake that the monsters faced by children and teens in horror texts targeted toward young readers often take the shape of the children's parents or other authority figures, including teachers, librarians, sports coaches, and principals. These figures represent forces that often desire to reshape or mold the child into something the society deems acceptable but that the child may view as objectionable. Part of the joy of the horror text for children and young adults is the opportunity to experience its disruption of and resistance against authority and to judge the moral law to which they are held accountable (often by people who fail to follow that code themselves).

Most frightening fictions today, especially those of a more literary class, strive to teach some sort of lesson (again, *The Monster* is a good example; at the very same time that the text undermines its own authority, it strives to teach its readers that, in many cases, one's fears are unfounded). These books regularly ask readers to examine their own humanity, forcing them to consider how they might act in the particular situation being considered. This does seem to make morality relative, but most of the texts considered here refrain from denying that there is a general moral code that determines right behavior from wrong (in fact, many depend squarely on the readers' or viewers' understanding of that division). In this, children's and young adult horror texts echo the horror novels and films that have been produced for adult readers over the last fifty years. Adult horror in the last few decades has especially placed behavior, choice, disobedience, and morality front and center, as in the *Saw* franchise, the spectacularly gruesome slasher films created in the 1980s referenced above, or Stephen King's *The Shining* and *Doctor Sleep* (it could be argued, however, that horror has done this all along; Mary Shelley's *Frankenstein*, for example, is largely about how Dr. Frankenstein morally fails in his choice to treat the monster that he erroneously chose to create inhumanely). Today's horror texts targeted toward children and young adults regularly ask the reader or viewer to function as a participant or critic, calling upon them to enter vicariously the world of the text and to make decisions about the characters' and their own behavior. In the novel *A Tale Dark and Grimm*, for example, there is an intrusive narrator who helps the reader move through the book and guesstimate what kind of decisions he or she would make if he or she were confronted by a similar frightening scenario. Through such an emphasis on personal responsibility and one's individual negotiation of the world, the texts echo the turn in the modern world toward the methods by which one must negotiate his or her individual identity while impressed upon by various external forces, some of which are actually in the child's best interests and some that would destroy him or her in favor of maintaining order. The literary horror examined in this volume concentrates especially on identity formation, considering the ways in which, as Charles Taylor describes in his book *Modern Social Imaginaries*, the modern self is "always socially embedded" (65). They concentrate on "identities in dialogue," "being inducted into a certain language." To again use *Coraline* as an example, the book is largely about one girl's social development and her negotiation with her parents to figure out her place in the family dynamic, a place that would allow her to coexist with them, to see herself as an important contributor in the family's life, and to avoid being devoured by either of their identities. Gaiman places concentrated emphasis on the importance of Coraline's individuality, which the text argues should be protected in the confrontation with the Other Mother, even as Coraline learns to appreciate and adopt what is valuable in her parents.

From books, films, and shows that contain dark elements, children and young adults also learn to realize that one being can be both evil and good at once, that a person must sometimes choose between turning toward the bad or turning toward the good. Think of the books that are considered children's classics. The best of them contain dark forces of one kind or another, as well as internal battles between the light and the dark: *The Lion, the Witch, and the Wardrobe*; *The Wizard of Oz*; *Alice's Adventures in Wonderland*; *Through the Looking-Glass*; *A Wrinkle in Time*; almost all of the Grimm's or Andersen's fairy tales; *The Lord of the Rings*; *Harry Potter*. In each of these landmark texts, darkness is often the catalyst that helps the good to evolve. Darkness is also rooted within many of the main characters. Harry Potter, for example, has to battle his own demons and eventually accept his own death in order to ascend into adulthood. In general, young readers, even if they are not drawn to the blatantly horrific, tend to be drawn to books that depend on a conflict with dark forces, as the list of widely accepted children's classics above attests.

Above all, as many of the essays in this volume argue, elements of horror can be viewed as beneficial for young readers and viewers because they encourage children to recognize that there are real dangers in the world they will have to confront, unveiling the terror in the familiar. "By the threats it presents to the everyday life of the viewer," Philip J. Nickel notes, "horror gives us a perspective on so-called common sense. It helps us to see that a notion of everyday life completely secure against threats cannot be possible, and that the security of common sense is a persistent illusion" (17). While children's and young adult horror often restores the order of the "normal" world, it also critiques that order and shows children and young adults that it is tenuous, fluid, and constantly under assault. The fantasy of horror offers young readers and viewers a dreamscape that parallels their reality, sometimes making it easier to cope with the monsters they must face in the real world; it is a proving ground of sorts, especially in much of the children's literature that seeks to elicit a visceral and psychological experience of terror. Much as Ofelia in del Toro's *Pan's Labyrinth* creates a horrifying fantasy world that mirrors her reality in recognizable ways (if one is willing to look), the creators of horror for children and young adults spawn monsters and monstrous human beings who test readers' abilities to overcome people, objects, and events that elicit visceral and psychological terror in their own lives—even if, sometimes, these monstrosities are unconquerable. In his essay on R. L. Stine's appeal, a response to an earlier essay on *Goosebumps* by Perry Nodelman, Roderick McGillis muses, "I wonder what it is that attracts them to these books?" He comes to this conclusion: "perhaps it is this: As so often in children's books, the plots show children coping with difficult and apparently dangerous situations alone, without their parents' help" (21). As McGillis goes on to explain, "The child's relative independence from adults is always a satisfying feature of children's books, addressing itself to the child reader's desire for control, even if this means facing threats in the form of monstrous creatures." In the realm of these texts, the child's desire for control can typically only be fulfilled, as Jackie Stallcup describes, by the child protagonist "developing adult-like characteristics themselves" (127). For some, the escape into horror is an escape that makes the reader or viewer feel alive. By forcing themselves to encounter that which frightens, readers and viewers, even the young, knowingly enter a space that asks them to call upon their wits and their physical resources.

The essays in this book seek to examine the productive intersection of the gothic horror genre and children's and young adult literature and culture, focusing on a broad assortment of narrative forms and extending the critical conversation about the gothic in children's and young adult literature and culture to focus more on the genre of gothic horror in its myriad manifestations in children's and young adult literature, television, and film. Why would two zombies falling in love and then falling into flesh-eating swoons elicit laughter from kindergartners? How do children read novels like Gaiman's spine-tingling *Coraline*, in which a girl and her Other Mother bargain over her eyes and, as the larger prize, her soul? Why have tweens and teenagers been drawn in droves to the world of Panem, where children's bodies and psyches are used as political weapons and where the kids themselves either die, become mutated monsters, or grow into ghostly shells of their former selves? The general progression of the collection moves from older texts either targeted toward younger readers or using aesthetics typically associated with books designed for younger readers to texts designed for older and more contemporary audiences. This progression demonstrates the ways in which horror texts targeting the very young differ from those whose intended audience are working their way through adolescence. It also shows how the appropriation and application of the gothic horror genre has both held steady and changed radically over time. We begin, then, in the past.

In the first essay in the volume, Justine Gieni examines the language and illustrations of Heinrich Hoffman's 1845 picturebook *Struwwelpeter*, a seminal text in the genre that, on the surface at least, makes explicit use of horrifying methods of childhood death and dismemberment as a means of cautioning young readers to behave according to the strictures of its era. In "Punishing the Abject Child: The Delight and Discipline of Body Horror in Heinrich Hoffman's *Struwwelpeter*," however, Gieni zeroes in on the transgressive nature of Hoffman's tales, concentrating specifically on the role of body horror in the text. Entering the debate about the book's appropriateness for child audiences, Gieni focuses especially on the violence committed against the child's body in the book, arguing that, through the "powers of horror," Hoffman satirizes the pedagogical didacticism of nineteenth-century German culture and empowers young readers, allowing them to experience the thrill of derisive laughter in the face of brutal authoritarianism. She also illuminatingly considers the publication, relevance, and reception of *Struwwelpeter* today, discussing how it has been rebranded as a text for "knowing" adult audiences with an emphasis more on its horror than its humor, as well as the implications of such a shift in the text's purported readership and thematic intentions.

In the next essay, "'A Wonderful Horrid Thing': Edward Gorey, Charles Dickens, and Drawing the Horror out of Childhood Death," A. Robin Hoffman considers the sinister books designed by Edward Gorey (many of which she claims were intended for a young audience) in relation to influences such as Hoffman's *Struwwelpeter* and Dickens's *The Old Curiosity Shop* and *Bleak House*. Hoffman argues that Gorey, by appropriating and reconceptualizing these texts' modes of representation, manages to provide an "anaesthetizing historical distance" between his modern readers and the representations of childhood death popular among Victorian audiences. Through a careful examination of his books' production methods, concentrating on their calculated appeal toward younger audiences, as well as his insistence on presenting childhood death as a subject of dark comedy, Hoffman asserts that what Gorey produces is at once an homage to Dickens's work and a perversion of Dickens's sentimentalized stories, mainly because of Gorey's more unequivocal representations of violence and his eradication of Christian symbolism that offered the promise of moral redemption in favor of a critique of mid-twentieth-century American representations of childhood. In the end, Hoffman recognizes Gorey's disruptive potential as he offers up, for both child and adult readers, a novel representation of childhood death, one that disempowers the mythologizing of textual children's demises as a means of conveying a particular social, philosophical, or political agenda. She also suggests that Gorey's portrayals of childhood death in his books serve as both a precursor to and an influence on the modern turn toward the comic gothic in many children's and young adult horror texts. In doing so, she provides us with a useful model for thinking about the methods of portraying and thinking about death and violence against children within the space of horror novels, films, or television shows targeted toward young audiences.

The following essay, "From Aggressive Wolf to Heteronormative Zombie: Performing Monstrosity and Masculinity in the Narrative Picturebook" by Rebecca A. Brown, examines the evolution of monstrous picturebooks, comparing the 1960s favorites *Where the Wild Things Are* and *There's a Nightmare in My Closet* to contemporary picturebooks that make vampires, Frankensteinian monsters, and zombies the protagonists and considering them in relation to boys' cultures dominant at the time of their publication. Brown concentrates especially on the role of the monstrous picturebook in young American boys' negotiations of identity formation, as well as their domestication of otherness. Brown argues that while Sendak's and Mayer's books served to socialize children to the normative behaviors of 1960s American culture and ultimately demonstrate children's ability to defeat or domesticate the monstrous, today's monstrous picturebooks ask young boys to identify with the monster—to find traits within themselves that they share with the monsters in the books' pages and to empathize with them. Brown ultimately shows, however, that despite their differences, both forms fixate on, challenge, and, in some cases, queer the boy's social and gendered identity development within their specific historical contexts. The claims made in her essay can be used to examine the performance of gender in other picturebooks and horror texts for children and young adults that utilize horror elements to focus explicitly on the masculine experience of American culture and identity formation.

In "'In the Darkest Zones': The Allure of Horror in Contemporary Revisionist Fairy-Tale Novels for Children," I focus specifically on the recent novels *Coraline* and *A Tale Dark and Grimm* as examples of gruesome, morally impactful modern fairy tales. I situate these particular books in relation to twentieth-century women authors' dark fairy-tale revisions that emphasize identity development and the current cultural moment, a time in which mainstream American culture is obsessed with the darker side of fairy tales and the resurgence and rehabilitation of the fairy tale. Both *Coraline* and *A Tale Dark and Grimm*, filled with violence, gore, and horror, hearken back to the literary fairy tales that precede them and concentrate on the idea that children must learn to conquer their demons in order to achieve self-awareness. As I argue, these novels illustrate that children can gain, through textual encounters with the horrific, an enhanced sense of self and the power of bravery. In the end, I argue that these books are excellent examples of the social importance of maintaining terror as part of the texture of modern fairy tales for young readers, especially those in which the pursuit of personal identity is at the apple's core.

From here, we turn the page from books to the silver screen. In his essay "Didactic Monstrosity and Postmodern Revisionism in Contemporary Children's Films," Peter C. Kunze investigates films for children that engage elements of horror, concentrating on the intersection between postmodernism and children's cinema. Closely examining two films in which the monstrous is a key aspect of the films' aesthetic, *Shrek* and *Monsters, Inc.*, Kunze studies the postmodern aspects of these films, considering their revisionary stance, their use of double address, and their allusive nature. As the essay progresses, he hones in on the narrative construction of the monster in these films and the processes by which they revise monstrosity. Kunze demonstrates, overall, that these films illustrate for the child viewer "the benefits of confronting the Other not to destroy it, but to appreciate it and work towards mutual understanding" and offers a useful methodology for thinking about the monster in children's books and films targeted toward the young that have been produced during the new millennium.

Turning to young adults, Nick Levey and Holly Harper's "Get It Together: Anxieties of Collective Responsibility in Contemporary Young Adult Horror Novels" begins fittingly with the line "If there's one thing you can depend upon during the zombie apocalypse, it's that you won't have to face it alone." In this essay, Levey and Harper examine the importance of group dynamics in contemporary teen novels that concentrate on surviving zombie invasions. Focusing on two recently published horror novels popular among teens, Charlie Higson's *The Enemy* and Michael Grant's *Gone*, Levey and Harper examine the "considerations of group consciousness and democratic dynamics" in the texts, noting that such attention to the group is a departure from previous teen novels that had focused more on negotiations of individual identity (this also marks a difference from the novels I examine in my essay, suggesting the different approach toward identity taken by those writing for older adolescents). For Levey and Harper, the importance of these particular novels and their treatment of the individual in relation to the group is twofold: they ask the characters therein to work through personal issues that are detrimental to the survival of the group and they call for social reevaluation. In the worlds of *The Enemy* and *Gone*, young adult readers experience a close encounter with monstrous humanity, one that allows them to vicariously experience how others deal with threats external to their circles, as well as the threats that lie within themselves and their own peer groups.

Janani Subramanian and Jorie Lagerwey continue the volume's focus on teen horror and the interrelationships functioning therein in "Teen Terrors: Race, Gender, and Horrifying Girlhood in *The Vampire Diaries*." Shifting the focus from zombie epidemics in books to vampire invasions on the small screen, Subramanian and Lagerwey contemplate the "raced and gendered contradictions of postfeminist girl culture" by concentrating on the character development of two of the show's main characters, Bonnie Bennett and Caroline Forbes. In doing so, Subramanian and Lagerwey consider how *The Vampire Diaries* employs monstrosity to consider and represent what coming of age means for girls of different racial identities, especially in melodramatic television series targeted toward teen audiences that have been produced in the postfeminist era. Through this, Subramanian and Lagerwey offer new insight into postfeminist horror designed for young viewers, especially the young females who find themselves fans of such shows and films.

Rounding out this deliberation of the qualities of monstrosity in texts targeted toward teenaged audiences, Emily Hiltz, in "Let the Games Begin: Hybrid Horror in *The Hunger Games* Trilogy," examines Suzanne Collins's monstrous "mutts" in her phenomenally popular series *The Hunger Games*. Hiltz is especially interested in Collins's characterization of human-animal hybrids, investigating the relationship between the political commentary at work in the novels and these "monsters," from the half-wolf, half-humans that nearly overtake Katniss at the Cornucopia in the first novel to the lizard-humans whispering her name throughout the viaducts beneath the city in the last. Hiltz focuses on the mutts as abject creatures, demonstrating the ways in which these uncanny monsters, quite literally making the familiar strange, are at once metaphors for the political control exerted by the Capitol, the rebels' resistance to the Capitol's power, and the disruption of natural order. She also concentrates on Katniss and Peeta as muttations, each of them reformed by warring entities in service of "the greater good." Hiltz emphasizes that Collins's mutts are designed to demonstrate the fine and wavering line between good and evil, calling into question the nature of monstrosity, especially as it relates to human behavior. Her location of monstrosity in the protagonists themselves especially offers a new way of thinking about teen dystopic novels that engage horror as a means of conveying identities assaulted by external forces.

The final essay in the collection, "Where Are the Scary Books? The Place of Scary Books for Children in School and Children's Libraries" by Kirsten Kowalewski, closes our study of children's horror from the perspective of a children's librarian (albeit one who runs the Website *Monster Librarian*). Kowalewski considers how "Librarians able to navigate the resources that fall into the category of scary books can be guides and partners for children interested in further exploration and extension of their knowledge." Noting that it can be rather difficult to find an appropriate title for a child who comes in asking for a "scary book" because of the methods by which frightening fictions are shelved in the children's collection, Kowalewski serves here as a guide, offering practical advice to librarians, educators, and parents who seek to point children in the right direction. Kowalewski argues that librarians' awareness of such titles is a matter of civic importance, noting that "aliterate," or disengaged readers, are less inclined to become involved citizens, educationally, politically, and professionally. As Kowalewski notes, titles in the gothic horror genre can serve as an enticement to young readers, luring them into the children's library. Kowalewski's essay serves as a thorough practical introduction to "scary books for kids," an excellent conclusion to our volume that makes its end, in actuality, a beginning, an entry point for those interested in promoting the horror genre among young readers.

As a whole, this essay collection seeks to consider horror texts for children with the respect such texts deserve, weighing the multitude of benefits they can provide for young readers and viewers. It refuses to write off the horror genre as campy or trite or deforming, instead recognizing that many of the texts categorized as "terrifying" are among those most widely read/viewed by children and young adults. It also considers how adult horror has been domesticated, with authors and screenwriters turning what once was utterly horrifying into safe, funny, and delightful novels and films, along with the impetus behind such reenvisioning of the adult horror novel or film as something appropriate for the young. Especially today, when dark novels, shows, and films targeted toward children and young adults are proliferating with wild abandon, understanding the methods by which such texts have traditionally operated, as well as how those methods have been challenged, abandoned, and appropriated in recent years, becomes all the more crucial.

As Dracula once so famously uttered, welcome to our house. Pull up a chair and crack open the spine of our book.

NOTES

1. The paradoxical appeal of horror, especially for adults, has been a subject of ongoing debate for many years, with several scholars weighing in on the emotional, psychological, and physiological appeal of horror. In her essay "The Paradox of Horror: Fear as a Positive Emotion," Katerina Bantanaki provides an excellent overview of this debate, examining the conflicting opinions of such scholars as Noël Carroll, Susan Feagin, Alex Neill, John Morreall, and Aaron Smuts. As Bantanaki notes in this overview, these scholars have gone back and forth over horror's attraction, debating the definition of horror and its qualifying characteristics. See, for example, Carroll's responses to Feagin's and Berys Gaut's critiques of his work in "Disgust or Fascination: A Response to Susan Feagin" and "Enjoying Horror Fictions: A Reply to Gaut," as well as Gaut's reply to Carroll in "The Enjoyment of Horror: A Response to Carroll." To read more about these specific scholars' takes on the paradox of horror, see, for example, Carroll's *The Philosophy of Horror: or, Paradoxes of the Heart*; Feagin's "Monsters, Disgust, and Fascination"; Gaut's "The Paradox of Horror"; Morreall's "Enjoying Negative Emotions in Fictions"; Neill's "On a Paradox of the Heart"; and Smuts's

"The Paradox of Painful Art." For examples of scholarship specifically targeted toward the examination of frightening literature and film designed for children and young adults, see the edited collection *The Gothic in Children's Literature: Haunting the Borders*; Katherine Shryock-Hood's dissertation "On Beyond Boo! Horror Literature for Children"; Geraldine Brennan, Kevin McCarron, and Kimberly Reynolds's volume *Frightening Fiction*; and Gregory Pepetone's *Hogwarts and All: Gothic Perspectives on Literature*.

2. Though some, for example, may not classify *The Hunger Games* as a horror text, it makes use of body horror, the grotesque, and the monster in much the same fashion as horror literature and film designed for adult consumption, hence its inclusion here.

3. As Victoria Nelson notes, many recent horror texts are "amazingly hybrid": "Proliferating across all storytelling media, Gothick horror has mated with noir, science fiction, comedy, romance, and erotic fiction" (8). This brand of horror also participates in the trend of making "Gothick characters flip their sex, species, and deep nature (most conspicuously, from evil to good)" (8).

4. For more on the frightening elements in fairy tales and their symbology of violence, see Marina Warner's *No Go the Bogeyman: Scaring, Lulling, and Making Mock* and Maria Tatar's *The Hard Facts of Grimm's Fairy Tales* or *Off with Their Heads!: Fairy Tales and the Culture of Childhood*. For a brief discussion of horror in American children's literature throughout the nineteenth century, see, for example, Charmette Kendrick's essay "The Goblins Will Get You: Horror in Children's Literature from the Nineteenth Century." Kendrick demonstrates, for example, that "Many scary stories written by nineteenth-century American authors [were] influenced by the Puritan ideal of instilling morals through fear and are much more graphic than those published in England" (21). She provides as an example the 1847 novel *The Children in the Wood* by Lawrence Lovechild, the plot of which, clearly indebted to fairy tales, "involv[es] a nobleman, his wife, and their two children—a 'gentle' girl and a 'delightful' little boy who lived long ago in Cornwall, England." The parents die and the children are taken in by their uncle, who wants to have his niece and nephew murdered so that he can control their fortune. The uncle hires two thugs to do the job, but they leave the babes in the woods to "fend for themselves" rather than murdering them outright; the children die, and the uncle drinks himself into bankruptcy, "finally perish[ing] in the woods as a beggar, where he is devoured by wolves and vultures" (22). As Kendrick notes, "Despite the subject matter and artwork, the book was lauded by critics of the day as being entirely suitable for the young. The *Boston Daily Advertiser* said that all stories in the series of Uncle William's Nursery Stories were 'interspersed with such sound morality that they may be read without danger by the tenderest mind.'" Whereas today the overt violence in a book like *The Children in the Wood* might give many adults pause, in the past it was looked upon as a teaching tool, just another weapon in a parent's socializing arsenal. The essay collection *The Gothic in Children's Literature: Haunting the Borders* is also an excellent resource on the threat of terror in the children's library over the centuries of children's publishing, as the essays therein seek to document how children "have always had a predilection for what we now categorize as the Gothic, for ghosts and goblins, haunting and horrors, fear and the pretence of fear" (2).

5. Katherine Shryock-Hood provides a fairly thorough discussion of the explosion of children's horror publishing in the 1980s and 1990s in her dissertation "On Beyond Boo!

Horror Literature for Children." See also Michael Wilson's essay "The Point of Horror: The Relationship Between Teenage Popular Horror Fiction and the Oral Repertoire" and Stephanie Loer's entry on "Horror Stories" in *Children's Books and Their Creators* for more on this phenomenon. For specific primary examples of this trend in children's and young adult publishing, see Christopher Pike's *Spooksville* series, the *Fear Street* series, the *Creepers* books by Bill Condon and Robert Hood, the *Scary Stories to Tell in the Dark* books by Alvin Schwartz, Lee Striker's *Hair Raisers*, and Johnathan Rand's *American Chillers*. With titles like *Night of the Living Dummy* (Stine *Goosebumps* #7, 1993) and *The Revenge of the Vampire Librarian* (Striker *Hair Raisers*, 1997), these books promised thrills, chills, and comedy all in one package. The titles of these particular books also suggest the interrelationship between film and text in these horror serials.

6. See Maria Tatar's *Off with Their Heads!* for a thorough description of the role of violence as a teaching tool, which she terms the "pedagogy of fear." Tatar points to the Grimm Brothers as masters of this pedagogy, demonstrating how they regularly amped up the violence in many of their tales to draw more attention to the lessons to be learned therein: "instead of disguising [violence] or blotting it out, they preserved and often intensified it, though usually only when scenes could be invested with a higher moral purpose" (5–6). To use the tale "Cinderella" as an example, in the first edition of *Children's and Household Tales* published in 1812, the two stepsisters are just exceptionally jealous; in the second, they have their eyes pecked out by birds (7). As this revision to "Cinderella" suggests, such brutal intimidation in service of a higher moral purpose usually relied on the text "pointing out the gruesome consequences of not following [societal rules]" (Shryock-Hood 3). From the gobbling up of the little girl in "Little Red Riding Hood," for instance, young readers were supposed to learn not to stray from the path; from the girl's dismemberment in "The Robber Bridegroom," they learned to trust their gut instincts; from "Bluebeard," they learned that curiosity often kills the cat.

7. See, for example, Perry Nodelman's essay "Ordinary Monstrosity" or Roderick McGillis's "R. L. Stine and the World of Child Gothic."

8. In an offhand conversation a year ago, my daughter's elementary librarian espoused this point of view, noting that she would not place *The Hunger Games* books or the *Divergent* series on the shelves of the book fair circulating through the school because she did not think it was appropriate reading for the age groups the fair was targeting (kindergarten through sixth grade). When I asked her why she thought so, she noted that the books were too gruesome, violent, and unsettling and that she thought it would make the problems with violence within the school worse rather than better.

9. Moreover, adults often make up a large population of the readers consuming these books. For more on this phenomenon, see, for example, the articles "'Twilight,' Take Me Away!: Teenage Vampires and the Mothers Who Love Them" (Em and Lo) and "Not Just a Teen Thing: Grown-ups in the Grip of 'Twilight'" (Meyer).

10. As Kendall Phillips notes in her assessment of the cultural appeal of certain horror films in *Projected Fears: Horror Films and American Culture*, the elements of horror in popular texts tend to resonate with "various anxieties existing in the broader culture" (7). She argues that truly successful horror films walk a fine line between the familiar and the shocking, using shock value to call attention to problems or anxieties in the familiar world

of the viewers; she terms this function of the horror text "resonant violation" (8). For more on horror films in particular as "collective nightmare," see Robin Wood's *Hollywood from Vietnam to Reagan . . . and Beyond*. For an example of criticism that reads the literary monster as a representation of cultural anxieties, see Judith Halberstam's "Technologies of Monstrosity: Bram Stoker's 'Dracula,'" which considers the representation of Dracula's characteristics in relation to the unfavorable portrayal of Jews in late nineteenth-century English popular and high cultures.

11. For a discussion of physiological responses to horror, see Susan Feagin, "Monsters, Disgust, and Fascination"; Alex Neill, "On a Paradox of the Heart"; John Morreall, "Enjoying Negative Emotion in Fictions"; and Katerina Batanaki, "The Paradox of Horror: Fear as a Positive Emotion."

12. Joseph Ledoux notes that the evolution of fear as an emotion is deeply linked to animals' and humans' perception of danger: "Fearful feelings [. . .] occur when a more basic neural system (the system that evolved to detect and respond to danger) functions in a brain that also has the capacity to be conscious of its own activities (LeDoux 1996). All animals (from bugs and worms to birds, lizards, pigeons, rats, monkeys, and people) are able to detect and respond to danger. Most animals in fact exist on both sides of the food chain, and their daily lives consist, in large part, of activities involved in finding food and avoiding becoming someone else's lunch. The ability to detect and respond to danger, then, is the function that the fear system evolved to perform, and the feelings of fear that occur when this system is active in a human brain (and perhaps some others) is a consequence of having this system plus a system for conscious awareness" (130–31).

13. Dickson concentrates on Carroll's argument that in art-horror, the reader/viewer is "in an analogous emotional state to that which fictional characters beset by monsters are described to be in" (Carroll *The Philosophy of Horror* 27). It should be noted that Dickson's focus is entirely on *Goosebumps*, which somewhat skews her perspective on children's horror in a general sense.

14. For other examples of the use of cannibalism in fairy tales and children's and young adult literature, see, for example, "Little Red Riding Hood," "Little Snow White," older versions of "Sleeping Beauty," "The Robber Bridegroom," "The Juniper Tree," "Beauty and the Beast," *Twilight*, *The Hunger Games*, *Coraline*, any number of teen zombie texts, *Where the Wild Things Are*, and the film *Monster House*. The use of cannibalism as a motif in these texts raises important questions about why food, and more particularly the girl objectified as food, is so crucial to each of the stories, as well as how young readers and viewers process the connection between the girl's body as an edible substance and the arguments about love, gender, and sexual politics in the texts.

15. Incidentally, the books treated in this volume tend to be more frightening and graphic than the films discussed. *The Hunger Games*, for example, was toned down some when it went to the screen, as the *were* nature of the wolves was not played up as much in the film as it was in the text. The directors did not emphasize as much as the novel that the wolves were fashioned out of the former, recently deceased tributes. Viewers also did not have to bear witness to the long devouring of Cato that readers are forced to endure in the book. When *Coraline* was translated from novel to screen, the terrifying qualities of the zombie-father under the bed and the weird older women in the flat's basement apartment were mitigated:

instead of the father being a disintegrating captive in the basement beneath an abandoned bedroom who tries to devour the young girl, he helps her find one of the marbles/lost souls she needs in order to beat the Other Mother at her own game; while the old women turn into a gross amalgamation of melting body parts in the book, in the movie they are made of candy. As these examples of books transformed for the screen demonstrate, when dealing with the horrific in children's culture, authors seem to be more willing to enter frightening territory than directors, perhaps because of pressure from censors and the ratings system.

16. Gaiman also notes that the use of horror in his novel *The Graveyard Book* is very calculated. As the interview describes, the novel opens with a "murderous knife: one that has just killed the family of the protagonist readers are about to meet. Gaiman was convinced that this wasn't too much for kids, and that they would keep reading. 'I wanted to make it very, very scary up front, because it's never that scary again,' Gaiman says" ("Kids' Book Club: A Graveyard Tour with Neil Gaiman").

17. As Julie Cross argues, "The use of humour can introduce and make palatable the elements of horror that Reynolds et al. (2001:3) believes are now aimed at readers as young as six or seven, and these texts often deal with children's deepest and unspoken fears" (59).

18. In a smaller number of horrific books that rely on humor, however, what is rendered funny is often deeply unsettling, the humor rebellious in nature. In Edward Gorey's sinisterly funny *The Gashlycrumb Tinies*, for example, in which twenty-six unassuming children are subjected to various demises, the children's deaths seem so outlandish and are treated in such an offhand manner that they tend to have the effect of generating laughter in both children and adults. Part of the appeal of *The Gashlycrumb Tinies* is laughing at that greatest fear of all, losing one's life, especially in an accident over which one has no control. As a result, however, the laughter the book produces can be viewed as deeply uncomfortable, the humor in the children's deaths linked to the author's desire to ridicule the socializing function in earlier children's books so valued by many children's literature enthusiasts. In *The Gashlycrumb Tinies*, Gorey underscores the ridiculousness of the rules children must deign to follow by punishing the children in his book for no apparent reason, which is, at once, hysterical and disturbing.

19. Del Toro has described the influence of fairy tales and children's fictions on the film. See, for example, his Fresh Air interview from January 2007 ("Oscar Nominee"), as well as the bonus material on the film's DVD, in which del Toro explains the influences of the film.

20. I must admit, here, that Ofelia is ultimately powerless against the Captain, who murders her at the entrance of her beloved labyrinth. This suggests that the fantasy world only has so much power. However, as del Toro argued in an NPR interview with Terri Gross, this fantasy world can be read as *real* ("Oscar Nominee"). Del Toro asserts that the fantasy world created by Ofelia, along with such worlds created by all of us, is as tangible as the concrete world where the creators reside. For del Toro, and in turn for his Ofelia (whom del Toro has noted is a deeply autobiographical character), it is not important whether or not she made up the Faun and the Underworld; what does matter is that she believes, with a fervor that is religious in flavor, that it exists, that she is entering her rightful kingdom as the daughter of her blood father, the king of the Underworld. To outsiders, Ofelia seems to function in a fantasy world that is fabricated; the Captain's inability to see the Faun suggests that he is

entirely a construct of Ofelia's imagination. The constructs of her imagination, however, allow both Ofelia and the film's viewers to realize that the real world is just as fabricated.

21. Philip J. Nickel has argued for a definition of "horror" that adds to Carroll's earlier definition of the term by "allow[ing] for horror with no specific monster and [. . .] for more 'realistic' monsters." In Nickel's view, "the threats that horror presents are not always fictional but can bleed into the actual world" (15).

22. Interestingly, *Coraline* was lauded after its publication, and Gaiman's novel *The Graveyard Book* won a Newbery Medal in 2009. Despite the darker subject matter of his books, Gaiman has remained relatively unchallenged among authors writing for the young who employ gothic and horror motifs within their work.

23. Coraline's revenge against the Other Mother can be read as a "revenge fantasy" against her own mother. As Julie Cross notes in her essay "Frightening and Funny: Humor and Horror in Children's Gothic Fiction," "such harmless acting out of vengeful fantasies can release negative feelings against those in authority and acts as a psychological safety-valve, letting out that which is normally repressed" (62).

24. For more on his view of children's moral education concerning evil, see the chapter of Guroian's book entitled "Evil and Redemption in *The Snow Queen* and *The Lion, the Witch, and the Wardrobe*."

25. For an assessment of the role of sex and violence in slasher films of the 1980s and 1990s, see Barry S. Sapolsky, Fred Molitor, and Sarah Luque's essay, "Sex and Violence in Slasher Films: Re-Examining the Assumptions," which compares the juxtaposition of sex and violence in slasher films of the 1980s and the revival of the genre in the mid-to late 1990s. See also David J. Hogan's *Dark Romance: Sexuality in the Horror Film* and Andrew Welsh's "On the Perils of Living Dangerously in the Slasher Horror Film: Gender Differences in the Association between Sexual Activity and Survival."

WORKS CITED

"100 Most Frequently Challenged Books: 1990–1999." *Missing: Find a Banned Book.* American Library Association, n.d. Web. 24 May 2014.

"About R. L." *The World of R. L. Stine.* 2014. Web. 13 May 2014.

Batanaki, Katerina. "The Paradox of Horror: Fear as a Positive Emotion." *Journal of Aesthetics & Art Criticism* 70.4 (Fall 2012): 383–92. Web. *Academic Search Elite.* 22 May 2014.

"Best Sellers: Children's Series." *New York Times,* 13 May 2014. Web. 13 May 2014.

Bird, Elizabeth. "Top 100 Picturebooks Poll Results." *School Library Journal,* 6 July 2012. Web. *ProQuest.* 13 May 2013.

"Brand New Fear Street Books in 2014." *RLStine.com,* 2014. Web. 13 May 2014.

Brennan, Geraldine, Kevin McCarron, and Kimberly Reynolds. *Frightening Fiction.* New York: Continuum, 2001. Print.

Carroll, Lewis. *Alice in Wonderland: A Norton Critical Edition.* Edited by Donald J. Gray. New York: Norton, 1992. Print.

Carroll, Noel. "Disgust or Fascination: A Response to Susan Feagin." *Philosophical Studies* 65 (1992): 85–90. Web. *Academic Search Elite*. 17 January 2014.

———. "Enjoying Horror Fictions: A Reply to Gaut," *The British Journal of Aesthetics* 35 (1995): 67–72. Web. *Academic Search Elite*. 29 January 2014.

———. *The Philosophy of Horror; or, Paradoxes of the Heart*. New York: Routledge, 1990. Print.

Cohen, Jeffrey J. "Preface." *Monster Theory: Reading Culture*. Minneapolis: U of Minnesota P, 1996. vii–xiii. *ebrary*. 1 May 2014.

Cross, Julie. "Frightening and Funny: Humor and Horror in Children's Gothic Fictions." *The Gothic in Children's Literature: Haunting the Borders*. Edited by Anna Jackson, Karen Coats, and Roderick McGillis. New York: Routledge, 2008. 57–76. Print.

Dickson, Randi. "Horror: To Gratify, Not Edify." *Language Arts* 76.2 (1998): 115–22. Print.

DiPucchio, Kelly. *Zombies in Love*. New York: Simon & Schuster, 2011. Print.

Dunleavy, M. P., and Sally Lodge. "Children's Writers Plumb the Depths of Fear." *Publisher's Weekly*, 27 March 1995, 28. Print.

Em and Lo. "'Twilight,' Take Me Away!" *New York*. 23 November 2009. *ProQuest*. Web. 29 May 2014.

Fahy, Thomas. "Introduction." *The Philosophy of Horror*. Edited by Thomas Fahy. Lexington: UP of Kentucky, 2010. 1–13. Print.

Feagin, Susan L. "Monsters, Disgust and Fascination." *Philosophical Studies* 65 (1992): 75–84. *Academic Search Elite*. Web. 17 January 2014.

Gaut, Berys. "The Enjoyment Theory of Horror: A Response to Carroll." *British Journal of Aesthetics* 35.3 (1995): 204+. *Literature Resource Center*. Web. 29 January 2014.

———. "The Paradox of Horror." *British Journal of Aesthetics* 33 (1995): 333–45. *Literature Resource Center*. Web. 29 January 2014.

Gaiman, Neil. *Coraline*. London: Bloomsbury, 2002. Print.

Gidwitz, Adam. *A Tale Dark and Grimm*. New York: Puffin, 2010. Print.

Gorey, Edward. *The Gashlycrumb Tinies*. New York: Simon and Schuster, 1963. Rpt. in *Amphigorey*. New York: Pedigree, 1972. Print.

———. *The Wuggly Ump*. Philadelphia: Lippincott, 1963. Rpt. in *Amphigorey*. New York: Pedigree, 1972. Print.

Guroian, Vigen. *Tending the Heart of Virtue: How Classic Stories Awaken a Child's Moral Imagination*. Oxford: Oxford UP, 1998. *ebrary*. Web. 5 May 2014.

Halberstam, Judith. "Technologies of Monstrosity: Bram Stoker's 'Dracula.' (Victorian Sexualities)." *Victorian Studies* 36.3 (1993): 333+. *Literature Resource Center*. Web. 29 May 2014.

Hogan, David J. *Dark Romance: Sexuality in the Horror Film*. Jefferson, NC: McFarland, 1997. Print.

Hood, Robert. "A Playground for Fear: Horror Fiction for Children." *Robert Hood*. Web. 22 May 2014.

"Horror." Def. *Oxford English Dictionary*. 2nd ed. 2014.

Jackson, Anna, Karen Coats, and Roderick McGillis. "Introduction." *The Gothic in Children's Literature: Haunting the Borders*. Edited by Anna Jackson, Karen Coats, and Roderick McGillis. New York: Routledge, 2008. 1–14. Print.

Kendrick, Charmette. "The Goblins Will Get You! Horror in Children's Literature from the Nineteenth Century." *Children and Libraries* (Spring 2009): 19–23. Print.

"Kids' Book Club: A Graveyard Tour with Neil Gaiman." *NPR*, 28 October 2011. Web. 29 May 2014.

Latham, Robert. *Consuming Youth: Vampires, Cyborgs, and the Culture of Consumption.* Chicago: U of Chicago P, 2002. *ebrary*. Web. 1 June 2014.

Ledoux, Joseph. "Cognitive-Emotional Interactions: Listen to the Brain." *Cognitive Neuroscience of Emotion*. Edited by Richard D. Lane and Lynn Nadel. New York: Oxford UP, 1999. *ebrary*. Web. 1 May 2014.

Loer, Stephanie. "Horror Stories." *Children's Books and Their Creators*. Edited by Anita Silvey. New York: Houghton Mifflin, 1995. 324–25. Print.

McGillis, Roderick. "R. L. Stine and the World of Child Gothic." *Bookbird* 33.3–4 (Fall–Winter 1995): 15–21. Print.

Meyer, Carla. "Not Just a Teen Thing: Grown-Ups also in Grip of 'Twilight.'" *Sacramento Bee*, 19 November 2009. *ProQuest*. Web. 29 May 2014.

Morreall, John. "Enjoying Negative Emotions in Fictions." *Philosophy and Literature* 9 (1985): 95–103. *ProjectMuse*. Web. 17 May 2014.

Neill, Alex. "On a Paradox of the Heart." *Philosophical Studies* 65 (1992): 53–65. *Academic Search Elite*. Web. 22 May 2014.

Nelson, Victoria. *Gothicka: Vampire Heroes, Human Gods, and the New Supernatural.* Cambridge, MA: Harvard UP, 2012. Print.

Nickel, Philip J. "Horror and the Idea of Everyday Life: On Skeptical Threats in *Psycho* and *The Birds*." *The Philosophy of Horror*. Edited by Thomas Fahy. Lexington: UP of Kentucky, 2010. 14–32. Print.

Nodelman, Perry. "Ordinary Monstrosity: The World of Goosebumps." *Children's Literature Association Quarterly* 22.3 (Fall 1997): 118–25. Print.

"Oscar Nominee Guillermo del Toro." *Fresh Air*. NPR, 24 January 2007. Web. 29 May 2014.

Pan's Labyrinth. Dir. Guillermo del Toro. Esperanto, 2006. DVD.

Pepetone, Gregory G. *Hogwarts and All: Gothic Perspectives on Literature*. New York: Peter Lang, 2012. Print.

Phillips, Kendall R. *Projected Fears: Horror Films and American Culture*. Westport, CT: Praeger, 2005. Print.

Poe, Edgar Allan. "The Tell-Tale Heart." *The Complete Works of Edgar Allan Poe: Centenary Edition*. Vol. 2. New York: Collier, 1903. 352–59. Print.

Roback, Diane. "For Children's Books in 2013, Divergent Led the Pack: Facts & Figures 2013." *Publishers Weekly* 261.11 (2014): 39–48. *ProQuest*. Web. 13 May 2014.

Sapolsky, Barry S., Fred Molitor, and Sarah Luque. "Sex and Violence in Slasher Films: Re-Examining the Assumptions." *Journalism and Mass Communication Quarterly* 80.1 (2003): 28–38. *MLA International Bibliography*. Web. 29 May 2014.

Sendak, Maurice. *Where the Wild Things Are*. New York: HarperCollins, 1988. Print.

Shryock-Hood, Katherine. "On Beyond Boo! Horror Literature for Children." Unpublished PhD diss., Indiana University of Pennsylvania, 2008.

Smuts, Aaron. "The Paradox of Painful Art." *Journal of Aesthetic Education* 41.3 (2007): 59–77. Web. *ProjectMuse*. 22 May 2014.

Stallcup, Jackie. "Power, Fear, and Children's Picturebooks." *Children's Literature* 30 (2002): 125–58. Print.

Stone, Jon, and Michael Smollin. *The Monster at the End of This Book*. New York: Sesame Workshop, 2012. Print.

Tatar, Maria. *Enchanted Hunters: The Power of Stories in Childhood*. New York: Norton, 2009. Print.

———. *The Hard Facts of Grimm's Fairy Tales*. Princeton: Princeton UP, 2003. Print.

———. *Off with Their Heads!: Fairy Tales and the Culture of Childhood*. Princeton: Princeton UP, 1992. Print.

Taylor, Charles. *Modern Social Imaginaries*. Durham, NC: Duke UP, 2004. Print.

"Top Ten Challenged Books List By Year: 2001–2013." *Missing: Find a Banned Book*. American Library Association, n.d. Web. 28 May 2014.

"Top 100 Banned/Challenged Books: 2000–2009." *Missing: Find a Banned Book*. American Library Association, n.d. Web. 28 May 2014.

Warner, Marina. *No Go the Bogeyman: Scaring, Lulling, and Making Mock*. New York: Random House, 2011. Print.

Welsh, Andrew. "On the Perils of Living Dangerously in the Slasher Horror Film: Gender Differences in the Association between Sexual Activity and Survival." *Sex Roles* 62.11–12 (2010): 762–73. *Academic Search Elite*. Web. 29 May 2014.

Wilson, Michael. "The Point of Horror: The Relationship between Teenage Popular Horror Fiction and the Oral Repertoire." *Children's Literature in Education* 31.1 (2000): 1–9. Print.

Wood, Robin. *Hollywood from Vietnam to Reagan . . . and Beyond*. New York: Columbia UP, 2003. Print.

Punishing the Abject Child

The Delight and Discipline of Body Horror in Heinrich Hoffmann's *Struwwelpeter*

JUSTINE GIENI

PUBLISHED IN 1845 BY DR. HEINRICH HOFFMANN, A GERMAN PSYCHIATRIST, the children's picture book *Struwwelpeter* features cautionary tales that inspire both fear and fascination. To a contemporary reading audience, the harsh lessons about etiquette, safety, and hygiene in Hoffmann's stories seem more suitable to gothic horror than the subject matter of children's literature. For example, in "The Story of Little Suck-a-Thumb," a boy's misdeed of thumb sucking precedes the excessively cruel and perverse punishment of having his thumbs cut off by the terrifying scissor-man. In other tales, a boy dies of starvation after refusing to eat his soup, and a girl burns to death after playing with matches. While the punishments seem unduly cruel in these tales, other stories exhibit punishments that are seemingly less severe: for instance, in the cover story of "Shock-headed Peter," there are no mortal consequences for the boy who has unkempt hair and nails, other than being scrutinized and shamed as a spectacle of the narrator's disgust. In another tale, "The Story of the Inky Boys," the seemingly antiracist lesson is upon first appearance ahead of its time, considering the historical context of early nineteenth-century Germany, in that the racist bullying of a group of boys is penalized. Yet upon closer scrutiny, this tale, like the others, reflects on the rigid norms of dominant culture: in this case, illustrating a racial hierarchy of white privilege in the equation of "blackness" with abject inferiority and punishment (Martin 152).[1]

Although the punishments vary in severity from story to story, Hoffmann's tales consistently draw upon children's anxieties about and fascination with the grotesque and transgressive as a means to both delight and horrify. In Hoffmann's representations of mutilated, degenerated, and monstrous child bodies, he utilizes abjection to construct his cautionary tales. Through exaggerated violence and graphic imagery of bloody, emaciated, and dirty child bodies, Hoffmann's work transgresses the conventional didacticism of children's books at this time. Indeed, as noted by Barbara Smith Chalou, while contemporary audiences often read Hoffmann's text as "the epitome of didacticism" in its overt message of cautioning children in propriety and obedience, Hoffmann's text is historically situated as a novelty for its "absence of didacticism" (72). Departing from the conventions of nineteenth-century children's literature, specifically the "heavy handed didactic books on the market" (24) such as *McGuffy's Eclectic Primer* (1836) and pedagogical chapbooks, Hoffmann's *Struwwelpeter* entertains and delights children through violent imagery (72). In this way, Hoffmann's tales of naughty and disobedient children occupy an ambiguous position in the literary canon, where the debate about its appropriateness for a child audience continues. At the heart of this debate is Hoffmann's representation of violence being inflicted on child victims. It is my argument that Hoffmann's use of violence is not gratuitous or pedagogical, but rather, a transgressive and satirical indictment of a historically and culturally specific social order. Indeed, through both humor and horror, Hoffmann satirizes the didacticism of nineteenth-century German culture by creating a counterdiscourse in children's literature; through exaggerated violence, Hoffmann mocks the heavy-handed pedagogical practices that sought to suppress the instinctual and subversive impulses of children in their creativity and rebellious nonconformity. To view Hoffmann's work as purely didactic is to underappreciate the text's subversive qualities. It is through the powers of horror that Hoffmann creates a text that exists in ambiguity, presenting its readers, both children and adults, with "merry tales and funny pictures" that not only horrify and delight, but also challenge the dominant social order.

The controversy surrounding Hoffmann's story collection continues into the present, as critics discuss the appropriateness of the work as children's literature and the ambiguity of its underlying message. Critics like Thomas Freeman have argued that the book uses violence to "frighten children into obedience" and "reinforce[s] already existing fears and violent tendencies" (817). Yet exaggerated violence, such as that found in fairy tales, is commonly depicted in children's literature, often to the delight of its readers. According to Lucy Rollin, children often enjoy characters who embody naughtiness and display "sadistic, aggressive, mischievious" and "id-driven" behavior (31). Indeed, one can see these qualities throughout children's literature, in the works of such authors as Roald Dahl and Maurice Sendak.

The enormous popularity of *Struwwelpeter* attests to the fascination that the tales have had, and continue to have, for generation after generation of readers. There is an undeniable appeal in the horrifying violence that Hoffmann invokes in his tales of disobedient children. And yet, contemporary critics like Thomas Freeman and Barbara Smith Chalou acknowledge there are potentially terrorizing aspects of the text, making it unsuitable for some children. Other critics, such as Bettina Hürlimann, suggest that the exagerrated quality of the illustrations minimizes children's anxieties, making it a suitable book for children of any age. According to Hürlimann, "The completely unrealistic way in which the book is illustrated produces a kind of symbolic hyper-reality which is far less dangerous for children than many of the photographic representations of similar happenings which they see daily in newspapers and magazines" (56). In this understanding, Hoffmann's exaggerated cartoonish illustrations minimize the potentially harmful depictions of violence that may terrify some children.

Adding to the critical discourse of *Struwwelpeter* studies, my reading focuses primarily on Hoffmann's use of gothic tropes: in particular, the many iterations of body horror in the text. Situating my reading in this critical discourse of *Struwwelpeter* studies, I underscore both the violence and the subversive pleasure of reading the text. In congruence with readings by Jack Zipes, Eva-Maria Metcalf, and Elizabeth Wesseling, I believe the text functions on two levels: on the surface level, the text functions as a set of cautionary tales designed to inform children about and discipline them into the rules and regulations of bourgeois German society (Zipes "Struwwelpeter and Classical Children's Literature"); however, a deeper reading of the text reveals its role as a subversive and farcical counterdiscourse to authoritarianism and conformity. As a result, the text occupies an ambiguous position by inspiring both fear and pleasure. When viewed in this duality, *Struwwelpeter* exemplifies Julia Kristeva's theory of abjection in *Powers of Horror*. Specifically, Hoffmann's emphasis on disciplining the material body and his gruesome depictions of punishment characterize his children's tales as body horror, where it is the corporeality of the human body that inspires feelings of dread, repulsion, and fear; yet as an abject or transgressive text, Hoffmann's tales also use horror to undermine and challenge socially sanctioned conformity by allowing child readers to face their fears through laughter at the over-the-top depictions of illness, morbidity, and monstrosity.

In its duality as an object of pleasure and pain, humor and horror, fascination and fear, Hoffmann's *Struwwelpeter* is an example of an "abject text" (Kristeva 18). In *Powers of Horror*, Kristeva describes an abject text as one wherein there is a confrontation between the subject and the abject Other, where "the aesthetic task" is "a descent into the foundations of the symbolic construct" (18). This confrontation between self and Other is described thus:

> the aesthetic task [. . .] amounts to retracing the fragile limits of the speaking being, closest to its dawn, to the bottomless "primacy" constituted by primal repression. Through that experience, which is nevertheless managed by the Other, "subject" and "object" push each other away, confront each other, collapse, and start again—insepa-rable, contaminated, condemned, at the boundary of what is assimi-lable, thinkable: abject. (18)

As a confrontation with that which threatens the borders of the subject, ab-jection is inherently frightening. As depicted in Hoffmann's illustrations, the abject child is one who experiences the breakdown of boundaries between clean and polluted, inside and outside, life and death, proper and improper, human and animal, self and Other. According to Kristeva, confrontation with the abject is both anxiety inducing and inexplicably fascinating. After all, the abject is that which is capable of disturbing "identity, system, or-der. What does not respect borders, positions, rules. The in-between, the ambiguous, the composite" (4). By occupying a position of ambiguity, the abject is closely associated with the principle of *jouissance*, that is, a feeling akin to pleasure or joyfulness but which exists at the border where pleasure crosses over into pain or angst. As Kristeva describes, we are drawn to the abject as it embodies both "condemnation and yearning" (10); we become the "fascinated victims" of the abject, "if not its submissive and willing ones" (9). By creating tales that blur the lines between propriety and the grotesque or transgressive, *Struwwelpeter* occupies an ambiguous position as an abject text that inspires both our fear and fascination.

In its depiction of cautionary tales, Hoffmann's text invokes the abject or monstrous child body, showing children what behaviors must be "thrust aside" (3) or rejected in creation of the "clean and proper" body (8), or what Zipes identifies as the culturally indoctrinated child ("The Perverse Delight" 165). Building from Zipes's reading of *Struwwelpeter* as exemplary of cul-tural indoctrination into the rules and values of bourgeois German soci-ety, my interpretation of Hoffmann's text highlights its subversive subtext. Indeed, when viewed as an abject text, *Struwwelpeter* exposes the violence of a rigid authoritarian society that censures the unruly, unkempt child as abject Other, repudiating and punishing him as a threat to the social conventions of nineteenth-century German society. Body horror becomes the means through which Hoffmann exposes the regulatory social practices that subdue children's instincts, desires, and willful rebellion. In Hoffmann's tales, authoritarian culture is characterized as a medical-patriarchal authority that he personifies through male "father" figures, who frequently take on supernatural or omnipotent power: the authoritative narrator who admonishes Shock-headed Peter, the Doctor who administers a "nasty physic" on Cruel Frederick, the Great Agrippa who dips Ned, Arthur, and William in ink, the tall Tailor who snips off Conrad's thumbs, and the angry father who scolds Fidgety Philip.[2] Hoffman, himself a physician and father, identified the purpose of his book as a means to delight his three-year-old son and to assuage the fears of children who visited his medical practice (Freeman 808). In fact, the subtitle "merry tales and funny pictures" emphasizes the authorial intent to entertain, rather than teach. However, according to Zipes, Hoffman's depictions reveal a sinister violence: specifically, the stories reflect a history of punishment and abuse from Hoffmann's father in his "sadomasochistic treatment of him" as a child (Zipes *Sticks and Stones* 153). In this regard, Zipes interprets the text's humor as concealing an underlying anxiety between father and son, as "Hoffmann tried to minimize the power that his father had held over him while also pursuing a new strategy to gain control over his own son" (153). Indeed, for many, it is not comfort, but rather fear and anxiety that frame the reception of the text in its portrayal of patriarchal authority, especially among today's readers who are particularly sensitive to the impact of media violence on children.

The authoritarian tone of the narrative is front and center, as evidenced in the prologue, where the structure of reward and punishment is clearly established:

> Naughty, romping girls and boys
> Tear their clothes and make a noise,
> Spoil their pinafores and frocks,
> And deserve no Christmas-box.
> Such as these shall never look
> At this pretty Picture book. (Hoffman)

The narrator's voice parrots the rigid, authoritarian tone of the patriarchal-medical establishment, where the intention of punishing "naughty" children, that is, children who exhibit qualities that are not affirmed by the status quo, is the surface message of the book. Notably, with the exception of

Harriet, the girl who plays with matches, the "naughty" children of the book are exclusively male. Whether Hoffmann thought the male protagonists would appeal more to his son, or if he was reflecting the more commonplace interest in boys' misbehavior, the tales explicitly depict male children, in particular, as troublesome and disruptive. Just as Fidgety Philip's parents implore him to "be a little gentleman," so too does Hoffmann's text reflect the commonplace socialization of child readers in the values, expectations, and customs of hegemonic masculinity.[3]

In her discussion of horror films, Barbara Creed reinforces the notion that horror can be a confrontation with the abject other: "the horror film attempts to bring about a confrontation with the abject [...] in order to eject the abject [...] to separate out the symbolic order from all that threatens its stability" (14). Like Frankenstein's monster that is banished to isolation and cursed by all of humankind, Hoffmann's children are admonished as monstrous and repulsive. Hoffmann's text invokes horror in this way, to illustrate the separation and purgation of abject qualities that threaten the stability of the status quo. By depicting the violent punishment of dirty, maimed, and monstrous children, Hoffmann exaggerates the horror of dominant social doctrines of obedience and ideological conformity. According to Kristeva, this obedience is aligned with the "Law of the Father," wherein the symbolic father separates child from mother and structures the social relations between the sexes. Kristeva indicates that abjection functions in this process to affirm patriarchal society by separating the sexes: "the masculine [...] confesses through its very relentlessness against the other, the feminine, that it is threatened by an asymmetrical, irrational, wily, uncontrollable power" (70). That which is "feminine" and "uncontrollable" is a threat to the boundaries of hegemonic masculinity, thus it is rejected and expelled to the borders of masculine identity. Notably, as Hoffmann's text illustrates, it is not only "the feminine" that threatens the symbolic order of authoritarian culture, but also there is a concerted effort to exclude and punish the "irrational, wily, uncontrollable" child. Indeed, Hoffmann's male protagonists transgress the boundaries of propriety through their appearance ("Shock-headed Peter"), disrespect of authority ("The Story of Augustus"; "The Story of Fidgety Philip"), and refusal to obey orders ("Little Suck-a-Thumb"). Set against the sociohistorical context of early nineteenth-century Germany, Hoffmann's stories mock the attempted indoctrination of boys to an ideology of conformity and discipline.[4]

When viewed from a perspective that acknowledges the satirical role of Hoffmann's violence, Hoffmann's tales become more than just cautionary tales about bad behavior; rather, Hoffmann exposes the dominant social order as an authoritarian system, where expressions of autonomy and creativity, particularly in the drives and desires of children, are repudiated by what Foucault calls "the punitive mechanics of power" (85). By looking more closely at three of Hoffmann's tales, "Shock-headed Peter," "The Tale of Little Suck-a-Thumb," and "The Story of Augustus," it is clear how Hoffmann's text satirizes the dictates of obedience and conformity that repudiate and pathologize nonconformist children through violent punishments. By highlighting patriarchal structures of the family and socio-medical discourses, my reading of *Struwwelpeter* reveals Hoffmann's satirical mocking of the underlying power structures of the nineteenth century that aimed to suppress children's curiosity and creativity.

According to Kristeva, the process of cultural evolution toward civilization is founded on the abjection of the "unclean and improper" body (72). Under the binary logic of the patriarchal symbolic order, the physical body is regulated by a set of prohibitions: "Through frustrations and prohibitions, this authority shapes the body into a territory having areas, orifices, points and lines, surfaces and hollows, where the archaic power of mastery and neglect, of the differentiation of proper-clean and improper-dirty, possible and impossible, is impressed and exerted" (72). This division between "proper-clean" and "improper-dirty" is aligned with the binary structure of the symbolic order. Urine, blood, sperm, and excrement, the discharges of the human body, are aligned with the "uncivilized." Strong odors, dirtiness, and substances expelled from the body are abjected as sources of shame and contempt. The fully symbolic body must bear "no traces of its debt to nature" (102). On the surface, Hoffmann's rhyme about "Shock-headed Peter" draws from the "uncivilized" appearance of a boy, whose unkempt hair and nails are deemed "dirty" and "sloven," teaches a lesson to children about proper hygiene (Hoffmann). However, implicit in Hoffmann's hygiene lesson is a challenge to the dictates of the "Father's Law."

In the illustration of Shock-headed Peter, the boy takes on an almost monstrous appearance, reminiscent of a freak-show spectacle. As both human and subhuman, Shock-headed Peter's appearance exemplifies the fear and fascination of body horror. Set on a pillory, the boy is displayed as a spectacular object who is scorned, feared, and ridiculed by the narrator (see figure 1.1). Disdained for "his nasty hair" and dirty fingernails "grimed as black as soot," Peter is objectified as an example of the improper-dirty body (Hoffmann). Indeed, the association between filth and depravity is evident in the narrator's gaze, which punishes the boy solely based on his appearance. Dirtiness, in this context, can be aligned with deviance and rebellion.

As noted by Wesseling, the child protagonists of Hoffmann's tales are often objectified by the authoritative narrator: "Shock-headed Peter does not get to speak a single line, nor do the other children in the stories that are to follow" (325). The narrator's voice is the sole authority guiding the child reader's perception of the characters in the story; in this way, the narrator's voice also represents paternal authority within the symbolic order. Hoffmann's narrator, whom Wesseling calls "the voice of authority" (325), implores the child readers to regard Peter as an object of disgust, a defiled body that must be repudiated in creation of the culturally indoctrinated child. In his authoritative position, the narrator also takes on a position of omnipotence to instill fear in the child readers. As Zipes suggests, "it is a voice that wants to oversee the children's reading panoptically and to make sure they learn from the horrific lessons" ("The Perverse Delight" 131). Rather than feel pity for or empathize with the filthy boy, the narrator implores child readers to dis-identify with Peter. Indeed, Peter's slovenly appearance is set in stark contrast to the "good" boys and girls who are addressed in the frontispiece to *Struwwelpeter* (Wesseling 324). On the one hand, for children who view Peter under the narrator's judgmental gaze, there is a delight in dis-identifying with Peter's appearance; that is, a pleasure derived from the external distinctions between self and Other. On the other hand, there will be child readers who recognize and identify themselves in the monstrosity of Peter's appearance, rather than disavow him. This recognition and familiarity with Peter's appearance is certain to cause a fright.

By defying convention through dirtiness, however, Peter's body is simultaneously an object of derision and a site of resistance. As Kristeva describes, that which is abject is excluded to the border of our identity, yet from this marginal position the abject "Other" still poses a threat: "from its place of banishment, the abject does not cease challenging its master" (2). Through his dirtiness and disheveled body, Shock-headed Peter occupies this position. In *Purity and Danger*, Mary Douglas discusses dirtiness as a symbolic threat to system and order: "If we can abstract pathogenicity and hygiene from our notion of dirt, we are left with the old definition of matter out of place [...]. Dirt is the by-product of a systematic ordering and classification of matter, in so far as ordering involves rejecting inappropriate elements" (35). As "matter out of place," Peter's unclean body symbolizes a threat to the systematic order of a "civilized" patriarchal society. Specifically, he embodies a masculinity that does not conform to the dictates of obedience

Just look at him! There he stands,
With his nasty hair and hands.
See! his nails are never cut;
They are grim'd as black as soot;
And the sloven, I declare,
Never once has comb'd his hair;
Any thing to me is sweeter
Than to see Shock-headed Peter.

1.1. *Struwwelpeter*, Shock-headed Peter

and self-denial. Rather, Peter's long hair and fingernails are reminiscent of a threatening (feminine) corporeality that jeopardizes the social order through its unstable boundaries.

The disturbing familiarity of Peter's unkempt body derives from the Freudian notion of "the uncanny," where "what is 'uncanny' is frightening precisely because it is not known and familiar" (Freud "The Uncanny" 220). The feeling of familiarity with that which is also dreadful relates to Peter's uncanny slovenliness, which is both familiar and repulsive. The taboo on uncleanliness furthers the horror and subversiveness derived from Peter's body. In *Totem and Taboo*, Freud defines taboo in relation to both "the uncanny" and the unclean: "The meaning of 'taboo,' as we see it, diverges in

two contrary directions. To us it means, on the one hand, 'sacred,' 'conse-
crated,' and on the other 'uncanny,' 'dangerous,' 'forbidden,' 'unclean'" (18).
By pushing the representation of the child body to extremes of filth and
depravity, Hoffmann creates a sense of abjection by rendering children's
disobedience in a graphic and disturbing form. Yet, it is the seeming ordi-
nariness of this disobedience and filth that is truly frightening, for it represents the readers' participation in transgressive, punishable, and somehow
pleasurable behavior.

As noted by Kelly Hurley in *The Gothic Body*, the spectator of body horror often identifies with the monster in recognition of repressed drives and
desires: "the horror text clothes the repressed contents of the unconscious
in phantasmatic narrative and spectacle, such that they may be both recognized and disavowed" (206). Under rigid social constraints, Peter's dirtiness embodies what is both feared and desired by children: that is, willful
disobedience of paternal authority. In this way, while the narrator demands
the child reader to disavow Peter's filthy body, there is also a counterforce of
recognition that connects Peter's disorderly appearance with a desirable, yet
taboo, rebelliousness. In other words, Peter embodies a desire to flout social
conventions and defy authority. The reader may experience this identification as a cathartic release, knowing that it is Peter, rather than "I," who is
punished.

Barbara Creed discusses this dual recognition of disgust and identification in the horror genre in relation to representations of bodily wastes:
"[Bodily wastes] in the horror film may invoke a response of disgust from
the audience situated as it is within the symbolic but at a more archaic
level the representation of bodily wastes may invoke pleasure in breaking
the taboo on filth" (74). By "breaking the taboo on filth," Hoffmann's child
protagonist offers a glimpse into the repressed drives and desires of "good"
nineteenth-century boys and girls, who were constrained by rigid sociocultural norms and expectations. As the narrator encourages children to shame
Peter for his filth and slovenliness, the counterforce of uncanny recognition enables the child reader to experience the abject Other as the source
of both horror and forbidden, cathartic pleasure. As identified by Kristeva,
"poetic catharsis" occurs in abject literature, where it functions as a release
for negative drives and desires (29). For Hoffmann's reading audience of
children, the expurgation of repressed desires that occurs as one reads the
book, views the illustrations, and finally distances oneself as spectator of,
rather than the object of, derision, there is a possiblity of pleasure to be
experienced in the child's reading of Hoffmann's text. Indeed, as Maria Tatar

argues, depictions of corporeal punishment in children's literature "may be more likely to give free reign to the transgressive impulses represented in the story than to curb them" (77). While the civilizing lessons of Hoffmann's tales may seem out-of-date with today's pedagogical methods, the endurance of *Struwwelpeter* in the canon of children's literature suggests that the tales continue to appeal to children's fascination with the grotesque and the macabre.

Arguably the most terrifying of Hoffmann's tales is "The Story of Little Suck-a-Thumb." In the story, Conrad fails to heed his mother's warning not to suck his thumbs; as a consequence, he faces the nightmarish reality of having his thumbs cut off by the "great, long, red-legged scissor-man" (Hoffmann). Wielding a pair of enormous scissors, the "great tall tailor" acts as an agent of paternal authority, doling out Conrad's punishment through mutilation (see figure 1.2). However, unlike the narrator in "Shock-headed Peter" who merely scolds Peter for his unkempt appearance, the scissor-man uses violence to teach Conrad a lesson. In his discussion of violence in *Struwwelpeter*, Thomas Freeman suggests that Hoffmann's tales invoke "some of the worst fears which can torment a child" (813); in the case of Conrad's punishment, Freeman, among other critics, has identified the psychoanalytic context of these fears to be a child's castration anxieties. In this sense, Conrad's thumb sucking is perceived as a thinly veiled substitute for the taboo behavior of childhood masturbation. As described in Freud's discussion of infantile sexuality, thumb sucking "is often combined with rubbing contact with certain senstive parts of the body, such as the breast and external genitals. It is by this road that many children go from thumb-sucking to masturbation" ("Three Essays" 181). Therefore, when Conrad is admonished for sucking his thumbs, the implicit interdiction is also against the more severe taboos of sexual impropriety and self-indulgence.

The modern reader of this tale is often struck by the disturbingly harsh punishment that Conrad is subjected to for sucking his thumbs; however, in the context of nineteenth-century German medical discourses, bodily mutilation as punishment of the child was not unheard of. In fact, to threaten a child with scissors in cases of child onanism was practiced, as evidenced by nineteenth-century child-rearing pedagogies. In his 1907 book *The Sexual Life of Our Times*, Iwan Bloch, a German dermatologist, describes the methods advocated by medical discourses:

According to the suggestion of Ultzmann, in the case of nursing infants and of small children, the hands may be confined in little bags or tied to the side of the bed. The methods of the older physicians, who appeared before the child armed with great knives and scissors, and threatened a painful operation, or even to cut off the genital organs, may often be found useful, and may effect a radical cure. The actual carrying out of small operations is also sometimes helpful. . . . Cages have even been provided for the genital organs to prevent masturbation, the key being kept by the father. (428)[5]

The lengthy description above suggests that Hoffmann's portrayal of the scissor-man was rooted in the actual medical practices of nineteenth-century Germany, and not merely the nightmarish fears of an imaginative child. The threat of castration was grounded in the practices of "black pedagogy," where a paternal authority, either the older physician or the father, takes up the position as overseer of the child's body. Patriarchal power is both literal and symbolically signified as the father holds "the key" to the child's caged sexuality, preventing him or her from engaging in self-pleasure.

Just as Shock-headed Peter violated the taboo against filth, Conrad commits a forbidden act when he engages in pseudo-masturbation by sucking his thumbs. According to Foucault in *The History of Sexuality*, the taboos surrounding the masturbating child emerged in the eighteenth century alongside the "pedagogization of children's sexuality" (104): "Educators and doctors combated children's onanism like an epidemic that needed to be eradicated" (106). By pathologizing masturbation, the authoritarian regime, which included "parents, families, educators, doctors, and eventually psychologists," took control over children's bodies (106). Onanism was perceived as self-indulgent, immoral, and pathological, posing a threat to the child's physical and moral constitution, as well as being a "collective danger" in the disintegration of society's moral codes of conduct (106). Hoffmann's text satirizes the "medio-sexual" discourses that aimed to create "a system of rules defining the permitted and the forbidden" in children's behavior (106). As a personification of this punitive authoritarianism, the scissor-man depicts the patriarchal-medical regime as a cold, demonic oppressor.

Conrad's thumb sucking is forbidden, in that it is an act that undermines the masculine ideal of being principled and proper. In its association with masturbation, thumb sucking was considered an act that conveyed weakness and perversity; it is the child engaging in autoerotic pleasure (Freud "Three Essays" 181). The taboo against thumb sucking is further reinforced for its association with a child's dependency on the mother in its association with breastfeeding. As Freud describes thumb sucking, he notes the

1.2. *Struwwelpeter*, The Scissor-Man

connection to the mother's breast: "the child's first and most vital activity, his sucking at his mother's breast, [...] must have familiarized him with this pleasure" (181). Conrad's thumb sucking instantiates his dependence on his mother, such that, when she leaves him on his own, his first action is to suck his thumbs despite her warning. Similar to the other "naughty" children of Hoffmann's storybook, Conrad allows his primitive drives and desires to take over. When viewed as a model of Freudian psychosexual development, Conrad's fixation on thumb sucking suggests his disobedience is directly related to his characterization as a neurotic child. Indeed, one might suggest that the entire catalog of Hoffmann's child protagonists could be pathologized in this manner.

Congruently, Conrad's transgression and punishment also recalls the psychosexual conflict of the Oedipus complex, which premises the son's incestuous attachment to his mother and subsequent rivalry with, and fear of being castrated by, his father (Freud "New Introductory" 86). According to Freud, in the phallic stage, the child fears punishment for his love of his mother: "the danger is the punishment of being castrated, of losing his genital organ," a threat that is reinforced by people "threaten[ing] him often enough with cutting off his penis during the phallic phase at the time of his early masturbation" (86). Here, it is the fantasy of a "jealous and cruel father" who intervenes in the mother-son attachment by threatening the child with

1.3. *Struwwelpeter,* Mother's Interdiction

castration. In this regard, Hoffmann's scissor-man is an uncanny double of the "jealous and cruel father," who carries through with his threat by castrating Conrad's thumbs.

To this reading of castration (anxiety) in the tale of "Little Suck-a-Thumb," there is also the troubling collusion of the mother. She indirectly participates in the violence enacted against her son, anticipating the event and leaving Conrad helpless against the scissor-man (see figure 1.3). One can interpret complicity in her words to Conrad following the mutilation, when she says, "I knew he'd come" (Hoffmann). The mother's actions leave her child vulnerable to the attack; her knowing the likelihood of Conrad's mutilation implies her approval of the abuse. From the perspective of Kleinian psychoanalysis, Conrad's mother personifies traits of the "bad mother" by abandoning her child. According to Melanie Klein, "the child needs to have its mother always with it not only to convince it that she is not dead but that she is not the 'bad,' attacking mother" ("The Psycho-analysis of Children" 249). In Kleinian theory, the male child projects its fears and anxieties onto the mother's body. For a boy, the "bad" mother threatens castration by being imagined as in possession of the phallus (Klein "Infantile" 436). Viewed from this perspective, the scissor-man not only embodies the "bad" father who violently punishes the naughty child, but also the "bad, attacking mother" who threatens her son with castration. Indeed, as depicted in figure 1.3, with her face obscured, Conrad's mother gives her warning, wielding a phallic umbrella in her hand—an ominous foreshadowing of the scissor-wielding tailor who will sever Conrad's thumbs.[6]

The final scene depicts Conrad, now thumbless, standing alone in an empty room, judged by the smugly smiling Janus mask in the archway (figure 1.4). Indeed, as Ben Parrot notes in his criticism of the story, the mask seems to suggest "happiness at the boy's suffering," as if it delights in Conrad's mutilation (333). One way to interpret the sinister smirk of the "all-seeing face" (333) is to align it with the always judging, always admonishing narrator, whose didacticism is aligned with malevolence and sadism. Like the narrator, rather than pity or console Conrad in his sadness, Conrad's own mother also seems cold, emotionally detached, and satisfied that her son has been justly punished.

The display of the bleeding and mutilated child's body is suggestive of sacrifice. Specifically, Conrad's sacrifice or symbolic castration marks his entry into the patriarchal symbolic order. Like circumcision, Conrad's castration of his thumbs is representative of his separation-individuation from the maternal figure. As Kristeva describes, circumcision "illuminates the rite in fundamental fashion [. . .]. [T]he other that circumcision carves out on his very sex, is the other sex, impure, defiled" (100). Conrad has undergone a rite of passage that has left him alone, suffering the melancholic loss of both his thumbs and the comforting security of maternal care.

Of all the stories in Hoffmann's book, the story of "Little Suck-a-Thumb" has garnered the most controversy, and has been omitted from some modern reissues (Parrot 333). Notably, this is the one tale in the entire collection that represents blood, as it drips from Conrad's thumbs (see figure 1.2). Although Conrad does not die like some of the other children in the storybook, by contemporary standards, "Little Suck-a-Thumb" is the most overtly violent and shocking in its gory punishment and sexual subtext. Although gory and gruesome, Hoffmann's illustrations exaggerate violence purposefully, to satirize the pathologizing patriarchal-medical regime that turns a child's innate sexual drives and attachment to his mother into a punishable

1.4. *Struwwelpeter*, Thumbless Conrad

crime. In addition, Hoffmann implicates parental indifference and cruelty as the basis of Conrad's suffering; the collusion of both the sadistic scissor-man and Conrad's mother suggest it is bad parenting, rather than childish indulgence, which is demonized in the story. While potentially frightening in its depiction of violence, this tale, like the others, also demonstrates the ambiguous pleasures of horror. With the scissor-man's exaggerated punishment and comically large scissors, there is a quality of what Tatar calls "surreal excess," which often appeals to a child audience (72). Indeed, while Hoffmann's story is framed as a didactic lesson not to indulge in pleasurable pastimes, the elaboration of Conrad's vice and the gory consequences are subversively satisfying to a child's sadistic joy of seeing the other punished. At the very least, the surreal imagery of Hoffmann's cartoon-like illustrations presents a degree of detachment from a child's everyday life.

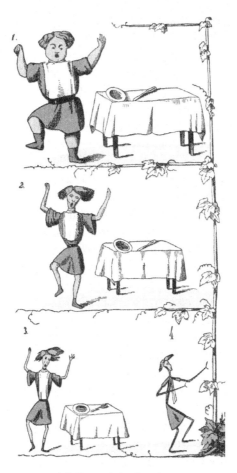

1.5. *Struwwelpeter,* Augustus

   Like Conrad, the child protagonist Augustus demonstrates a troublesome disobedience that is met with parental neglect and indifference. In
the story, Augustus, once a healthy eater, decides that he no longer wants
to eat his soup. The narrator's voice leads the reader to view Augustus's behavior as "naughty" and a "sin" when he refuses to eat. Little reason is given
to Augustus's self-starvation other than that he views the soup as "nasty."
Every day, Augustus refuses to eat the soup, until on the fifth day, he dies
of starvation (see figure 1.5). This tale, like the others, punishes the child
protagonist for his dissent against authority. Like "Shock-headed Peter," and
"Little Suck-a-Thumb," Augustus enacts his rebellion through bodily resistance: in this case, a hunger strike. Through his willful display of protest,

Augustus engages in the self-destruction of his own body as he chooses to waste away rather than eat what is given to him. However, rather than view Augustus in the way that the narrator insists, as a "naughty," selfish, self-indulgent boy, my reading emphasizes Augustus as yet another rebellious child, subversively pursuing self-assertion. One way to view Augustus's self-inflicted hunger is through the lens of male anorexia, which like its female counterpart, embodies dissatisfaction with authoritarian social controls by engaging in symptomatic behavior: namely, a willful act of self-starvation.

In studies of eating disorders, theorists like Susie Orbach and Hilde Bruch understand anorexic behavior to be a highly symbolic act of protest against societal expectations and a means of self-assertion. As Susie Orbach identifies in *Hunger Strike*, eating disorders "contain within them protest, accommodation, despair: an attempt to engage as well as an attempt to reject exclusion" (vii). Although Orbach and Bruch focus primarily on female anorexics, one can situate the male child of Hoffmann's tale in relation to this sense of powerlessness and the ineffectuality of the marginalized subject constrained by patriarchal norms. Indeed, Orbach goes on to identify the exclusive arena of men's sociopolitical power as the source of the anorexic's bodily protest, where eating disorders are a "powerful signal of distress expressing women's experience of patriarchal society" (vii). Like the female anorexic, Augustus's anorexia can be viewed as an act of protest against authoritarian power, which attempts to control and constrain the child's body—in this case, by continually ignoring Augustus's desire for something more, for something different. Indeed, like the female anorexic who is silenced and excluded from participating as an active subject within patriarchal culture, the child protagonists of Hoffmann's narrative react in ways that are symptomatic of their resistance against authority.

As a form of protest, anorexic behavior is not only an expression of anger and despair against oppression, but also a subversive means to assert one's self and regain power. In *The Golden Cage*, Hilde Bruch identifies anorexia as a means for a child to gain power against his or her parents and reject conformity. For Bruch, "excessive conformity on the part of the child, always fitting in, always doing what is expected" comes at the price of the child's autonomy (89). If the child realizes the "deficiencies" of conformity and desires self-assertion, extreme weight loss may become a means through which the child can reclaim a sense of self: "the weight loss accomplishes much: the parents are drawn back into being protective, not demanding, toward the child who for the first time experiences that she has power and is in control" (89). Through self-starvation, the anorexic child asserts a sense of self that has, until this point, been suppressed. According to Bruch, parental despotism, in particular, excessive control of the child's life and decision making, is instrumental in the development of an eating disorder. When a child is "deprived by her parents of the right to live her own life" and when parents "direct the child in every respect" the results can mean tragic, even mortal, consequences for the child (37). According to Bruch, overbearing parents who control and constrain their child's self-expression and who place unrealistic expectations onto their child are identified as the source of the child's symptomatic self-destruction (37). Constrained in this way, the child takes control of its body by refusing to eat. Through its body, the child expresses its unhappiness and conflict with authority by engaging in self-starvation. Through Bruch's connection between ineffective parenting and childhood eating disorders, one can identify the source of Augustus's conflict to be not the dissatisfactory soup, but rather his dissatisfactory parents, who refuse to acknowledge his desire and need for autonomy.

As an example of abjection, the anorexic's body demonstrates the subject's attempt to create boundaries and establish a sense of identity. Disgust for food, such as that which Kristeva describes in *The Powers of Horror*, functions as a formation of identity by establishing boundaries of the self:

> *nausea* makes me balk at that milk cream, separates me from the mother and father who proffer it. "I" want none of that element . . . "I" do not want to listen, "I" do not assimilate it, "I" expel it. But since food is not an "other" for "me," who am only in their desire, I expel *myself*, I spit *myself* out, I abject *myself* within the same motion through which "I" claim to establish *myself*. (3)

In a similar way, Augustus's assertion that the soup is "nasty" and his refusal to eat what is given to him demonstrates an attempt to shore up his identity against the parental, authoritarian forces that tell him what to do. He no longer wants to eat and drink "as he was told" (Hoffmann). In this way, Augustus's disgust demonstrates more than his wastefulness or finicky appetite; rather, through starvation, Augustus asserts his autonomy from domineering social structures.

Like Shock-headed Peter's willful display of his unkempt hair and dirty fingernails and Conrad's disobedient act of sucking his thumbs, Augustus also communicates his dissent through his body. By using his body to signify a message of unhappiness and conflict with authority, Hoffmann's tale presents a counterdiscourse of rebellion, albeit a passive, self-destructive form of resistance. In Metcalf's reading of Hoffmann's tales, she identifies a "spirit of revolt" that exists as a subtext against the book's overt didacticism. Metcalf identifies characters like Augustus, who "model[s] the possibility of resistance," as an example of the text's appeal as a subversive source of "subliminal enjoyment" that children "derived from its presentation" (212). Taken further, I would suggest that the child characters of Hoffmann's stories do more than demonstrate a subversive resistance against authority: they indict these authoritarian figures of abuse and neglect. As evidenced in the illustrations of Augustus that represent his rapid decline in health from plump and robust to a stick figure, Hoffmann not only creates a comic exaggeration of Augustus's emaciation, but also a subversive challenge to the dictates of an oppressive authoritarian culture.

Over one hundred and sixty years have passed since Hoffmann published his collection of children's tales. In this time, *Struwwelpeter* has remained a source of controversy, sparking debate among parents, educators, and academics regarding its disturbing depictions of violence against children. Often the subject of scholarly conferences and collections, including a special issue of *The Lion and the Unicorn* in 1996, in recent years Hoffmann's tales have emerged as the site of modern parodies and adapations. Notably, when contemporary authors adapt Hoffmann's work, consideration of the intended audience is paramount. References to the book range from Harold Begbie's *The Political Struwwelpeter* (2010) to episodes of *Family Guy* and *The Office*, and include a junk opera, "Shock-headed Peter" performed by the Tiger Lilies (1998), and David Kaplan's short film *Little Suck-a-Thumb* (1992). Often, these modern adaptations of *Struwwelpeter* capture some of the original satirical elements to appeal to adult audiences. Newly illustrated versions have been released by Bob Staake (2005), Sanya Glisic (2010), Sarita Vendetta (1999), and a German-language rerelease by Fil Atak (2009). When intended for children, the disturbing violence of Hoffmann's original illustrations is subdued by twenty-first-century illustrators in highly stylized and whimsical drawings, such as in Staake's or Fil Atak's versons. Other versions, such as Vendetta's, come with an explicit warning: "this children's book is not for children!" Indeed, there is a significant shift in modern versions to address the appropriate audience of Hoffmann's tales as adult or mature readers, those who, purportedly, can view the text with detachment and understand its intended humor.

While contemporary audiences are often shocked by the violence and sadistic didacticism of *Struwwelpeter*, this perception reveals as much, if not more, about culture today as it does about nineteenth-century German society. Contemporary children's literature reflects our modern-day sensibilities, rejecting graphically violent depictions of corporeal punishment and the overt didacticism of nineteenth-century texts. Heightened concern about age-appropriate subject matter and the effects of media violence on children have added to *Struwwelpeter's* controversial inclusion in the children's literary canon. As critics like Metcalf, Chalou, and Zipes attest, contemporary reading audiences often focus more on the horror than the humor of the text, failing to percieve the historical context of Hoffmann's comical rebellion as a satire of violent pedagogy.

Whether considered a source of horror, humor, or morbid fascination, Hoffmann's tales have remained a part of popular culture, occupying an ambiguous position as both a beloved classic of children's literature and a monument to the violent pedagogical practices of times past. Hoffmann's tales function satirically and subversively, as a source of both pleasure and fright. As an abject text, the tales of *Struwwelpeter* depict frightful violence, yet do so purposefully. By depicting the conflicts and anxieties between authoritarian figures and willful children, Hoffmann not only satirizes the rigid authoritarianism of nineteenth-century culture through depictions of exaggerated violence and frightful figures like the scissor-man, but also provides a subversive vision of willful disobedience as depicted by unruly child protagonists. During this time in the nineteenth century, German children experienced the strict discipline of authoritarian figures, including parents (both mother and father), doctors, and later psychologists, as well as the social and legislative powers of their country. These authorities attempted to control the child through corporeal punishment and through didactic instruction. As a piece of children's literature, *Struwwelpeter* humorously satirizes this rigid didacticism through depictions of exaggerated violence and farcical, over-the-top punishments. Yet beyond the humor of the text, Hoffmann's use of body horror, in his depictions of mutilated, malformed, and abject bodies of children, reveals a culture constrained by conformity and discipline and holds it up to derision.

As a monument of violent pedagogy, *Struwwelpeter* reveals more than just the prescribed values of conformity and obedience; when deconstructed, one can see the contradictions of a culture that punishes and pathologizes the unruly child as a scapegoat for its own transgressions. By punishing and repudiating abject children, Peter, Conrad, and Augustus among others, who attempt to assert autonomy through self-expression, Hoffmann's text reveals how it is not the children, but rather the mechanisms of power that are revealed as the truly "monstrous" creation of pedagogical practices. To punish children who embody creativity, pleasure seeking, and liberated self-expression, Hoffmann indirectly indicts authoritarian culture as the real source of horror.

NOTES

1. Michelle H. Martin discusses the racial ideology implicit in Hoffmann's "The Story of the Inky Boys," wherein she argues that the "explicitly anti-racist" message of punishing the boys for teasing "Black-a-moor" for his racial difference is "off-set by the text's implicit racism that erases Black-a-Moor's subjectivity and humanness" (152).

2. The medical-patriarchal system developed in relation to modern social organization. According to Jeroen Jansz, in the nineteenth century, there was a "dramatic expansion of attempts to monitor and control the populace." In Germany, medicalized discipline intensified in response to a growing social intolerance of "deviant" behavior. As Jansz argues, the "institutionalization" of children at this time corresponded with "modern social organization," which sought to "re-educat[e]" deviant children in the dictates of the dominant social order (24–26).

3. Children's literature has provided a powerful vehicle through which patriarchal values have been transmitted; in regards to conventions of sexuality and gender, children's literature has been used to "condition [children] to assume and accept arbitrary sex roles" (Zipes *Don't Bet on the Prince* 3). For male children, which Hoffmann's text seems to implicitly address, hegemonic masculinity is associated with traits of power, authority, conformity, and self-control. Conflict arises when Hoffmann's disobedient boys do not conform to hegemonic masculinity, such as when they disobey their fathers' authority and commit willful displays of nonconformity and self-indulgence.

4. Joachim J. Savelsberg discusses the ideological formation of Hoffmann's text in relation to the "spread of German nationalism" in the first half of the nineteenth century. Savelsberg suggests a connection between the "civilizing control messages of *Struwwelpeter*" and the emerging social organization of Germany as a modern bourgeois society (191).

5. Although Bloch is describing disciplinary practices of the early twentieth century, sixty years after Hoffmann first published the *Struwwelpeter*, such practices were seen in Germany as early as the eighteenth century. See Alice Miller, *For Your Own Good* for more information about the methods of "black pedagogy."

6. In *Family Guy*, "Little Suck-a-Thumb" is reimagined as a German bedtime story where it is the mother who cuts off her son's thumbs.

WORKS CITED

Begbie, Harold. *The Political Struwwelpeter*. Charleston, NC: Nabu P, 2010. Print.

Blackmore, Susan. *The Meme Machine*. Oxford: Oxford UP, 1999. Print.

Bloch, Iwan. *The Sexual Life of Our Times in Its Relation to Modern Civilization*. London: Rebman, 1909. Print.

Bruch, Hilde. *The Golden Cage: The Enigma of Anorexia Nervosa*. Cambridge MA: Harvard UP, 2001. Print.

"Business Guy." *Family Guy*. Television, 30 minutes. Season 8: Episode 9. FOX.

Chalou, Barbara Smith. *Struwwelpeter: Humor or Horror?* Lanham, MD: Lexington, 2007. Print.

Creed, Barbara. *The Monstrous-Feminine: Film, Feminism, Psychoanalysis*. New York: Routledge, 1993. Print.

Douglas, Mary. *Purity and Danger: An Analysis of Concept of Pollution and Taboo*. New York: 1966. Print.

Fil, Atak. *Der Struwwelpeter*. Zurich: Kein & Aber, 2009. Print.

Foucault, Michel. *The History of Sexuality*. Vol. 1. Translated by Robert Hurley. New York: Vintage, 1990. Print.

Freeman, Thomas. "Heinrich Hoffmann's *Struwwelpeter*: An Inquiry into the Effects of Violence in Children's Literature." *Journal of Popular Culture* 10.4 (1977): 808–20. *EBSCOhost*. Web. 3 July 2013.

Freud, Sigmund. "New Introductory Lectures on Psycho-Analysis" (1933). Translated by James Strachey. *The Standard Edition of the Complete Psychological Works of Sigmund Freud*. Vol. XXII (1932–1936): New Introductory Lectures on Psycho-Analysis and Other Works, 1–182. *PEP Web Archive*. Web. 3 July 2013.

——. "Three Essays Contributions to the Sexual Theory" (1905). Translated by James Strachey. *The Standard Edition of the Complete Psychological Works of Sigmund Freud*. Vol. VII (1901–1905): A Case of Hysteria. 123–46. *PEP Web Archive*. Web. 3 July 2013.

——. "Totem and Taboo: Some Points of Agreement between the Mental Lives of Savages and Neurotics" (1913). Translated by James Strachey. *The Standard Edition of the Complete Psychological Works of Sigmund Freud*. Vol. XIII (1913–1914): Totem and Taboo and Other Works, vii–162. *PEP Web Archive*. Web. 3 July 2013.

——. "The Uncanny." (1919). Translated by James Strachey. *The Standard Edition of the Complete Psychological Works of Sigmund Freud*. Vol. XVII (1917–1919): An Infantile Neurosis and Other Works, 217–56. *PEP Web Archive*. Web. 3 July 2013.

Glisic, Sanya. *Struwwelpeter*. Chicago: Spudnik P, 2011. Print.

Hoffmann, Dr. Heinrich. *Struwwelpeter: Merry Tales and Funny Pictures*. New York: Frederick Warne & Co. The Project Gutenberg EBook, 2004. Web. 3 July 2013.

Hurley, Kelly. *The Gothic Body: Sexuality, Materialism, and Degeneration at the Fin de Siècle*. Cambridge: Cambridge UP, 1996. Print.

Hürlimann, Bettina. *Three Centuries of Children's Books in Europe*. London: Oxford UP, 1967. Print.

Jansz, Jeroen, ed. "Psychology and Society: An Overview." *A Social History of Psychology*. Edited by Peter van Drunen and Jeroen Jansz. Oxford: Wiley-Blackwell, 2003. Print.

Kaplan, David. *Little Suck-a-Thumb*. Film. Malaprop Productions, 2009. Print.

Klein, Melanie. "Infantile Anxiety-Situations Reflected in a Work of Art and in the Creative Impulses." *International Journal of Psycho-Analysis* 10 (1929): 436–43. *PEP Web Archive*. Web. 3 July 2013.

———. "The Psycho-Analysis of Children." *International Psycho-Analytical Library* 22 (1939): 1–379. *PEP Web Archive*. 3 July 2013.

Kristeva, Julia. *Powers of Horror: An Essay on Abjection*. Translated by L. S. Roudiez. New York: Columbia UP, 1982. Print.

Martin, Michelle H. "'Hey, Who's the Kid with the Green Umbrella?': Re-evaluating the Black-a-Moor and Little Black Sambo." *The Lion and the Unicorn* 22.2 (1998): 147–62. *EBSCOhost*. Web. 3 July 2013.

Metcalf, Eva-Maria. "Civilizing Manners and Mocking Morality: Dr. Heinrich Hoffmann's *Struwwelpeter*." *The Lion and the Unicorn* 20.2 (1996): 201–16. *EBSCOhost*. Web. 3 July 2013.

Miller, Alice. *For Your Own Good: Hidden Cruelty in Child-Rearing and the Roots of Violence*. Translated by Hildegarde Hannum and Hunter Hannum. New York: Farrar, Straus and Giroux, 2002. *EBSCOhost*. Web. 3 July 2013.

Orbach, Susie. *Hunger Strike: The Anorectic's Struggle as a Metaphor for Our Age* (1986). London: Karnac, 2005. Print.

Parrot, Ben. "Aesthetic Tension: The Text-Image Relationship in Heinrich Hoffmann's *Struwwelpeter*." *Monatshefe* 102.3 (2010): 326–39. *EBSCOhost*. Web. 3 July 2013.

Rollin, Lucy. "Uncanny Mickey Mouse and His Domestication." *Psychoanalysis Responses to Children's Literature*. Edited by Lucy Rollin and Mark I. West. Jefferson, NC: McFarland & Co., 1999. 31–44. Print.

Savelsberg, Joachim J. "*Struwwelpeter* at One Hundred and Fifty: Norms, Control and Discipline in the Civilizing Process." *The Lion and the Unicorn* 20.2 (1996): 181–200. *EBSCOhost*. Web. 3 July 2013.

Staake, Bob. *Struwwelpeter and Other Disturbing Yet Cautionary Tales*. Seattle, WA: Fantagraphics, 2006. Print.

"Take Your Daughter to Work Day." *The Office*. Television: Mindy Kaling. 30 minutes, NBC. 16 March 2006.

Tatar, Maria. "'Violent Delights' in Children's Literature." *Why We Watch: The Attractions of Violent Entertainment*. Edited by Jeffrey Goldstein. New York: Oxford UP, 1998. Print.

Tiger Lilies. *Shock-headed Peter*. Audio recording. *NVC Arts/Warner Classics*. 1998.

Vendetta, Sarita (Illustrator). *Struwwelpeter: Fearful Stories and Vile Pictures to Instruct Good Little Folks*. Port Townsend, WA: Feral House, 1999. Print.

Wesseling, Elizabeth. "Visual Narrativity in the Picture Book: Heinrich Hoffmann's *Der Struwwelpeter*." *Children's Literature in Education: An International Quarterly* 35.4 (2004): 319–46. *EBSCOhost*. Web. 3 July 2013.

Zipes, Jack. "The Perverse Delight of Shock-headed Peter." *Theater* 30.2 (2000): 129–43. *EBSCOhost*. Web. 3 July 2013.

———. "*Struwwelpeter* and Classical Children's Literature." *The Lion and the Unicorn* 20.2 (1996): v–vi. *EBSCOhost*. Web. 3 July 2013.

———. *Sticks and Stones: The Troublesome Success of Children's Literature from Slovenly Peter to Harry Potter*. New York: Routledge, 2001. Print.

———. *Don't Bet on the Prince*. New York: Routledge, 1987. Print.

Zornado, Joseph. *Inventing the Child: Culture, Ideology, and the Story of Childhood*. New York: Garland, 2001. Print.

"A Wonderful Horrid Thing"

Edward Gorey, Charles Dickens, and Drawing the Horror out of Childhood Death

A. ROBIN HOFFMAN

IN 1992, STEPHEN SCHIFF FAMOUSLY OPENED A *NEW YORKER* PROFILE BY observing that "Many of Edward Gorey's most fervent fans think he's (a) English and (b) dead" (136). Schiff's introduction succinctly conveys how aspects of Gorey's visual and verbal style unite with subject matter to produce books that belie their American, mid-twentieth-century origins. Many people have observed that his work alludes to or invokes nineteenth-century tropes and themes, leading Mark Rusch to characterize Gorey's world as a "grotesquely constructed interpretation of Victorian England" (445). Gorey himself confirms this impression: in interviews conducted over several decades, his references to nineteenth-century novels and engravings are both persistent and enthusiastic, with Charles Dickens singled out for particular praise.[1] The influence of Dickens and his illustrators sometimes manifests directly in Gorey's work as borrowed motifs and compositions.[2] But equally significant points of divergence from his models allow Gorey to highlight Victorian idiosyncrasies still relevant to modern audiences. This is especially true with respect to the recurring scenes of childhood death in both oeuvres, a theme Dick Cavett described to Gorey as "the beset-upon child, the murdered child, the abused child" (Gorey "Cavett" 54). The shift from sentimentality to ghoulishness is most clearly illuminated by two books that were produced early in Gorey's nearly fifty-year career, but remain among his most popular productions. *The Hapless Child* (1961), which biographer Alexander Theroux called "the seminal Gorey tale" (3), recounts the tragic history of Charlotte Sophia, who expires unrecognized in her long-lost father's arms. *The Gashlycrumb Tinies* (1963) is a widely read parody of abecedarian primers full of sinister scenes. Gothic modes have more recently become "mainstream" in children's media, but Gorey has long been presenting young audiences with dire threats to their fictional peers.[3] By deftly managing a dialogue between past and present modes of representation and between textual and visual traditions, Gorey introduces an anesthetizing historical distance that (literally) draws the horror out of the trope of Victorian childhood death.

The Tinies and Charlotte Sophia join foregone legions of dying fictional children in Gorey's perversion of Victorian literary tradition. In *Death Sentences*, Garrett Stewart memorably observed that "characters die more often, more slowly, and more vocally in the Victorian age than ever before or since," and children occupied a great number of those deathbeds (8). Since Charles Dickens contributed so much to the death count, he is a natural lightning rod for discussions of childhood death in nineteenth-century settings. As Peter Coveney has pointed out, the frequency with which later and lesser voices produced variations on the theme of child morbidity has led to his name being used as an umbrella for this literary trope and its nineteenth-century ubiquity (161). Gorey himself once recalled reading as a child "a wonderful horrid thing called *Child Stories from Dickens*. It was all the deaths" ("The Connection" 224).[4] Both he and Dickens recognized that "the child makes the ideal victim in a genre that is absolutely dependent on masses of qualified victims" (Büssing xvi). For the latter, that genre was sentimental fiction. For Gorey, this genre is Victorian melodrama mixed with violence, and with enough humor to qualify it as black comedy. Thus, Gorey's nominally sadistic treatment of childhood death can be understood as a precursor to the modern trend in "comic Gothic texts for young readers" (Cross 71).[5]

Although the capacity for satirizing childhood death appeared among the Victorians, prompting Oscar Wilde's notoriously glib reaction to Little Nell's death in *The Old Curiosity Shop*,[6] it has also tended to coalesce around more overtly didactic narratives for children: Heinrich Hoffmann's *Struwwelpeter* (translated into English in the 1840s), Harry Graham's *Ruthless Rhymes for Heartless Homes* (1899), and Hilaire Belloc's *Cautionary Tales for Children* (1907). Gorey was certainly familiar with such satirical forms, since he had designed illustrations for a reissue of *Cautionary Tales* (published posthumously in 2002). Similarly, *The Gashlycrumb Tinies* features twenty-six child deaths in thirteen rhymed couplets, starting with "A is for Amy who fell down the stairs" and proceeding to "Z is for Zillah who drank too much gin" without pausing for remorse. The abecedarian frame contrasts ludicrously with the litany of lives cut short. Gorey also appears to quote Hoffmann's portrayal of Pauline in *Struwwelpeter*, who plays disastrously with matches, in his drawing of "R is for Rhoda consumed by a fire." As George Bodmer has pointed out, *The Gashlycrumb Tinies* is clearly a descendant of these texts; he goes on to assert that "while Gorey is using the appearance of children's books he is actually satirizing the genre" (115). Indeed, Gorey's books have prompted hand-wringing over incongruities between formal audience cues and confrontational content. Gorey himself complained to his sometime-collaborator Peter Neumeyer that "at least half of my books have been written, albeit vaguely, for children" but he struggled to find publishers who would market "those things for children that [. . .] turn out to be totally unsuitable for children according to everyone else" (qtd. in Neumeyer 89, 140). However, Kevin Shortsleeve has convincingly argued that Gorey's works may be considered suitable for children if we acknowledge the historical context of such judgment calls—they reflect instability in age-based audience distinctions (30).[7] Although the late Victorians worked to establish and develop children's literature as distinct from that produced for adults, an effort predicated upon increasing recognition of a "special" status for childhood, Jarlath Killeen and others have demonstrated that this cultural shift did not necessarily improve conditions for children, either in reality or in sensational fiction.[8] This incongruity was succinctly noted by John Leech in a cartoon that appeared in *Punch* in 1849 depicting "Useful Sunday Literature for the Masses—or, Murder Made Familiar."[9] Dickens's books were vulnerable to this criticism. Like contemporary broadsheets, these books were undoubtedly enjoyed by families. But they also included precisely the sort of elements—violence, crime, death, and filth—that were targeted by the eponymous John Bowdler. These same ingredients for horror have since been used to declare Gorey unsuitable for child readers (Stallcup 125). But rather than accept such Romantic assumptions about child audiences and horror, I argue that Gorey has resurrected mid-nineteenth-century aesthetics for his readers.[10]

As a result, Gorey himself has sometimes been pegged as the "child-hater" figure that frequently appears in comic gothic texts for young readers, from the abusive adults populating many of Roald Dahl's novels (which began to appear contemporaneously with Gorey's) to the villains of Lemony Snicket's *A Series of Unfortunate Events* (Cross 59–61). As he admitted to Robert Dahlin, "I've been murdering children in books for years" (Gorey "Conversations" 40). But Gorey's cool detachment contrasts sharply with the attitude of the self-described child-murderer with whom he has often been compared. While writing the death of Little Nell, Charles Dickens lamented in a letter to William Macready that "I am slowly murdering that poor child, and grow wretched over it. It wrings my heart" (180). Clearly, context separates Gorey from Dickens even as a Romantic veneer of precious vulnerability links many of their abused child characters, particularly those with claims to the upper classes. Gorey's work is framed by a secularized American society wherein parents sought child-rearing advice from empirical research and experts like Dr. Spock rather than comfort from religious figures and the promise of spiritual rewards for their children's suffering or their own bereavement.[11] In *Anxious Parents: A History of Modern Child-rearing in America*, Peter Stearns has most thoroughly documented how improvements in health care achieved through the first part of the twentieth century led American adults to invest even more heavily in their fewer offspring, both emotionally and economically, and to feel more responsibility for shaping a healthy and happy childhood in the midst of unprecedented prosperity after World War II—with corresponding spikes in parental anxiety. Beyond the feelings of revulsion or disgust that are conventionally associated with horror media (Botting 124), Tony Magistrale and Michael Morrison cogently point out that American horror as a genre can be best understood as "contemporary social satire that reveals—and often critiques—the collective cultural fears and personal anxieties of everyday life" (3). In order to unpack Gorey's satire, I will first dissect the iconology and materiality of Gorey's book designs, so as to map them within a history of printing technology and book illustration. After identifying important similarities to mid-nineteenth-century illustrated serial novels, I can then show how Gorey's representations of dying children both depend upon and are distinguished from those in Dickens's novels featuring child characters. Significantly, Dickens allotted only the occasional postmortem portrayal to his illustrators, and always reserved the actual moment of death for verbal description. Gorey, however, relies heavily on text-image relationships to produce modern representations of childhood death that subvert their own Victorian modes of expression and reflect disillusionment about the ideals of child protectionism popularized in America by the early 1960s.

Although he is perhaps better known for his visual stamp than his verbal eloquence, Gorey's ability to work as both writer and illustrator has allowed him to take intertextual liberties within the small weird books that constitute his best-known representations of childhood death. His images cooperate with text and design to produce ironic versions of the sentimental scenes that dominate popular visions of Victorian literature. In first glances at *The Hapless Child* or *The Gashlycrumb Tinies*, we appear to be flipping through an album of captioned images. Unlike, for instance, Gorey's *L'Heure Bleu* (1975) with its acrobatic text placement and blue highlights, or the shifting page layouts of his *The Iron Tonic* (1969) and *The Awdrey-Gore Legacy* (1972), these books are composed of a line of text placed just beneath a black-and-white illustration, with substantial margins on all sides. However, closer inspection reveals a more sophisticated text-image relationship that incorporates the materiality of the book as a whole. In most obvious contrast to those of Dickens, Gorey's representations of dying children are narrated through iconotexts—helpfully defined by Kristin Hallberg as "an inseparable entity of word and image, which cooperate to convey a message" (qtd. in Nikolajeva and Scott 6)—that depend on a greater proportion of visual information.[12] However, I refrain from saying that Gorey's representations are more "visual" or "pictorial" than Dickens's because this fallacious distinction obscures Gorey's holistic approach to book design. Similarly, I here avoid the popular term "picture book" because it shifts emphasis to the visual aspects rather than insisting upon iconotextual unity and interpenetration.[13]

The widespread confusion about Gorey's own biography was fostered primarily by the drawing style and production methods utilized in *The Hapless Child* and *The Gashlycrumb Tinies*, which unite to evoke pre-photomechanical reproductive technology. They are some of his most thorough attempts to mimic the visual effects produced by outdated printing technology and its constraints, including hand-lettering, small size, wide margins, and other framing elements.[14] He often confirmed his viewers' impression of looking at older images, professing, "Mostly what it is, is nineteenth-century wood and steel engraved illustration" (Gorey "Cavett" 61). Perhaps the most striking and overt means by which Gorey "dates" his work to this era is through the use of a black-and-white color scheme. Illustrated books were routinely printed in black and white through the middle of the nineteenth century while the mechanical details of color printing were explored, perfected, and brought within the bounds of economy. Like his predecessors, Gorey attributed some of his resistance to color to simple production costs as dictated by Doubleday publishing: "if nobody knew who you were ... they weren't going to publish books in color" (Wilkin "Mr Earbrass" 36). While it is still true that colored printing is more expensive than monochrome, his behavior elsewhere belies this kowtowing to publishers. In one instance, Gorey personally hand watercolored the tutus on the covers of eleven hundred copies of *The Lavender Leotard* (1973) "because the printer couldn't manage the exact shade of the real skirt belonging to the New York

City Ballet" (Hodenfield 2). Clearly he would rather expend great personal effort than allow technical difficulties to countermand his artistic choices, and dissimulation lurks in his bottom-line explanation.

Beyond the simple use of black and white, Gorey cultivates a resemblance to engravings by means of exhaustive cross-hatching. He is notorious for lavishing hours upon elaborate wallpaper designs, for example, although his earlier books tend to be more intricate than those that follow. The opening scene of *The Hapless Child*, which features two intricate wallpaper designs as well as a floral carpet, drapery folds, and wood grain on both panelling and a bookshelf, is representative of this signature style element. It also prompted him to temporarily stop work on the book because he "couldn't face the notion of drawing any more wallpaper" (Gorey qtd. in Neumeyer 86). In fact, it is a rarity to find so-called white space on the page; in a later scene in the life of Charlotte Sophia, only her cheeks and the candle flame are free from ink, while even the bare wall behind her has been painstakingly inked into shadow. A hallmark of Gorey's aesthetic is self-evident labor that contrasts sharply with the constraints of his predecessors. When producing the often-shadowy illustrations for the original serial publication of *Oliver Twist* (1837–1839), George Cruikshank had no choice but to scratch a vast collection of marks onto a plate. These were carefully etched so that they would not collapse together and print as an inky pool. Browne exploited a mechanical process in the "dark plates" of *Bleak House* (1851–1853), but the limitations were similar. The preponderance of marks, and their formal character, is also reminiscent of wood-engravings like those that were part of the original serial publication of *The Old Curiosity Shop* (1840–1841, under the title *Master Humphrey's Clock*).[15] The designers' lines, even when interpreted by proficient engravers like Ebenezer Landells or the Dalziel brothers, necessarily bent to the limitations of the engravers' tools.[16] They are quite distinct from the more fluid lines permitted by etching, which are in turn more constrained than the lines and washes possible with lithography, which came into wide popular use after 1900. Gorey's detailed lines, although reproduced by modern offset processes, conspicuously imitate those that were made possible by technological innovations in engraving around the turn of the previous century.

It is doubtful that Gorey would have the time or patience to practice "cross-hatching as a way of life" if he did not work on such a small scale (C. Stevens 131). In the early 1990s he confirmed his preference for small size to Clifford Ross, and also noted that he was resistant to the usual practice of reproducing work "smaller than the original for better effect" (Gorey qtd. in

Ross 29). This preference for drawing to the size of reproduction, which is redolent of the printmaker's mentality, is so strong that he occasionally even reversed convention by having his work enlarged in order to avoid working on more than six linear inches (Gorey "Mind's Eye" 89). He composes his images on the scale of book illustrations rather than posters or even folio albums. This is a particularly important consideration when attempting to locate Gorey's work in a technological history. He has never claimed, as he has with his infrequent use of color, that economic and technical pressures restrained him. The small size that characterizes his books—very much in line with limits imposed on Victorian illustrators by boxwood and/or expensive copper and steel plates—seems to be a design choice rather than a compulsion. The size of the illustrations is consistent within each book, and among the books no illustration measures more than four inches by five. It should be noted, however, that some of his books now appear only, or most accessibly, in a larger anthologized form: the *Amphigorey* (1972); *Amphigorey, Too* (1975); and *Amphigorey, Also* (1983) collections. These coffee-table-sized books reproduce at least two pages from the books' first editions per anthology page so that more illustrations with text can be seen in one spread. The pictures are slightly reduced in size and a great deal of white space disappears in the process: although the generous margins are mostly preserved, the blank versos of each illustrated page are gone. In an interview, Gorey admitted that "he doesn't particularly like the *Amphigorey* anthologies because 'the originals were carefully designed as small books'" (Dyer 121).[17] This economizing move dramatically distorts the original designs and elides one of the ways that Gorey frames his narratives about dying children with nineteenth-century ideas about childhood.

Some of the (apparently) anachronistic features of Gorey's book design conveniently duplicate as markers for a child audience. For instance, I have noted that their small scale recalls a time when the cost of producing illustrations tended to limit their size. But as Jackie Stallcup has pointed out, this can also signal intended audience, since *The Gashlycrumb Tinies* seems designed for little hands to hold (Stallcup 125). A similar pair of readings can be applied to Gorey's use of hand-lettering. Because engravings and etchings could not be printed at the same time as letterpress, hand-lettered titles like the often-ironic ones that captioned the illustrations for *Dombey and Son* (1846–1848) and *Bleak House* were inscribed directly on the plate with the image. Gorey obviously had no such restrictions, but *The Hapless Child* is lettered differently from *The Gashlycrumb Tinies*, and still another script appears in other works like *The Pious Infant* (1966). In today's age of digital and offset reproductive processes, permitting the free combination of letterpress with images, the rarity of hand-lettering suggests antiquity. However, children's books are one area of publishing where hand-lettering has conspicuously persisted to the present day.[18] Birnbaum and Forrester also point out that *The Gashlycrumb Tinies* is unpaginated, as children's books often are, because they can be consumed in one sitting and do not need to be indexed ("Composite Art"). However, the illustrated pages of serial publications like Dickens's novels were also unpaginated because they were routinely printed separately (via intaglio methods) and tucked into the wrappers rather than interleaved with the letterpress. These pages usually had blank reverses and, thanks as well to the "titles" included below the image, could be detached from the text entirely—a stroll through London's Portobello Market today reveals the brisk trade in Victorian book illustrations that have been repackaged as wall art. The punctuation, as well as the blank versos, further isolate each image: in *The Hapless Child* each image is accompanied by one full-stop sentence, while *The Gashlycrumb Tinies* has no punctuation at all. Although the rhyming format of the latter does provide some of the cohesion accomplished in the former by a narrative thread, we have a subtle bibliographic joke here. These books strongly resemble a bound collection of engravings sans the serialized text: a Dickens novel without the Dickens, as it were, and as twentieth-century children often experience him. As Patricia Crain has pointed out, children's books, including alphabet books in particular, have long served as "conservators of the low": a site for preserving the cultural past as it is expunged by "middle-class gentility" (75). Gorey here extends that truism by offering less-evolved forms of print culture for still-evolving humans.

Gorey's use of modern printing methods to produce the visual effects of archaic printing technology seems to have been at least occasionally successful; Stephen Schiff concluded that "the drawings have the nostalgic feel of nineteenth-century engravings" (143).[19] And it is this sense of transplantation from the past, rather than purposeful deviation from conventional illustration, which is most illuminating. Sometimes Gorey was forced to find a new commercial pathway in order to bring his projects to completion, but he did so less for the sake of a new form of bookmaking than in the interest of appealing to a specialized market. He once recalled, "Nobody would touch my book proposals. So I said to hell with it . . . and published them myself under my own imprint, the Fantod Press. I did all of the work myself, the drawings, the texts in hand lettering, the layout, the covers. Most were printed in editions of about 200" (Gorey qtd. in Theroux 11). His forays into independent publishing via the Fantod Press, which produced the first edition of *The Pious Infant* in book form,[20] were usually motivated by content rather than format: *The Beastly Baby* (1962) was the Fantod Press's first publication, and some bookstores refused to carry the horrifying tale, which culminates (happily) in the title character's death (Gorey "Cavett" 62). As we now reconsider Gorey's allusions to Charles Dickens's illustrated novels and the nineteenth-century trope of childhood death, we can see how the page layouts and elements of book design interact with twentieth-century American attitudes to render childhood death an object of dark comedy.

As we have already noted, Gorey had the advantage of being both writer and illustrator. Dickens, however, spent a significant portion of his career overcoming his inability to produce visual representations of the scenes and characters that he conceived. He wrote to John Forster that "I don't invent it—really do not—*but see it*, and write it down" (305, emphasis in original). Although they were channeled through verbal forms, Dickens's narrative methods were shaped by earlier graphic satirists like William Hogarth, the eighteenth-century designer of *The Rake's Progress* (ca. 1735) and other hugely successful fine print series. So he was attuned to the same traditions of visual storytelling from which his own future illustrators emerged.[21] Michael Steig has identified a number of illustrations in Dickens novels crammed with significant iconographic details, some of which expanded on the text in the Hogarthian tradition.[22] At the same time, Dickens's highly visual prose was explicitly compared to Hogarth's paintings and satirical engravings, with which he was known to be familiar (Harvey 51). So Dickens did not design the illustrations that accompanied the original publications of his prose as Edward Lear, or his fellow novelist William Thackeray, had done. But thanks to improving reproduction technologies and a compliant sidekick in the young and unformed Hablot Knight Browne,[23] he was nonetheless instrumental in reversing the hierarchy of author and illustrator during the nineteenth century. Despite his well-documented debt to a visual tradition of graphic satire, and the effort he expended overseeing "everything but the actual execution of the illustrations to his works," in the long run Dickens rearranged the playing field rather than leveling it (Cohen 5).[24]

The illustrations that received Dickens's most concentrated attention, and were among the most famous, were often those of child characters. He was exacting in his specifications about the scenes portraying Little Nell, Paul Dombey, and Oliver Twist. However, he consistently reserved the actual moment of childhood deaths for himself (when it was described at all), as with Jo's death in George's Shooting Gallery, or the chapter titled "What the Waves Were Always Saying" that recounts Paul Dombey's death. Nell deserves specific mention here because Dickens was very involved in designing her postmortem portrait, while her actual death occurs within a narrative gap. Illustrators in the nineteenth century were constantly striving to produce images that did more than simply replicate the text, and Dickens's crew was no exception. At work on *The Old Curiosity Shop*, Browne struggled to illustrate the chosen text with images that accurately represented the story "without giving it away" (Cohen 8). This was of particular concern because illustrations would often be enclosed at the beginning of the serial number rather than inserted alongside (or after) the corresponding passage in the text. In a significantly similar fashion, Gorey's illustrations of children typically represent them on the cusp of death: they are explicitly doomed, but as yet physically unharmed. Kate in *The Gashlycrumb Tinies* is a notorious exception to this tendency. Her portrayal with an axe buried in her belly is all the more shocking for its frank representation of a messy death amid other Tinies who are oblivious to an imminent demise, *verbally* detailed. More important, Victorian readers' anxiety about imperiled children hinged much more upon plot than the prospective shock of corporeal damage. Gorey, however, relies on word-image interactions to infuse those images of doomed children with "a sense that something dreadful is just about to happen" in the familiar mode of "traditional horror" (Reynolds 3). His iconotexts shift Dickensian death from sentimentality to horror via two distinguishing characteristics: the explicit evocation of violence and the erasure of a morally redemptive (Christian) context.

In this section, I will focus on the striking contrasts between representations of Little Nell from *The Old Curiosity Shop*, and the horror-infused illustrations featuring her Gorey-designed doppelgangers: Clara in *The Gashlycrumb Tinies* and Charlotte Sophia in *The Hapless Child*. Beyond her demographic resemblance to Little Nell, Charlotte Sophia has perhaps the best claim to comparison with Dickens's children. Charlotte's loss of her high-status birthright is the initial tragedy of *The Hapless Child*, and it reduces her, like Oliver Twist, to the mean circumstances of Dickens's waifs. In the four bedroom scenes associated with these girl characters (figures 2.1–2.4), we can see most clearly how Gorey has reimagined childhood death as a source of horror rather than spiritual inspiration.

Julia Thomas has documented a Victorian fascination with deathbed scenes, among which Little Nell's is a *locus classicus*.[25] But although Gorey clearly draws on a Victorian love of the deathbed for inspiration, he also vehemently rebels against the narrow confines of a literal (or literary) bed.

Instead, his child characters impale themselves, swallow hazardous substances, or succumb to the elements. In *The Hapless Child* Charlotte Sophia is run down by a motorist and dies almost literally in the gutter. The Grim Reaper pays as little heed to sex as setting; in *The Gashlycrumb Tinies*, thirteen boys and thirteen girls (their ominous numbers conveniently falling from an equal division of the letters in the alphabet) perish in an orgy of thesaurus offerings. Allusions to violence are explicit and unrelenting throughout *The Gashlycrumb Tinies*. However, it should be noted that descriptive passages such as "F is for Fanny sucked dry by a leech" and "Y is for Yorick whose head was knocked in" are not accompanied by appropriately grisly illustrations. Only Rhoda, "consumed by a fire," and Kate, "struck by an ax," are actually shown in the process of annihilation, while equally violent deaths, such as those of "Titus, who flew into bits" and "Prue trampled flat in a brawl," occur offstage in the readers' heads. Thus does Gorey simultaneously align himself with Dickens—who accorded the author the right to actually "murder" child characters—and set himself apart from a writer who confined himself to deathbed scenes so pious and prim as to become a cliché. In *The Hapless Child* and *The Gashlycrumb Tinies*, we encounter representations of childhood death that could never be confused with sleep because they wreak such havoc upon the children's bodies. However, this slippage was characteristic of childhood deaths in Victorian literature, as when the bystanders at Nell's deathbed "did not know that she was dead, at first" (559).

The illustration of Nell's deathbed, designed for *The Old Curiosity Shop* by George Cattermole, and that of Clara, who "wasted away" on the third page of *The Gashlycrumb Tinies*, merit close comparison because the latter is clearly an allusion to what was an iconic scene of Victorian childhood death. Even if a modern viewer is unfamiliar with the original Dickens illustration (as most modern readers are[26]), Clara corresponds to "the popular idea of Dickens's children" as described by Coveney, albeit in reinterpreted form (161). While both Nell and Clara recline on their deathbeds (figures 2.1 and 2.3), Nell's face conveys serenity, Clara's a staring grotesqueness that recalls the work of Charles Addams. Furthermore, the former's postmortem portrait is crammed with iconographic significance—an hourglass, an open window, the probably religious book clasped in her hand—that would have allowed readers to deduce her sainted postmortem status even without the text. By contrast, although the wallpaper around her sick bed certainly is elaborate, Clara has no other accoutrements to reward viewers with careful looking. Her surroundings signal neither death nor the hope of an afterlife.

Clara's nonviolent death, marked only by uneasy emphasis on her eyes (and by extension the viewer's), serves to heighten the contrast between the other Tinies' violent ends and their nonviolent Victorian precedents, not least because it occurs so near the beginning of the book. She is almost the only one who conforms to Judith Plotz's generalization about the nineteenth century: "When children die in literature, they are assimilated to fixity, usually perishing in ways that makes them clean, quiet, immobile, and permanent" (3). Gorey's Tinies and Charlotte Sophia are transfixed only by fear, revulsion, or impending death, and are often conspicuously sullied by bodily fluids or other forms of filth along the way.

Gorey's heavily marked and shadowed style of inscription allows him to clearly communicate that these child characters are surrounded by both literal and figurative darkness. This same iconographic message appears in Dickens's novels: Nell's pale white face peers out again and again as Browne exploited this visual trick at Dickens's behest throughout *The Old Curiosity Shop* and later novels (Cohen 136–37, 165).[27] However, Samuel Williams designed one of the most lauded examples of this sentimental representation of childhood since he stepped in to provide the famous illustration of "Nell in Bed" (figure 2.1) for *The Old Curiosity Shop* when Browne was unable to do so. Both contemporary and modern critics have dwelt upon the contrasts initiated in this scene and sustained throughout the novel between the purely innocent Nell and the "mob" who accost her throughout her long journey to another illustrated scene of "Nell in Bed"—her postmortem portrait. J. R. Harvey has pointed out that Dickens adjusted later editions of the text to heighten these contrasts, very likely in response to Thomas Hood's review of the first number: "Look at the Artist's picture of the Child, asleep in her little bed, surrounded, or rather mobbed, by ancient armour and arms, antique furniture, and relics sacred or profane, hideous or grotesque:—it is like an Allegory of the peace and innocence of Childhood in the midst of Violence, Superstition, and all the hateful or hurtful Passions of the world" (Harvey 122–25; Hood 887–88). Accordingly, Williams's design preserves a halo of light around Nell's head while assorted threatening articles lurk in the surrounding shadows, as threatening human figures like Quilp are subsequently wont to do. Dickens's children are forces for good overpowered by the corrupt society that surrounds them.

As in Dickens's novels, in Gorey's illustrated books children's pale, vulnerable faces appear to shine amid their dark, hostile surroundings. Isolated and often physically shrinking from an ominous atmosphere, these characters communicate their experience of horror to the audience, which

2.1. Samuel Williams, "Nell in Bed" from *Master Humphrey's Clock* (later *The Old Curiosity Shop*)

brings the surrounding text under the umbrella of Tzvetan Todorov's classic definition of the genre (33). However, the relationship Gorey constructs between his work and the tradition of illustration associated with Dickens that also features heavily marked backgrounds is one of conspicuously frustrated expectations. Where Browne filled his scenes with emblematic details such as pictures on the walls, derived from the tradition of Hogarthian satire, Gorey has reduced this scene to its central action and actors, cropping and eliminating telling details. Although he lavishes just as many marks upon the scene, he fills the white space with intricate carpet and wallpaper patterns rather than investing it with iconographic messages. Charlotte Sophia's various environments are so sterile and uninviting as to turn her peripatetic. Her bedroom (figure 2.2), like that of Clara in *The Gashlycrumb Tinies* (figure 2.3), is insistently blank in comparison to that of Dickens's wandering Little Nell (figure 2.1). Merely "pin-sized" creatures in most backgrounds point to the hostility of Charlotte Sophia's environments (Theroux 11), while the generic threat is communicated via pervasive shadows. Similarly, the "low" quality of Charlotte Sophia's abode with the drunken brute is confirmed by a pornographic poster on the wall: a paltry imitation of Browne's habitual use of adverts and wall art as emblematic details.

At night she lay awake weeping and weeping.

2.2. Edward Gorey, "At night she lay awake weeping and weeping"
[Charlotte Sophia's bedroom] in *The Hapless Child*

When Browne and Williams framed white-faced children with threatening figures, they were participating in Dickens's larger program of social
reform. The author was and is extremely prominent among the nineteenth-
century community of artists and authors who made use of a Romantic
view of innocent childhood in the interest of promoting social and moral
improvement, drawing attention to the plights and fates of poor children.
Much has been made of Dickens's own youthful experience working in a
blacking warehouse, and his preoccupation with child exploitation, particularly in work environments, is of a piece with his propensity for portraying
"good" threatened children.[28] As in the classic image of "Oliver asking for
more" (which George Cruikshank illustrated to critical acclaim) or his portrayal of Jo in *Bleak House*, Dickens emphasized the vulnerability of poor
children as part of a larger mission against poverty and misery. The sentimental virtue attached to childhood did half the work in arousing sympathy.

C is for CLARA who wasted away

2.3. Edward Gorey, "C is for Clara who wasted away" in *The Gashlycrumb Tinies; or, After the Outing*

For just that reason, they are almost always accorded good Christian deaths. They are effectively better off dead because death lifts them out of their miserable lives and into their shining afterlives as angels or heavenly denizens. While there are certain unorthodox elements about many of Dickens's portrayals, the basic Christian or religious context is consistent.[29] Nell's actual deathbed (figure 2.4) is not only practically inside a church but the illustration is strewn with details that render it a "sacred space," including the carved representation of the Virgin and Child on her headboard.[30] The final illustration of Little Nell is her apotheosis, as was common in representations of childhood death at the time (Steward 128). Nell's is one of the most memorable virtuous child deaths in a Dickens novel largely because it is so protracted; Paul Dombey is led away into a Sunday School print, and Jo expires in the midst of repeating the Lord's Prayer. These Christian elements are often obscured or lost in the twentieth century's version of Dickens's childhood deaths, but they are the most obvious points of connection with evangelical childhood deaths that predate, give rise to, and coexist with Dickens's.[31]

Barry Westburg prefaced the nineteenth-century bestseller *The History of the Fairchild Family* (Part I, 1818) with the claim that Mrs. Mary Sherwood dramatically "shaped the frame of mind we think of as characteristically Victorian" through her novel's preoccupation with childhood mor(t)ality and its climactic focus on the death of the virtuous Charles Trueman (vi). It is also simply the most successful of a huge number of publications produced by the Religious Tract Society (RTS) throughout the nineteenth century. Founded in 1799, the RTS was producing over a million tracts a year less than a decade later, and in addition it eventually oversaw the publication of periodicals and magazines like the *Boys' Own Paper*. From the 1820s onward, many RTS books were bound with engraved illustrations,[32] and some related religious tracts included woodcuts with standardized deathbed scenes. Elisabeth Jay has characterized a number of these types of stories, such as *The Dairyman's Daughter* by the Reverend Leigh Richmond, as being "in effect long drawn-out death bed scenes" (117). Laurence Lerner more specifically observes the frequency with which dying children metamorphose into angels in both nonfiction and novels (100–103).[33] Since childhood death was a profitable subject, Dickens rather pointedly incorporated more children and killed one off in *Dombey and Son* so as to recover from the slump in popularity that accompanied the adult-populated *Martin Chuzzlewit* published the year prior (Cockshut 150). Just as broadsheet printers slotted crudely precut figures into generic representations of recurring events like hangings,[34] the mere outlines of a child were sufficient to arouse the appropriately sentimental response. Mid-century, both Mrs. Sherwood and Dickens were singled out for their exploitation of the trope: Charlotte Yonge described the former as "first in the field of pious slaughter" (308), while the *Saturday Review* sardonically reported that no one but Dickens "can offer to the public so large a stock of death-beds adapted for either sex and for any age, from five and twenty downwards . . . there never was a man to whom the King of Terrors was so useful as a lay figure" ("Mr Dickens" 475). Dickens's contributions came to serve as the truly Victorian representatives, with irritatingly virtuous children populating secular novels as well as evangelical texts (e.g., the headmaster's "favourite pupil" in *The Old Curiosity Shop* or even Tiny Tim).

Gorey demonstrated his own direct familiarity with evangelical works by parodying them and even directly quoting *The Fairchild Family* in *The Pious Infant*.[35] Gorey hews so closely to the original as to bend his own name into the suitably matronly pseudonym of "Mrs. Regera Dowdy" for this publication. But even with such concrete cues, he runs the risks assumed by all who

2.4. George Cattermole, "Nell at Rest" from *Master Humphrey's Clock*

traffic in allusion, risks that are potentially heightened by disparate knowledge bases between child and adult audiences.[36] As Elizabeth Thiel points out in her discussion of graphic (and abridged) adaptations of *Oliver Twist*, twenty-first-century audiences may more readily associate the word "Dickensian" with "conditions of poverty" or "traditional images of Christmas" than with sentimental childhood death (144). However, the availability of adaptations, such as the graphic novels discussed by Thiel, along with Dickens's continued presence on school syllabi, suggest that twenty-first-century children are still exposed to his version of childhood. Moreover, Gorey can assume mainstream familiarity with the history of sentimental representations of childhood because Dickens helped popularize it, in addition to enduring as a vehicle for dissemination. As part of his and other Victorians' legacy, the assumption that children occupy a "sacred" social position deserving of particular protection is now a staple in political campaigns. This attitude has persisted in the face of postwar secularization within American popular media, including increasing numbers of books about children that at least nominally approached them from a scientific perspective, such as Spock's bestselling *Baby and Child Care* (1946).[37]

As Gorey wrote, illustrated, and designed his small books in America in the early 1960s, he clearly constructed his scenes of childhood death with different goals and preoccupations than Dickens did. Perhaps most conspicuously, he eschewed much of Dickens's moral mission by routinely depicting middle-class and aristocratic children rather than good-hearted working-class figures like Jo and Tiny Tim, or even analogues of the fellow travelers whom Oliver Twist, David Copperfield, and Nicholas Nickleby meet during their "low" periods. Such figures would have extended the archaism of Gorey's narratives because the intervening century had wrought dramatic changes in the socioeconomic status of children as a group: motivated by concerns about their vulnerability for exploitation, legal measures protected even poor children from the tyranny of paid labor that had so haunted Dickens. The child welfare movements of the nineteenth and early twentieth centuries had eventually succeeded in assuring the opportunity for social advancement through schooling, at least nominally. As Viviana Zelizer documents in *Pricing the Priceless Child*, by the interwar period, it was a nearly universally held opinion in both America and the United Kingdom that education was the only appropriate "work" for young people. Instead of producing goods, children became invaluable "goods" themselves as the public and their own parents invested in their future productivity. This situation was paradoxically exacerbated within American families after World War II, when the standards of middle-class living—including higher education and domestic comforts—became more accessible than ever before.[38] Scholars of children's media and the history of childhood have linked children's privileged social status within post–WWII American society directly with this buoyant market and the increased emphasis on consumption that it engendered. Not only were the children of the "baby boom" targeted directly by enterprising manufacturers, but the relative comfort of American households enabled adults to construct a vision of childhood as free of both labor and cares.[39] This led, in turn, to a tremendous psychic and financial burden on American parents. For all of their increasing relief from the terrors of infant mortality and devastating childhood diseases, the benefits were, as Peter Stearns compellingly argues, not as dramatic as might have been imagined. Instead, parents faced intense pressure to seize the opportunity to "really do a proper job for the first time in history" of providing the happy childhood to which everyone was "naturally" entitled (Stearns *Guaranteed* 179, 198). Paula Fass has rather bluntly argued that in the middle of the twentieth century, "the [American] middle-class family" took steps to protect its investment and "began to crack down on its kids, consciously (if not completely successfully) circumscribing their range of choices, patrolling their behavior, and supervising their activities [. . .]. The reasons for this combined economics and psychology in a potent blend of fear and hope" (11). By the time that Gorey began work on *The Hapless Child* and *The Gashlycrumb Tinies*, American society had reconstituted the Victorians' fascination with children's moral superiority as an increasingly paranoid preoccupation with ensuring their welfare.

In short, the "priceless child" that Gorey represented in both *The Hapless Child* and *The Gashlycrumb Tinies* derives more of its value from the literal economy than a moral one. *Safe* children justified substituting faith in technological progress for that of Christian redemption. However, children in post–WWII America still endured a situation not unlike that of their peers from the prior century: rhetoric about children's vulnerability, and even active efforts to intercede on their collective behalf, stood in contrast with the persistent reality that children could be the victims of abuse and injury. Twentieth-century Americans just enjoyed the privilege of having the specter of Dickensian children to look back upon. The archaic format of Gorey's books ironically reinforces the comforting illusion that progress has relegated child endangerment to the past, so that the myth shatters under the pressure. Indeed, Gorey was hardly the only twentieth-century artist to offer a sardonic take on the sentimentalizing Victorian view of childhood, or to be inspired by parodic interventions from the fin de siècle. Sabine Büssing and others have pointed out that the Romantic image of childhood has been increasingly exploited in horror fiction and films like *Rosemary's Baby* and the work of Stephen King. Not coincidentally, the trend first becomes noticeable in the early 1960s in America, and includes both children as victims (whose purity exacerbates the horror of what befalls them) and as monsters who effectively use the adult presumption of childhood innocence as a disguise.[40]

There is little reason to think that children could be entirely shielded from advertising for politicians or other forms of adult media, much less from the real-life adult behavior and anxieties that help shape the ambivalent representation of children. To the contrary, children would be ideally situated to recognize that autonomy is sacrificed in exchange for moving "from participation to protection" within society (Qvortrup 6); as Michael Grossberg has shown, children's bids for political, economic, and social rights throughout the twentieth century have often been made in response to "caretaking" measures officially established on their behalf (20–21). Furthermore, the much-ballyhooed educational mandate is itself potentially oppressive, as Zelizer has more recently pointed out, because it obstructs compensation for labor that children perform in familial situations, and largely ignores nonstandard career trajectories.[41] Certainly, schooling is often perceived by reluctant pupils as anything but liberating, necessitating public rhetoric addressed to them directly.[42] Since tensions between text and subtext are embedded in form, I join Julie Cross in crediting younger readers with at least the potential to detect and decipher widely disseminated cultural codes in works like Gorey's, whether or not they have read Dickens in the original (58). Child readers may learn generic conventions of Victorian cultural production from Gorey's works themselves. He generates the ambience of allusion through deviation from current convention—for instance, with old-fashioned names and dress—and also through formal emphasis on the text's own stylization. Verbal and visual elements like rhyme (in *The Gashlycrumb Tinies*), rigidly consistent sentence structure (in *The Hapless Child*), and conspicuous draftsmanship in both books prompt even young readers to infer traditional habits of expression governing the representation of child characters in Gorey's work.

Whether or not a reader (whether child or adult) can identify Gorey's stereotypes as specifically Victorian, the cumulative effect is an anesthetizing aesthetic distance from the horrific violence threaded through both books and the brief lives of their protagonists. Precisely because child-character "types" have been so useful to sentimental fiction, religious tracts, and horror, Henry Clump of *The Pious Infant* shares with Charlotte Sophia, all of the Tinies, and Paul Dombey the defining characteristic of dullness. It is impossible to conceive of actually weeping over the deaths of such undistinguished lumps. One final means by which Gorey cultivates an old-fashioned appearance in his books about children is by using simplified and/or exaggerated forms associated with early Victorian illustrators—and of course, Dickens's flair for satire and caricature is legendary. The one shared characteristic of all the victims is youth. Although Gorey's children are not exactly caricatures, in keeping with the satirical predispositions and enabling constraints of Dickens's illustrators, Gorey simplifies the forms of the children's faces to the point that they might all be siblings. This is perhaps most apparent in the frontispiece of *The Gashlycrumb Tinies*, where the indistinguishable children are usefully lined up for comparison. They are truly stock figures; Gorey has reused Charlotte Sophia's cowering posture for Xerxes's reaction to an approaching band of ravenous mice. Dickens's illustrators paid little more attention to distinguishing facial features of children: as deadlines pressed down upon Dickens's "*Clock* Works" team and multiple artists were employed, portrayals of Nell varied depending on whether the rendering hand belonged to Williams, Cattermole, or Browne (Allingham). In both sentimental stories and horror, "the child" is valued as a tool for evoking the socially codified reactions to children. Who the child characters are is less important than what happens to them. There is no particular need for Gorey to provide his childish victims with more than a name, much less a history. In fact, as Büssing points out, "the lack of individual traits and qualities have been more and more emphasized and elaborated" because "the stylized depiction of the child in fact fulfills requirements essential to the effectiveness of horror literature": that of creating an aesthetic distance from content that is otherwise taboo or unpalatable (xiv). Thus, within their respective settings, Gorey's children do not receive protection any more than Dickens's child characters do, with similarly lethal but more horrifying results. But in Gorey's *Hapless Child* and *Tinies*, that content is specifically framed by the tradition of Victorian melodrama, so that the gothic elements become comic by satirically exaggerating and repeating the original.

Although Dickens's child characters did far more than simply die—David Copperfield and Pip do get to grow up a bit—the linkage between Dickens and representations of childhood death is so pervasive and iconic that his legend is summoned even when visual rather than verbal comparisons would seem appropriate. Beyond the nineteenth-century book design that frames his compositions with a Victorian context, I have shown that Gorey's visual representations of children have much in common with those of Dickens and confirm that we are, at least superficially, expected to understand them as precious "Romantic" children. Their names and dress further confirm the impression created by the draftsmanship. But Gorey shows his debt to engraving by exploiting iconographic elements that have heretofore gone unidentified, as well as unappreciated for their role in both construing and managing the horrifying aspects of Gorey's comic gothic productions.

For all of Gorey's children, death definitively ends their stories. The concluding image of *The Pious Infant* focuses on the grave, and Henry Clump has no apotheosis, no representation of either body or soul making the journey, belying his earlier assurances to his sister that "When I die I shall go up to heaven like that bird." *The Gashlycrumb Tinies* concludes with a collection of unmarked graves, so that the endpiece suggests either the untended resting places of the Tinies, or their fundamental lack of distinction, and in any event confirms that the stories go no further. Rather than a full rhyme for each Tiny (as in other cautionary tales) we have half a couplet

that can stand alone syntactically and, above all, offers neither explanation nor moral conclusion to complete the scene of childhood death. Even
Charlotte Sophia's father does not recognize her, creating dramatic irony
that is never narratively redeemed. However, we should resist a tendency
to see Gorey's works as deficient or subtractive, by comparison with Dickens's. Gorey himself once said, "I think of my books as Victorian novels all
scrunched up" (qtd. in Wilkin *Ascending Peculiarity* 239). This helpfully
suggests that he is compressing rather than eliminating narrative elements,
and invoking dynamic nineteenth-century text-image relationships derived
from the traditions of graphic satire. Readers are confronted with brevity
when they reach the text. So they may either turn the page to white space
or linger over images that yield a mass of marks without apparent iconographic significance. However, that blankness is precisely the point. It stands
in contrast with a rich history of finding profound social meaning in threats
to child characters and childhood death. Masterfully exploiting the power
of context, Gorey's drain on meaning transforms the hope of redemption
into the horror of wasted potential.

NOTES

1. There are many instances of his professed enthusiasm for Dickens. See particularly
Ross, 37, and Gorey, "The Connection," 223–24.

2. For example, Gorey has clearly drawn on Hablot Knight Browne's illustration of
"Changes at Home" in *David Copperfield* in an early frame from *The Pious Infant*: in both
cases the armchair's back visually and literally excludes the small, doomed boy from a scene
of maternal domestic comfort (Dickens *David Copperfield* n.p. [facing 94]; Gorey *Pious
Infant* n.p.).

3. For an overview of these recent developments, see Jackson, Coats, and McGillis, 1–14,
and Reynolds 1–18.

4. See J. Walker McSpadden, *Child Stories from Dickens*, illus. Ethel Everett (London:
George G. Harrap & Co., 1934).

5. Julie Cross also suggests that "the parody of melodrama [. . .] is itself strongly associated with the Gothic" (68–69).

6. See Marcia Muelder, "Laughing at the Death of Little Nell: Sentimental Art and
Sentimental People," *American Philosophical Quarterly* 26.4 (October 1989): 269–82.

7. Similarly, Gorey philosophically concluded that "In the long run I don't think it matters, because children eventually find what is for them" (qtd. in Neumeyer 89).

8. See Killeen's chapter on "The Horror of Childhood" (60–91). He thoughtfully documents the Victorian "general cultural fixation on killing the child as a means of protecting
her" (63).

9. Jennifer Thorn usefully discusses this image and its social context at some length in her introduction to *Writing British Infanticide: Child-murder, Gender, and Print, 1722–1859*, ed. Jennifer Thorn (Newark: University of Delaware Press, 2003), 13–17.

10. I have argued elsewhere that *The Gashlycrumb Tinies* is susceptible to categorization as horror for children; this essay draws on work previously published as "G Is for Gorey Who Kills Children," *Studies in Weird Fiction* 27 (Spring 2005): 23–32.

11. I understand that the term "secularization" is important but variously defined and deployed among sociologists and historians of religion (see "The Development of Secularisation as an Historical Concept," Brown and Snape, particularly 3–5). I use it in the simplest popular sense, as Bryan Wilson did in 1966 when describing some recent developments in America and the United Kingdom: "the declining social significance of religion" (14).

12. Although several critics have conducted semiotic explorations of narrative images, their relevance to the present discussion is limited by their emphasis on graphic forms. See Nodelman and Bader as well as David Lewis, *Reading Contemporary Picturebooks* (London: Routledge, 2001) and William Moebius, "Introduction to Picturebook Codes," *Word and Image* 2.2 (1986): 141–58.

13. The term "composite art" presents similar difficulties; see particularly Birnbaum and Forrester. Joseph Schwarz's "composite text" comes nearer the mark, although he too tends to treat the visual and verbal elements of children's picturebooks as cooperative or parallel phenomena rather than unified. See his *Ways of the Illustrator: Visual Communication in Children's Literature* (Chicago: American Library Association, 1982), 13–14.

14. Theroux assembled a similar list, drawing a similar conclusion: "With their hand-lettering, queer layouts, their framed and ornate borders, the small books seem frightfully old-fashioned and biscuity, as if they had bepressed out and printed in suspiciously limited editions in the cellar of some creepy railway warehouse in nineteenth century England" (2).

15. Originally, Dickens planned to write a series of stories to be published in a weekly periodical, all narrated by the eponymous "Master Humphrey." However, this plan was abandoned shortly after starting the first piece, which grew into *The Old Curiosity Shop* and was subsequently published as an independent novel. I will use that title henceforth, and all citations refer to the Clarendon Press edition, which reproduces each illustration in its original location on the page.

16. For a good overview of the publishing technologies and constraints experienced by Dickens's illustrators, see Cohen 5. For a particularly detailed discussion of Dickens's efforts to control his illustrators' output, see also J. Stevens and Allingham.

17. See Edward Gorey, *The Gashlycrumb Tinies, or, After the Outing* in *Amphigorey* (New York: Perigee, 1972); and Edward Gorey, *The Hapless Child* in *Amphigorey Too* (New York: Perigee, 1975).

18. Wanda Gág is sometimes credited for reviving this practice in America with the child-oriented *Millions of Cats* (1928); see Bader 34.

19. Nodelman points out that black and white often cues nostalgia (67).

20. *The Pious Infant* was first published in a format similar to that reproduced in *Amphigorey, Too*, with four images per page. However, each unit of iconotext (one sentence with one image) was enclosed by a frame and numbered sequentially outside that frame

in a manner evoking page breaks. See Edward Gorey, "The Pious Infant," *Evergreen Review* 9.35 (March 1965): 22–25.

21. On Dickens as influenced by graphic satire, see Harvey, "Chapter 3: Brueghel to Dickens: Graphic Satire and the Novel," 44–75.

22. See Steig, "Chapter 1: Dickens and Browne: Illustration, Collaboration, and Iconography," 1–23.

23. As Cohen points out, Browne was quite clearly selected by Dickens because he possessed these qualities (5). Harvey observes that "The great advantage of the actual illustrator, Hablot Browne, was his unformedness and transparency: he was ready to let Dickens's imagination work through him" (175). See also Steig 24–25.

24. See also J. Stevens and Allingham.

25. See especially Thomas 79–80 and 91–93.

26. As Sarah Solberg points out, most of Dickens's contemporary readers, not to mention those in the twentieth century, consumed his books without any illustrations at all (133). Similarly, Cohen notes that "Between 1916 and 1937, no editions of Dickens's collected novels appeared with the original illustrations" (234). There were practical as well as artistic reasons for including illustrations with serial publication: visual cues aided readers' memories between monthly issues, not to mention the simple market forces in effect. But when the entire text was collected into a single volume, illustrations were often eliminated entirely. Although Gorey surely knows the names of Dickens's original illustrators, much of *his* audience does not, and Solberg has rightly warned us against mistaking a growing scholarly field for a rediscovered context (134–35).

27. Killeen points to a critical history cementing Nell's status as an iconic "lonely and beleaguered child, wandering lost through the terrifying forests of the world" (Harry Stone qtd. in Killeen 66). But neither he nor those he surveys consider how her visual representation complements the verbal construction of her environment and its threats.

28. See especially Coveney 116–19 and 158–59 and Spilka 169–73. Killeen also asserts that "Charles Dickens is a central figure in the propagation of the modern myth of childhood as a zone of innocence besieged by malevolent Gothic threats from the family and from social, religious and political institutions" (62).

29. See Lerner 94 and Cockshut 136. See also Margarete Holubetz, "Death-bed Scenes in Victorian Fiction," *English Studies* 1 (1986): 14–34.

30. See Cockshut 142–43 and Landow "'At Rest (Nell dead)' by George Cattermole." See also Angela Gawel, "Subordinating the Other: Illustrations in Dickens's *Old Curiosity Shop*," *Metaphor and Symbolic Activity* 8.3 (1993): 175. Cohen describes these religious markers as "hackneyed" (129).

31. For an overview of such scenes of childhood death, see Samuel Pickering Jr., *The Moral Tradition in English Fiction: 1785–1850* (Hanover: UP of New England, 1976), 107–22.

32. For an overview of the RTS and the form of its periodicals, see Dennis Butts and Pat Garrett, ed. and intro., *From the Dairyman's Daughter to Worrals of the WAAF: The Religious Tract Society* (Cambridge: Lutterworth Press, 2006), especially 8.

33. See also Plotz 17.

34. For a discussion of this phenomenon and examples, see Tom Gretton, *Murders and Moralities: English Catchpenny Prints 1800–1860* (London: British Museum Press, 1980), 21–22 and 48.

35. Henry Clump's final words—"I am happy!"—echo those of Charles Trueman in *The Fairchild Family*. Gorey recalled having read the novel as a child (Ross 37).

36. For an efficient discussion of these risks and rewards, see Peter Hunt, "What Do We Lose When We Lose Allusion? Experience and Understanding Stories," *Signal* 57 (1988): 212–22.

37. In 1961, the Baptist minister Harvey Cox famously published *The Secular City* and declared American culture to be fully secularized, with religion no longer serving a distinct social function. Both sociologists and historians of religion have challenged this view in recent years, documenting the persistence and periodic resurgence of religious faith and practice in America through the twentieth century and into the twenty-first. For a brief overview of the current state of these discussions, see Brown and Snape 3–4; for a more extended version, see Frank Lambert, *Religion in American Politics: A Short History* (Princeton: Princeton UP, 2008). Although other historians—such as the influential Hugh McLeod—have also identified the 1960s as a decisive break between the Christian past and a secular future (Brown and Snape 10), Cox's characterization is probably best understood as an exaggeration of a genuine trend in American mainstream media in the years immediately following World War II.

38. For an efficient summary of these developments, see George Brown Tindall and David E. Shi, *America: A Narrative History*, 5th ed. (New York: W. W. Norton, 1999), 1424–25. See also Eric F. Goldman, *The Crucial Decade—and After: America, 1945–1960* (New York: Vintage Books, 1960); David Halberstam, *The Fifties* (New York: Villard Books, 1993); and William Manchester, *The Glory and the Dream: A Narrative History of America, 1932–1972* (Boston: Little Brown, 1974).

39. For the marketing of consumer goods to and for children, see Shirley R. Steinberg and Joe L. Kincheloe, eds., *Kinderculture: The Corporate Construction of Childhood* (Boulder, CO: Westview Press, 1997), and Gary Cross, *Kids' Stuff: Toys and the Changing World of American Childhood* (Cambridge, MA: Harvard UP, 1999). For the psychological effects of American consumerism on children and families, see Stearns (especially *Guaranteed* 201–2) and Zelizer as well as D. R. John, "Consumer Socialization of Children: A Retrospective Look at Twenty-Five Years of Research," *Journal of Consumer Research* 26.3 (1999): 183–213. For a representative example of a cluster of polemics published in response to the consumerist tendencies of the 1970s and 1980s, which include reference to mid-century origins for those trends, see Marie Winn, *Children without Childhood* (New York: Pantheon, 1983).

40. Many scholars have documented how ambivalence about the special status of children increased from the Romantic era to the late twentieth century. See Büssing; Zelizer; Karen J. Renner, ed., *The "Evil Child" in Literature, Film and Popular Culture* (New York: Routledge, 2013); Ellen Pifer, *Demon or Doll: Images of the Child in Contemporary Writing and Culture* (Charlottesville: UP of Virginia, 2000); and Anne Higonnet, *Pictures of Innocence: The History and Crisis of Ideal Childhood* (London: Thames and Hudson, 1998). In his work on *Hollywood from Vietnam to Reagan*, Robin Wood has most prominently discussed "the Terrible Child" in horror films, linking it to a "unifying master figure: The Family," which was seen to be under threat in 1960s America (83).

41. In this supplement to her original work in *Pricing the Priceless Child*, Zelizer points to several forms of "work"—namely, "household caring and immigrant enterprises" ("Revisited" 184)—that children perform without compensation as a prompt to examine

the nuances and limitations of dominant conceptions of child labor, including corresponding resistance to it.

42. The War Advertising Council was formed during World War II in order to bolster the
image of the advertising industry and its clients during a period of reduced consumption.
In 1945 the renamed "Ad Council" turned to producing "Public Service Announcements"
designed to promote social agendas; for a brief history of the Ad Council, see Robert H.
Wicks, *Understanding Audiences: Learning to Use the Media Constructively* (New York:
Routledge, 2000), 61–68; for an extended discussion of the Ad Council's place in mid-
century advertising more generally, see Dawn Spring, *Advertising in the Age of Persuasion:
Building Brand America, 1941–1961* (New York: Palgrave Macmillan, 2011). In the 1960s,
some of the Ad Council's campaigns for print, radio, and television responded to observers
who perceived a crisis in school attendance and youth compliance with the educational
mandate. For the social history of this trend and public responses to it, see Sherman Dorn,
Creating the Dropout: An Institutional and Social History of School Failure (Westport, CT:
Praeger, 1996).

WORKS CITED

Allingham, Philip V. "*The Old Curiosity Shop* Illustrated: A Team Effort by 'The *Clock
Works*.'" *Victorian Web*. 4 January 2006. Web. 5 March 2007.

Bader, Barbara. *American Picturebooks: From Noah's Ark to the Beast Within*. New York:
Macmillan, 1976. Print.

Birnbaum, David J., and Sibelan E. S. Forrester. "The Composite Art of Edward Gorey's *The
Gashlycrumb Tinies*." Unpublished manuscript distributed by authors. 24 June 2006. TS.

Bodmer, George. "The Post-Modern Alphabet: Extending the Limits of the Contemporary
Alphabet Book, from Seuss to Gorey." *Children's Literature Association Quarterly* 14
(1989): 115–17. *Project Muse*. Web. 4 January 2006.

Botting, Fred. "Horror." *The Handbook to Gothic Literature*. Edited by Marie Mulvey-
Roberts. New York: New York UP, 1998. 124–31. Print.

Brown, Callum G., and Michael Snape. "Conceptualising Secularisation 1974–2010: The
Influence of Hugh McLeod." *Secularisation in the Christian World*. Farnham, Surrey:
Ashgate, 2010. 1–12. Print.

Büssing, Sabine. *Aliens in the Home: The Child in Horror Fiction*. New York: Greenwood,
1987. Print.

Cockshut, A. O. J. "Children's Death in Dickens: A Chapter in the History of Taste."
Representations of Childhood Death. Edited by Gillian Avery and Kimberley Reynolds.
London: Macmillan Press, 2000. 133–54. Print.

Cohen, Jane R. *Charles Dickens and His Original Illustrators*. Columbus: Ohio State UP,
1980. Print.

Coveney, Peter. *The Image of Childhood: The Individual and Society, a Study of the Theme in
English Literature*. Baltimore: Penguin Books, 1967. Print. Rpt. and rev. *Poor Monkey: The
Child in Literature*. London: Rockliff, 1957. Print.

Crain, Patricia. *The Story of A: The Alphabetization of America from* The New England
Primer *to* The Scarlet Letter. Stanford: Stanford UP, 2000. Print.

Cross, Julie. "Frightening and Funny: Humour in Children's Gothic Fiction." *The Gothic in Children's Literature: Haunting the Borders*. Edited by Anna Jackson, Karen Coats, and Roderick McGillis. New York: Routledge, 2008. 57–76. Print.

Dickens, Charles. *Bleak House*. 1853. Edited by Stephen Gill. Oxford: Oxford UP, 1998. Print.

———. *David Copperfield*. 1850. Edited by Nina Burgis. Oxford: Clarendon Press, 1981. Print.

———. *Dombey and Son*. 1848. Edited by Alan Horsman. Oxford: Clarendon Press, 1974. Print.

———. Letter to William Macready. 6 January 1841. *The Letters of Charles Dickens*. Edited by Madeline House and Graham Storey. Vol. 2. Oxford: Clarendon Press, 1969. 180. Print.

———. *Oliver Twist*. 1838. Edited by Kathleen Tillotson. Oxford: Clarendon Press, 1966. Print.

———. *The Old Curiosity Shop*. 1841. Edited by Elizabeth Brennan. Oxford: Clarendon Press, 1997. Print.

Dyer, Richard. "The Poison Penman." 1 April 1984. Wilkin, *Ascending Peculiarity*, 110–25.

Fass, Paula. "The Child-Centered Family? New Rules in Postwar America." *Reinventing Childhood after World War II*. Edited by Paula S. Fass and Michael Grossberg. Philadelphia: U of Pennsylvania P, 2012. 1–18. Print.

Forster, John. *The Life of Charles Dickens*. 1872–1873. The Memorial Edition. 2 Vols. Edited by B. W. Matz. London: Chapman and Hall, 1911. Print.

Gorey, Edward. *The Gashlycrumb Tinies, or, After the Outing* in *Amphigorey*. New York: Perigee, 1972. N.p. Print.

———. *The Gashlycrumb Tinies; or, After the Outing*. New York: Simon and Schuster, 1963. N.p. Print.

———. *The Hapless Child*. New York: I. Obolensky, 1961. N.p. Print.

———. *The Hapless Child* in *Amphigorey Too*. New York: Perigee, 1975. N.p. Print.

———. Interview by Christopher Lydon. "The Connection." 26 November 1998. Wilkin, *Ascending Peculiarity*, 216–27.

———. Interview by Dick Cavett. "*The Dick Cavett Show* with Edward Gorey." 30 November 1977. Wilkin, *Ascending Peculiarity*, 50–65.

———. Interview by Jean Martin. "The Mind's Eye: Writers Who Draw." July–August 1980. Wilkin, *Ascending Peculiarity*, 86–91.

———. Interview by Robert Dahlin. "Conversations with Writers: Edward Gorey." 1977. Wilkin, *Ascending Peculiarity*, 24–49.

——— [Mrs. Regera Dowdy]. *The Pious Infant* in *Amphigorey*. New York: Perigee, 1972. N.p. Print.

Grossberg, Michael. "Liberation and Caretaking: Fighting over Children's Rights in Postwar America." *Reinventing Childhood after World War II*. Edited by Paula S. Fass and Michael Grossberg. Philadelphia: U of Pennsylvania P, 2012. 19–37. Print.

Harvey, J. R. *Victorian Novelists and Their Illustrators*. London: Sidgwick and Jackson, 1970. Print.

Hodenfield, Jan. "And 'G' Is for Gorey Who Here Tells His Story." 10 January 1973. Wilkin, *Ascending Peculiarity* 2–5.

Hoffmann, Heinrich. *Struwwelpeter*. 1845. New York: Dover, 1995. N.p. Print.

Hood, Thomas. "Master Humphrey's Clock. By 'Boz.' Vol. I." *Athenaeum* 680 (7 November 1840): 887–88. *British Periodicals*. Web. 12 April 2013.

Jackson, Anna, Karen Coats, and Roderick McGillis, eds. *The Gothic in Children's Literature: Haunting the Borders*. New York: Routledge, 2008. 1–14. Print.

Jay, Elisabeth. "'Ye careless, thoughtless, worldly parents, tremble while you read this history!': The Use and Abuse of the Dying Child in the Evangelical Tradition." *Representations of Childhood Death*. Edited by Gillian Avery and Kimberley Reynolds. London: Macmillan Press, 2000. 111–32. Print.

Killeen, Jarlath. *Gothic Literature, 1825–1914*. Cardiff: U of Wales P, 2009. Print.

Landow, George P. "'At Rest (Nell dead)' by George Cattermole." *Victorian Web*. 4 January 2006. Web. 4 January 2006.

Lerner, Laurence. *Angels and Absences: Child Deaths in the Nineteenth Century*. Nashville, TN: Vanderbilt UP, 1997. Print.

Magistrale, Tony, and Michael Morrison, eds. *A Dark Night's Dreaming: Contemporary American Horror Fiction*. Columbia: U of South Carolina P, 1996. Print.

"Mr. Dickens." *Saturday Review of Politics, Literature, Science and Art* 5.132 (8 May 1858): 474–75. *British Periodicals*. Web. 20 April 2013.

Neumeyer Peter F., ed. *Floating Worlds: The Letters of Edward Gorey and Peter F. Neumeyer*. San Francisco: Pomegranate, 2011. Print.

Nikolajeva, Maria, and Carole Scott. *How Picturebooks Work*. New York: Garland Publishing, 2001. Print.

Nodelman, Perry. *Words about Pictures: The Narrative Art of Children's Picture Books*. Athens: U of Georgia P, 1988. Print.

Plotz, Judith. "Literary Ways of Killing a Child: The 19th Century Practice." *Aspects and Issues in the History of Children's Literature*. Edited by Maria Nikolajeva. Westport, CT: Greenwood Press, 1995. 1–24. Print.

Qvortrup, Jens. "Varieties of Childhood." *Studies in Modern Childhood: Society, Agency, Culture*. Edited by Jens Qvortrup. New York: Palgrave Macmillan, 2005. 1–20. Print.

Reynolds, Kimberley. Introduction. *Frightening Fiction*. Edited by Kimberley Reynolds, Geraldine Brennan, and Kevin McCarron. London: Continuum, 2001. 1–18. Print.

Ross, Clifford. "Interview with Edward Gorey." *The World of Edward Gorey*. Edited by Clifford Ross and Karen Wilkin. New York: Harry N. Abrams, 1996. 9–41. Print.

Rusch, Mark T. "The Deranged Episode: Ironic Dissimulation in the Domestic Scenes of Edward Gorey's Short Stories." *International Journal of Comic Art* 6.2 (Fall 2004): 445–54. Print.

Schiff, Stephen. "Edward Gorey and the Tao of Nonsense." 9 November 1992. Wilkin, *Ascending Peculiarity*, 136–57. Print.

Shortsleeve, Kevin. "Edward Gorey, Children's Literature, and Nonsense Verse." *Children's Literature Association Quarterly* 27.1 (2002): 27–39. *Project Muse*. Web. 3 May 2013.

Solberg, Sarah. "Dickens and Illustration: A Matter of Perspective." *Journal of Narrative Technique* 10 (Spring 1980): 128–37. Print.

Spilka, Mark. "On the Enrichment of Poor Monkeys by Myth and Dream; or, How Dickens Rousseauisticized and Pre-Freudianized Victorian Views of Childhood." *Sexuality and Victorian Literature*. Edited by Don Richard Cox. Knoxville: U of Tennessee P, 1984. 161–79. Print. Tennessee Studies in Literature 27.

Stallcup, Jackie. "Power, Fear, and Children's Picture Books." *Children's Literature* 30 (2002): 125–58. Print.

Stearns, Peter N. *Anxious Parents: A History of Modern Child-rearing in America*. New York: New York UP, 2003.

———. *Satisfaction Not Guaranteed: Dilemmas of Progress in Modern Society*. New York: New York UP, 2012.

Steig, Michael. *Dickens and Phiz*. Bloomington: Indiana UP, 1978. Print.

Stevens, Carol. "An American Original." January/February 1988. Wilkin, *Ascending Peculiarity*, 126–35. Print.

Stevens, Joan. "'Woodcuts Dropped into the Text': The Illustrations in *The Old Curiosity Shop* and *Barnaby Rudge*." *Studies in Bibliography* 20 (1967): 113–34. Print.

Steward, James Christen. *The New Child: British Art and the Origins of Modern Childhood, 1730–1830*. Berkeley: University Art Museum and Pacific Film Archive, 1995. Print.

Stewart, Garrett. *Death Sentences: Styles of Dying in British Fiction*. Cambridge, MA: Harvard UP, 1984. Print.

Theroux, Alexander. *The Strange Case of Edward Gorey*. Seattle, WA: Fantagraphic Books, 2000. Print.

Thiel, Elizabeth. "Downsizing Dickens: Adaptations of *Oliver Twist* for the Child Reader." *Adapting Canonical Texts in Children's Literature*. Edited by Anja Müller. London: Bloomsbury, 2013. 143–62. Print.

Thomas, Julia. "Happy Endings: Death and Domesticity in Victorian Illustration." *Reading Victorian Illustration, 1855–1875: Spoils of the Lumber Room*. Edited by Paul Goldman and Simon Cooke. Surrey: Ashgate, 2012. 79–96. Print.

Todorov, Tzvetan. *The Fantastic: A Structural Approach to a Literary Genre*. Cleveland, OH: P of Case Western Reserve U, 1973. Print.

Westburg, Barry. Preface. *The History of the Fairchild Family, Part I*. By Mrs. Mary Sherwood. 1818. Edited by Barry Westburg. New York: Garland Publishing, 1977. Print.

Wilkin, Karen, ed. *Ascending Peculiarity: Edward Gorey on Edward Gorey*. New York: Harcourt Brace, 2001. Print.

———. "Mr. Earbrass Jots Down a Few Visual Notes." *The World of Edward Gorey*. Edited by Clifford Ross and Karen Wilkin. New York: Harry N. Abrams, 1996. 43–111. Print.

Wood, Robin. *Hollywood from Vietnam to Reagan*. New York: Columbia UP, 1986. Print.

Yonge, Charlotte M. "Children's Literature of the Last Century: Didactic Fiction." *Macmillan's Magazine* 20 (August 1869): 302–10. *British Periodicals*. Web. 4 June 2011.

Zelizer, Viviana. *Pricing the Priceless Child: The Changing Social Value of Children*. New York: Basic Books, 1985. Print.

———. "The Priceless Child Revisited." *Studies in Modern Childhood: Society, Agency, Culture*. Edited by Jens Qvortrup. New York: Palgrave Macmillan, 2005. 184–200. Print.

From Aggressive Wolf to Heteronormative Zombie

Performing Monstrosity and Masculinity in the Narrative Picturebook

REBECCA A. BROWN

SINCE THE PUBLICATION OF MAURICE SENDAK'S *WHERE THE WILD Things Are* and Mercer Mayer's *There's a Nightmare in My Closet* in the 1960s, monsters have increasingly overrun the pages of American-authored narrative picturebooks.[1] They have terrorized family cellars in Dick Gackenbach's *Harry and the Terrible Whatzit* (1977), and they have haunted children's bedrooms in James Howe's *There's a Monster under My Bed* (1986). Beginning in the 1970s, vampires, werewolves, mummies, zombies, and Frankensteinian monsters gradually invaded picturebooks alongside corporally animalistic and/or hybrid creatures, the bunyip, hippogriff, and phoenix appearing in books like *Dragons, Unicorns, and Other Magical Beasts* (1966).[2] This incursion of recognizable monsters does not solely attest to millennial anxiety, the oft-cited rationale for literary (and later filmic) gothic propagation. In fact, this infiltration also relates to at least two other factors: the contemporary gothic's ability to traverse "disciplinary boundaries to be absorbed into all forms of media" (Spooner 23), including picturebooks, and "new writers [in children's literature] need[ing] to carve out their own cultural space in the marketplace" due to the "highly competitive" nature of the field and other children's media (Allan 3).[3]

Monstrous picturebooks, a term I use to describe densely intertextual works that depict empowered children confronting monsters in domestic spaces and other familiar settings, reinforce the gothic's cultural diffusion and engage with monsters' literary and visual symbolism. Judith/Jack Halberstam writes, "Monsters are meaning machines. They can represent gender, race, nationality, class, and sexuality in one body" (21–22).[4] Although some monstrous picturebooks channel the Romantic, Victorian, and horror-film anxieties Halberstam addresses, the five books I examine in this essay primarily underscore the monster's significance for reimagining boys' gendered and social identities within Cold War and millennial domestic contexts. Since these works are intended for younger audiences, they often downplay monsters' most terrifying physical attributes. With notable exceptions, the artists bestow their creations with rounded bodies, curious eyes, and fewer pointy edges than their filmic and literary counterparts.[5] Yet, these books are still attuned to the transformative possibilities that monsters innately possess. Echoing Halberstam's emphasis on bodies as sites of monstrous meaning, Kerry Mallan explains the intersections between masculinity and embodiment: "Despite the complex and changing definitions and redefinitions of manhood that have occurred over the centuries, paradigms and parodies of masculinity are always embodied, and hence masculinity needs to be understood as being coterminous with the body's physique and physicality" (16). The five works I examine expose normative masculinity as a corporal and behavioral performance by depicting confrontations between boys and monsters and melding boys' and monsters' bodies.[6]

This essay begins by analyzing *Where the Wild Things Are* (1963) and *There's a Nightmare in My Closet* (1968). Then I investigate three twenty-first-century picturebooks featuring vampires, Frankensteinian creatures, and zombies. Using filmic, literary, and sociocultural contexts, I demonstrate how boys in narrative picturebooks utilize monsters both to expose conventional masculinity as a performance and to create fluid individual, social, and gendered identities within domestic and social settings. The 1960s picturebooks, which feature human children confronting and defeating imaginary creatures, reveal the protagonists' abilities to amass and deploy knowledge so as to perform canny,[7] masculine, independent identities. In contrast, the characters in the twenty-first-century picturebooks collapse the child as monster metaphor because, literally and visually, they are vampires, Frankensteinian creatures, and zombies. These amalgamated male protagonists, in turn, have more complex social and gendered identities, especially since the works incorporate external forces, including family and romantic partners, as well as more densely layered narrative and filmic allusions.

The "controversy" Maurice Sendak's *Where the Wild Things Are* incited in 1963 has been well documented within the field of children's literature, but the book's connection to American visual culture trends remains relatively unexplored.[8] As Perry Nodelman explains, the picturebook provoked outrage "because the depiction of monsters was perceived to be a new and unsettling idea" (*The Hidden Adult* 120). Nodelman additionally underscores the issue's paradoxical nature by declaring that fairy tales had long since portrayed "children confronting monstrous horrific beings." Nonetheless, "In the early 1960s the field of children's literature was constructed around then currently powerful educational and psychological assumptions that made such depictions of monstrosity outmoded and counterproductive" (120–21). Kenneth Kidd draws out the implications of Nodelman's discussion by stating that the literary critic "suggest[s]" Sendak's work highlights the idea "that childhood can be monstrous, and usefully so" (*Freud in Oz* 130–31). I wish to further expand these ideas by considering the book's sociocultural context. As David Lewis explains, "Just as the chapbook could ingest almost anything that came its way, so the picture book seems to be able to assimilate almost any kind of text, allowing for the fact that it is first and foremost a form for young children" (12). The picturebook also "hybridise[s]" "with games and toys" and has been compared to cinema, theater, and/or comic books through its incorporation of these genres' formalist/narrative/visual features (20). While "Monster Culture," as I discuss below, is not inherently "a form for young children," there are, nonetheless notable resonances between this trend and *Where the Wild Things Are* that reveal significant connections between masculinity and monstrosity.

David Skal defines "Monster Culture" as "a phenomenon of horror-movie hoopla that began in the late fifties and continued into the mid-sixties" (266).[9] As he elaborates, "In Monster Culture, the participatory rituals surrounding the movies were every bit as important as the films themselves. [. . .] Most important, monsters materialized in the living room for the first time—not just reflected light in the movie theatres, but now a light *source*, a glowing electronic fireplace around which a generation could huddle and shudder and share" (Skal 266–67). Skal's examination posits monsters' domestic invasions as culturally sanctioned by 1950s media; their living room materializations may have united the younger generations, but adolescents were by no means the only ones watching. Nonetheless, the "participatory rituals" he refers to were generally linked to Cold War boy culture. In highlighting the "sex-segregated" nature of play in the 1950s and early 1960s, Steven Mintz writes, "While boys read war comics and horror comics like *Tales from the Crypt*, girls read romance comics and comics about Wonder Woman and Polly Pigtails" (*Huck's Raft* 284). One of the rituals Skal addresses, the fan magazine *Famous Monsters of Film Land* (founded in 1958), offered an implicitly male audience many black-and-white images of monsters and monstrosity to devour alongside *Tales from the Crypt* and horror comics.[10] Other Monster Culture rites included Aurora Plastics' models of Universal's famous creatures—"rigid plastic simulacra of the Wolf Man, Frankenstein's monster, and Dracula" (Skal 274)—which allowed the "intended" audience of "pubescent boys" to construct their own creatures (Skal 277).

Unlike Aurora Plastics' monsters and the creatures featured in *Famous Monsters*, Max's Wild Things have no specific contemporary predecessors. Instead they are animalistically "hybrid" beings (Ball 171–72), the offspring of mythology's and antiquity's ogres (Warner 150).[11] As a horde, they menace the boy at the beginning and end of his imaginary island visit. In order to discipline the Wild Things, Max harnesses his own physical and emotional beastliness by engaging in a "wild rumpus" and other playfully violent activities. If, as Skal claims, "Kids [in the late 1950s and early 1960s] were making monsters of their own," referring implicitly to the Aurora Models and explicitly to television show hosts' penchant for "interrupting and intercutting" horror films (268), Max, although prepubescent, channels these impulses by mentally constructing his own creatures and participating in his own childish monster movie. Whereas American youths found comfort in a threatening Cold War world through their "resurrect[ed]" monsters (Skal 278), Sendak's protagonist seeks solace from his domestic existence in his dreamscape where he can play with beasts, behave like a wild thing without social repercussions, and create his own securely domestic conclusion.

In the context of Monster Culture, Max might also be read as a werewolf, an idea Nodelman and Kidd imply in their analyses of Sendak's book.[12] The werewolf, although a folkloric creature, was, like the vampire, prevalent in Hammer films, American International Pictures' horror movies, and horror comics.[13] As Kimberley McMahon-Coleman and Roslyn Weaver contend, "lupine shapeshifting [can be connected] to male aggression and uncontrolled, unprovoked violence" (42), but "shapeshifting [also] offers space for resisting or reframing gender stereotypes" (45). The conclusion of Sendak's story affirms these notions by exposing the child's aggressive, violent masculinity throughout the book as a performance reliant upon his shapeshifting—that is, donning the white wolf suit. Nodelman claims that, in contrast to femininity, "Masculinity is often understood as *not* being a form of dress—as resistance to the act of putting on costumes or being repressed by conventional roles" ("Making Boys Appear" 1). As he further contends, this is because "Masculinity is taken to be somehow natural and free—the state one achieves by resisting societal norms and being one's true self" ("Making

Boys Appear" 1). These perceptive remarks can also be read as socioculturally inflected in Sendak's work, since the Cold War era was "marked
by anxiety over masculinity and intense hostility toward homosexuality";
consequently, "boy culture emphasized toughness and aggression" (Mintz
282–83).

Taking these various theoretical stances into consideration, Max's wolf
suit allows him to perform conventional aggressive masculinity throughout
the book, redirecting his anger toward his mother at his Wild Things. Monstrosity and masculinity are predicated upon visibility, yet they are simultaneously subject to invisibility, masculinity due to its pervasiveness (Nodelman "Making Boys Appear" 1), monstrosity due to its marginality. The picturebook, with its overwhelming emphasis on images, consistently makes
these attributes visible through the boy's performance, reinforcing the idea
that his authoritarian behavior is neither natural nor free. Max's costume
and the theatrics it engenders also expose two other essential features of
conventional masculinity: the child temporarily relinquishes his implicitly
middle-class status, and he demonstrates that whiteness can be nonnormative. At the end of *Where the Wild Things Are*, the boy's unsheathed head
juxtaposed against the costume encompassing his body transforms his animalistic performance into a more "domesticated" one (Nodelman "Making
Boys Appear" 7). The illustration of Max smiling, about to eat his supper,
likewise suggests the child, both in and out of his costume, wakeful in his
bedroom, is readily able to reprise his performance within his dreamscape
when he wishes. At his most monstrous, then, Max exposes normative masculinity as a social construct in respect to gender, social class, and even race/
ethnicity. At his least monstrous, he de-naturalizes associations among boyhood, aggression, violence, and power, demonstrating that both maternal
care and his own creativity productively structure his burgeoning middle-
class identity.[14]

Mercer Mayer's *There's a Nightmare in My Closet* (1968) elaborates performances of normative masculinity through a child's confrontation with
monsters in equally compelling ways.[15] *Nightmare* takes place in the name-
less boy protagonist's bedroom, suggesting that the unfolding scenario
could occur in any middle-class, white, male child's most private domain. In
the initial doublespread, the frightened youth lies in bed; a toy shotgun and
cannon rests across his body, aimed at the closet door to protect him from
the imaginary creature hiding within its depths. This fictional bedroom,
with boys' toys and plentiful space to play, relates to post–World War II
ideas about imagination as well as gender identity. Amy Ogata explains, "the

playroom—along with other spaces in the dwelling, such as the bedroom—reflected not only consensus that play was beneficial but also confidence that a dedicated space designed for play might cultivate individuality and imagination" (133). In particular, "the child's bedroom was given new attention for its spatial and psychological potential as an incubator of the child's fragile ego and gender identity, and as a place where creative energy might originate" (139).[16] The text on Mayer's opening doublespread states, "There used to be a nightmare in my closet," proclaiming that the child's imaginative capacities have been fully developed in this domestic space because he has produced and defeated a nightmare born in the womb-like closet. Simultaneously, the opening line implies that the bedroom will contribute to the boy's fluid identity, a blending of feminine (creator) and masculine (defeater).[17]

Initially, Mayer's child is the antithesis of Max; although he is physically normative, he does not embody "stereotypical constructions" of masculine behavior such as "independen[ce], competitive[ness], directive[ness], persisten[ce], and active[ness]" (Crisp and Hiller 203). The subsequent doublespreads, though, chart his performative transformation. On the night the child "decided to get rid of [. . .] [his] nightmare once and for all," he dons a four-star general's helmet, the highest military ranking of the period. He amasses his two queen's guards beside him and aims his phallic extensions of power, a popgun and miniature cannon, at the closet door.[18] Mallan writes, "War has provided an ideal mise-en-scène for the staging of masculinity. The warring male body signifies the masculine ideal of control, dominance, and mastery, and battle becomes the ultimate test of manhood, summarily sorting out the weak and the cowardly from the strong and heroic" (16–17). By "playing war" the child performs dominance, mastery, and middle-class masculinity when he confronts the large spotted monster tiptoeing through his bedroom. After intimidating the terrified creature with his threat—"Go away, Nightmare, or I'll shoot you"—the youth stands in front of his adversary, shooting it with his toy gun. Similar to Max, whose costume enables him to quiet and control the Wild Things, the boy's toys serve as props that contribute to his sustained bodily and behavioral masculine performance. Likewise, Mayer's child's anger and aggression is both transhistorical and socioculturally specific, which establishes a compelling connection to military play in the Cold War years. As Mintz notes, "Cold War children's culture sought to prepare the young for a particular conception for the future: a future in which boys would be prepared to defend the United States from threats of freedom [. . .]. Thus the emphasis in boy culture on mock gun-play and battles between cowboys and Indians" ("The Changing Face" 43). In this context, defeating his nightmare with a toy gun, cannon, and soldiers is tantamount to growing up, that is, becoming a middle-class male adult who embodies and perpetuates hegemonic masculinity so that he can impose expected characteristics and behaviors of a normative social order upon "the other."

Yet, Mayer's child reveals that his military play is another performance, since he quickly alters his role after shooting his Nightmare. Taking off his helmet and placing his gun aside as his anger diffuses, the child maintains his position of authority as he tucks the creature into bed. These nurturing gestures may be read as gender-neutral rather than conventionally masculine or feminine, since either a mother or a father might engage in this type of performance. The penultimate doublespread, portraying the child and Nightmare in bed together, reveals another reason why the two beings are so aptly paired. Not only does the confrontation with the monster expose the performance of normative masculinity, but the creature is also integral to developing the child's psychic and gendered identity. Similarly, Max's retention of the wolf suit at the conclusion of *Where the Wild Things Are* reinforces the idea that embracing monstrosity is essential to the formation of his selfhood.[19]

Sendak's and Mayer's books engage with transformations in 1950s and 1960s American visual culture that reaffirm boys' socioculturally sanctioned connections to monsters and their protagonists' confrontations with horrific creatures simultaneously mark the children as "canny." Anna Jackson performs a Freudian-inspired etymological investigation of the term to conclude that "Canny is a word which has increasingly come to mean a cleverness that is not just about knowing things, but is about a particular sort of capability, the capability to manipulate people and events in your own self-interest. It is to do with self-possession—a self-possession that makes you capable of acting powerfully in and on the world" (159).[20] Sendak's and Mayer's protagonists utilize their costumes, props, and their imaginations to tame Wild Things and confront and defeat nightmares. Although both boys emulate adult behavior, Max demonstrates his gender fluidity by reproducing his mother's verbal threat to quiet the Wild Things (sending them to bed without supper), and Mayer's child expertly performs as an adult tucking a child-Nightmare into bed, they frequently act independently "in and on their [imaginary and domestic] worlds" without adult intervention. Their knowledge, both innate and empirical, enables them to "manipulate" the outcomes of their confrontations with imaginary monsters. Consequently, they foster the self-possession that allows them to act powerfully by ridding their imaginary and domestic environments of these threats while simultaneously cultivating their transforming identities. Mayer's and Sendak's boys also reveal that the whiteness and middle-classness that structure normative masculinity are subject to as much performance as gender itself.

The monster children I discuss in the remainder of this essay, narrative inheritors of literary and filmic pasts, also amass and deploy knowledge so as to perform as canny children. However, their monstrosity differs from their predecessors' in at least a few important respects. Victoria Carrington, in her investigation of contemporary gothic toys and gothic literacy, contends, "Contemporary childhoods are not lived in a glow of innocence and sequential development. Often, there is no 'innocence' to recapture. Instead, these childhoods are lived in the glow of digital technologies, unrelenting 24/7 global media, and the positive and negative effects of globalization and family and community change" (306).²¹ *The Sleepless Little Vampire, Frankie Stein*, and *Zombie in Love* offer a retreat from the notion of the corrupted twenty-first-century child who has lost its innocence due to excess knowledge and experience—sexual or otherwise. These works depict vampire, Frankensteinian, and zombie children/adolescents navigating implicitly middle-class conservative familial, romantic, and domestic contexts. Due to the characters' densely woven filmic and literary allusions, they might initially seem to embody a loss or lack of innocence; instead, their physical monstrosity is tempered by their nonaggressive behavior, which distinguishes them from Sendak's and Mayer's protagonists.

Importantly, the three books might be linked to "the boys' movement" and "its centerpiece, the 'boy crisis'" that began to garner public attention in the late 1990s. "Therapists," including Michael Gurian and William Pollack, expound on contemporary boyhood through their "manuals" and other writings by reenvisioning the conventional behaviors and attributes associated with masculinity (Kidd *Making American Boys* 167). Some of these writers proffer reactionary responses to the supposed emasculation wrought by feminism. As Kidd explains, "The new boyology [. . .] takes issue with [a variety of discourses, including] feminism and feminization by appealing to a mythic understanding of masculinity's wild essence" (*Making American Boys* 169). Kidd synthesizes these critics' stances by writing, "Whatever their claims about the boy's fundamental nature, the new boyologists simultaneously assume that the boy's behavior can be altered to some degree. Character can apparently be shaped, even as the wildness of boys is immutable" (169). The three picturebooks I examine do not explicitly engage with this "contemporary crisis," but they implicitly offer a response to these various cultural critics by reconstructing, queering, and making normative masculinity strange through performance.

Stephen King underscores children's attraction to vampires when he remarks, "I've always wondered if the appeal of the vampire myth for children doesn't lie partly in the simple fact that vampires get to sleep all day and stay up all night" (351).[22] Fictional and filmic incarnations of child vampires, such as the diminutive killer Claudia in *Interview with the Vampire* (1976, 1994) and the romantic Eli in *Let the Right One In* (2004, 2008), frequently revel in the nightlife while simultaneously revealing another potential site of attraction: the monster's queerness. As a creature who rarely distinguishes between male and female victims, who often possesses a transformative body, and who is never bound by socially constructed gender roles, the vampire has been read as a queer figure par excellence.[23] In Richard Egielski's picturebook *The Sleepless Little Vampire* (2011), a child vampire, who physically and behaviorally subverts normative constructions of masculinity and femininity, realizes it cannot sleep because it is a creature of the night. The book can be read as a parody of Pat Hutchins's *Good-Night, Owl!* (1972), in which the gender-ambiguous bird's attempts to slumber during the day are foiled by the noisy animals that inhabit the same tree. Unlike the owl, the sleepless monster ascends to canniness by *temporarily* performing[24] conventional masculinity to tame the other creatures that encroach upon its domestic space. Consequently, the vampire child offers a more complex challenge to normative masculinity than Sendak's and Mayer's protagonists due to its queerness, and its failure to execute innately vampiric actions such as blood-sucking and physical mobility, despite its literal monstrosity.

The book's opening doublespread reveals a small, framed illustration of an exceptionally white child vampire in a Victorian nightgown clutching a Frankensteinian doll. Its nightgown, tuft of hair, bulbous eyes, Nosferatu ears, and large feet imply gender ambiguity. Significantly, neither the written text nor the peritextual material engender the vampire through masculine or feminine pronouns. These details reinforce a definition of the term queer based on "sexual ambigu[ity], protean[ness], and corporal illegi[bility]" (Bruhm "Michael Jackson's" 158). The vampire's domestic space complements these ideas, particularly because its bedroom differs from those in Sendak's and Mayer's books. In the first doublespread, the vampire stares directly at the reader from the confines of its mausoleum; it sleeps on top of a coffin, with the comforts of a soft pillow, a blue-patterned blanket, and a floral stained-glass window. In subsequent pages, the frame increasingly widens, *Wild Things*–style from recto to verso, revealing that the monster's mausoleum is located within a graveyard. Mair Rigby explains that "Gothic texts are replete with marginal spaces" and that such "liminal spaces are never entirely exterior to the normal world, but can be recognized as constituting places of *difference*." Consequently, they can "be considered ambivalent sites of queer possibility, critical power and danger, because, away from the hegemony of dominant institutions, sexual subjects are least stable" (46). The graveyard, a liminal site of death, becomes a site of celebratory queer possibility in Egielski's book. In this place of multifarious difference, the vampire's knowledge about itself will blossom rather than decay and die.[25]

The first doublespread's text introduces the vampire's sleeping problem, linking the creature's inability to sleep to the publicly private nature of the graveyard: "Why can't I sleep? / What could it be? / Is it—." The next doublespread, depicting a large, colorful arachnid staring at the monster, completes this question—"the spider spitting? / THOOP!—THOOP!" Egielski's book parodies Hutchins's book by replacing the nocturnal bird of prey (the owl) with a nocturnal monster whose literary and filmic predecessors prey upon humans and by employing alliteration and onomatopoeia, techniques that engage the child listener's ear. However, Egielski's substitution of a spider spitting for Hutchins's buzzing bees creates a distinctively gothic effect. Gothic stories and horror films channel noise through descriptions of tempestuous weather, ghostly footsteps, rattling chains, and beasts howling in the nighttime sky.[26] Gothicized noise, in turn, blurs boundaries between inside and outside, as well as between open and enclosed spaces, thereby rendering physical, geographical, and corporeal sites vulnerable to invasion. In Hutchins's and Egielski's books, animals and supernatural creatures' bodies, as well as their associated sounds increasingly infiltrate the owl's and the vampire's homes, encroaching upon their space in disruptive auditory and physical ways. In Egielski's book, these sounds not only convey a sense of gothic nostalgia tied to Rice's vampire works and even *Dark Shadows* (1966–1971, 1991, 2012), but also expose the child's difference from the other creatures in the graveyard.

Over the next several doublespreads, the frame surrounding the vampire expands to reveal cockroaches, bats, a werewolf, a blue witch, skeletons, and ghosts disrupting the child's sleep. The text introduces each new creature with appropriate onomatopoetic and alliterative phrases such as "the bats flitting? / FLAPPITY—FLAP!" and "the werewolf bawling? / AWHOO!—AWHOO!" Consequently, the book maintains its verbal homage to

Goodnight, Owl! by substituting familiar gothicized figures for bees, squirrels, crows, a woodpecker, starlings, jays, cuckoos, sparrows, robins, and doves. Spooner explains that the gothic is "profoundly concerned with its own past, self-referentially dependent on traces of other stories, familiar images and narrative structures, intertextual allusions." She further asserts, "If this could be said to be true of a great many kinds of literature or film, then Gothic has a greater degree of self-consciousness about its nature, cannibalistically consuming the dead body of its own tradition" (10). *The Sleepless Little Vampire* and the next two books I discuss heighten this gothicized self-consciousness. The monstrous picturebook, especially Egielski's work, is not only concerned with the past of the picturebook (Hutchins; Sendak), but also with narrative and filmic gothic/horror imagery to such a self-conscious degree that it *may* surpass that of YA and adult-oriented gothic texts, specifically because of its uniquely visual and verbal nature.[27] There are several ways that *The Sleepless Little Vampire* exemplifies these ideas. The book is, for instance, a pictorial homage to "The Monster Mash" that, while pillaging imagery from older cartoons, including Betty Boop's "Minnie the Moocher" (1932) as well as the Disney's "The Dancing Skeletons" (1929), also resembles a danse macabre.[28] Since the vampire, unlike many other adult and child vampires in filmic and literary works, does not consume human (or even animal) blood, but visually ingests the spectacles that surround it, the monster may be said to "cannibalistically consume the dead body of its own [adult and child gothic] tradition" in an unconventional way.

In addition to watching the unfolding gothic theatrics, the child also engages with its own queer gothic tradition because of its attachment to its Frankensteinian doll. As the pairing between the vampire and the toy reinforce, Mary Shelley's renowned creature and the English literary vampire, John Polidori's creation, were born out of the infamous 1816 Villa Diodati literary gathering.[29] They are creatures who enter the literary imaginary at the same time; they are also male monsters who actively pursue male victims, performing queer desire within public spaces.[30] In Egielski's book, the green-skinned doll physically highlights the vampire's gender-ambiguous mode of dress and physical features because it wears pants, a shirt, large black shoes, and has short boyish hair. In contrast to Max's and Mayer's child's violently masculine guns, toy soldiers, and wolf suit, the vampire's Frankensteinian doll is a cuddly, occasionally sentient object that provides the child with comfort during its domestic invasion. The toy, in short, does not engender the child, but rather reinforces another definition of queer that is essential to the book's undermining of normative boyhood: "the term *queer* in its more traditional sense [. . .] indicate[s] a deviation from the 'normal'" (Bruhm and Hurley x). In short, the child is queer because of its gender ambiguity (physically and behaviorally), its asexualized desire for the doll, and because it does not cohere to normative vampirism.

Despite its multilayered queering of the norm, the child nonetheless briefly performs normative masculinity in order to gain control of its surroundings. When the vampire confronts new monsters and supernatural entities, the questions it initially poses ("the cockroaches crawling?") increasingly become exclamatory statements ("That's loud, but so are— / the skeletons clacking!"), thereby revealing its increasing intellectual and verbal power. A vital transformation occurs in the picturebook's plot when the child articulates the reason for its sleeplessness: "No! / That's not it. / Don't you see? / It wasn't *bedtime* yet for me." This canny declaration halts all the movement in the illustration. Werewolf, skeletons, witch, bats, spider, ghosts, and cockroaches stare at the vampire in befuddlement, as if they have been robbed of their agency by the creature's rhyming statement. This idea is paradoxical, considering the child's relative physical stasis, which is an inversion of the literary and filmic vampire's threatening mobility. For instance, Lord Ruthven in Polidori's "The Vampyre" (1819) invades English drawing rooms and travels to Greece to victimize peasants. Mobility, including supernatural speed, flying, and floating likewise characterizes filmic vampires, as Ken Gelder and others have shown.[31] The sleepless vampire's confined movements—the child is always depicted in the book's recto, within or near its mausoleum—serve as a stylistic and thematic homage to *Where the Wild Things Are*. The recto also serves as Max's sanctioned space of domesticity that he does not move from until he arrives at the Wild Things' island. But whereas Max's physical mobility within his house and at the island affirms his masculine performance and associates him with the Wild Things, the vampire child's near immobility helps disassociate it from its literary and filmic vampiric predecessors' power, even as the child channels their queerness and power.

The child's ascension into canniness, its articulation of its nocturnal nature, grants the monster verbal and social authority over the other graveyard residents. To demonstrate this change, the vampire shouts, "GOOD MORNING, NIGHT CREATURES!" in the book's only unframed doublespread. This benevolent, contradictory greeting disappears on the subsequent page when the vampire declares, "Now, I don't want to hear a peep! / Everyone go—." The doublespread's frame reappears to visually reinforce the vampire's "control" and "mastery" over these creatures. Here, the child temporarily performs as conventionally masculine—in both behavior and appearance. Kimberly Reynolds, in her discussion of masculinity, maintains, "It seems that it is not the fact of being male that provokes masculine behavior, but the condition of power" (99). Like a king lording over his minions, the vampire stands on the second step of its mausoleum, facing the reader, right hand slightly raised. Its inwardly arched eyebrows combined with its open pink mouth and sharp fangs present a sufficiently threatening image to ensure that the other animal and paranormal creatures retire. This appropriation of power combined with the child's physical metamorphosis magnifies the book's intertextuality by paying homage to Sendak's and Mayer's protagonists who either verbally mesmerize their monsters into slumber or fall asleep with them in bed.

After demonstrating its ability to act powerfully upon its graveyard world, the book's final doublespread shifts the narrative to a predictably restful conclusion. The verso, entirely white for the first time in the book, completes the previous doublespread's phrase "Everybody go—" with the words "to sleep." This verb amplifies the vampire's newfound control over its surroundings and inhabitants, even as the child sheds its performance of normative masculinity. Juxtaposed against the white background, the vampire's own whiteness becomes especially relevant at this narrative juncture. White, as Richard Dyer has explored, not only has compelling racial and ethnic significations, but also bears cultural associations with death (207). Of the vampire, Dyer explains, "The horror of vampirisim is expressed in colour: ghastly white, disgustingly cadaverous, without the blood of life that would give colour" (210). The sleepless vampire is, like other literary and filmic vampires, an un-dead creature, who is ethnically ambiguous, but the visually consuming child rewrites whiteness as a sign of livelihood rather than of death. Sleep, an approximation to death for vampires, is also recast in this respect, as an essential and productive act that offers a final connection to gothic queerness. William Hughes and Andrew Smith explain, "The tempting 'queerness' that Gothic presents is [. . .] that of assimilation to the alternative, acceptance of the valid claims of heterodoxies that might be, variously, cultural, theological, political or, indeed, sexual" (2). The vampire's attainment of sleep is a conventional child activity, necessary for development and well-being, that is queered, per Smith's definition, because it shows the acceptance of a cultural heterodoxy—that the fictional child may fall asleep during the daylight even as the child reading the book is forced to fall asleep at night.

Frankie Stein (2007), written by Lola M. Schaefer and illustrated by Kevan Atteberry, mines Mary Shelley's *Frankenstein* (1818) as well as the novel's filmic incarnations to produce an inverted monstrous tale.[32] Through extensive visual and textual parodying, Schaefer and Atteberry not only depict the titular character's identity formation, but also rewrite what Laura P. Claridge refers to as "the resultant real subject of" Shelley's novel: "the failure of human beings to 'parent' their offspring in such a way that they will be able to take part in society rather than retreat into themselves" (14). Victor Frankenstein utilizes science and alchemy to transform dead matter into a live adult-child, yet he abandons his horrific creation. By watching the DeLacey family from a distance, the monster acquires language, along with the knowledge that his longing for a loving family will never be fulfilled due to his abhorrent physical features. Halberstam, Claridge, and other critics highlight examples of family dysfunction within the novel aside from Victor and his offspring's, but *Frankie Stein*, like several filmic adaptations of Shelley's novel, omits the Walton and Victor frame story as well as Victor's extended and adopted family. Because it focuses only on the child and his immediate family, the book illustrates that Frankie Stein's ascension to canniness and his creation of a masculine identity is shaped by domestic confrontations with his parents' otherness. These engagements result in his perpetuation of monstrous familial traditions that occur by paradoxically embracing and defamiliarizing normative boyhood behaviors and attributes.

The book's opening doublespread reveals constructions of masculinity and femininity integral to the book's remaking of monstrosity. Frankie is an adorable bald white baby in a bassinette, covered with a ghoulish blanket. Despite the disconcerting accoutrement, Frankie epitomizes healthy boy human normalcy because of his physicality and his name. His egg-shaped cranium suggests his youth and fragility, in addition to starkly contrasting the shape of his father's head. Mr. Frank N. Stein, who grips the bassinette with one hand and waves to his son with the other, is an amalgam of monstrous masculine traits. The father's rectangular head, green skin, purple unibrow, and purple hair illustrate the visual and familial dissonance between father and son. Frankie's mother, Mrs. Frank N. Stein, further highlights these disparities. Her green skin implies a genetic connection to her husband, and her absent first name initially suggests that she is merely his possession. The book reinforces this relationship by visually coding her as an homage to James Whale's Bride of Frankenstein, clad in a full-length white dress, with rippling sleeves, and a bouffant of black hair marked by two white streaks. This initial family grouping links the parents' gender roles to their physical monstrosity, highlights Frankie's otherness within his home, and parodies the heteronormative family gathering around a newborn baby's bassinette. The monster's birth is rewritten as a celebration rather than a disavowal, despite the visual differences between figures.

The second doublespread reinforces the book's inversion of monstrosity by highlighting the importance of skin within gothic narratives. Halberstam explains that in Shelley's novel the monster's skin serves as a visual marker of monstrosity, and vision, in turn, affirms knowledge and fear of the monstrous (39). However, Frankie's smooth, peach-colored skin serves as a sign of humanness and thus constitutes a form of monstrosity within a monstrous household that is, as his father states, not "scary like us." The contrast between the parents' and the child's bodies exposes monsters' skin as a site of racial and ethnic difference and specifically revises these significations in Frankenstein stories, plays, and films. Elizabeth Young explains, "The Frankenstein story of monstrous sons and haunted fathers throws U.S. racial formations into high relief" (7): "The English story of a monster made in a European laboratory [...] has as domestic a claim on American literary culture as that of the slave in his cabin" (8). As these statements imply, Young's analysis begins with an investigation of the interconnections between nineteenth-century African Americans, in fiction and culture, and Mary Shelley's monster; she then explores written and visual twentieth-century works that revamp these monstrous and racial connections alongside their attendant queer overtones, particularly as evinced in James Whale's renowned films. *Frankie Stein* thus contributes to the *Frankenstein* genealogy and the monstrous picturebook lineage, in part, through its recasting of whiteness. Max's white wolf suit enables his alpha male performance, making hegemonic masculinity overtly visible and nonnormative, and Mayer's child expertly performs middle-class male whiteness, while the Little Vampire's white visage simultaneously erases ethnic ambiguity and highlights productive living death. In contrast, Frankie's whiteness becomes increasingly visible in his home and is eventually embraced as a form of "positive" monstrosity. Before this acceptance of monstrosity can occur though, Mrs. Stein suggests that she and her husband help their child perpetuate the family's visual and behavioral monstrous traditions. Consequently, she demonstrates parents' complex role in constructing their child's identity and highlights one of the book's most potent distinctions from Sendak's and Mayer's works. Frankie's very present mother and father mark him as a Lockean tabula rasa, but their failed efforts to overhaul his looks and behaviors[33] reinforce the idea that "masculinity" and in this case monstrosity are "at least partially [...] learned as part of socialization" (Reynolds 98).

After several failed attempts to enact a makeover, Frankie's mother and father take "the family tree from the closet," thereby making the Stein family's lineage visible. Mr. Stein ambles toward his son holding a small tree in his enormous hands, each of its brown branches laden with black, white, and greenish photographs of family members. By literalizing the family tree, the illustration highlights the symbolic undertones of monstrous growth. Instructively, Mr. and Mrs. Stein relay the exploits of three different family members to their son: Uncle Franklin (whose "laugh turns men to stone"), Great-granddaddy Frank the Gripper (who "can hold the attention of an entire town"), and Grandmother Frances (who is "always full of surprises"). The pictures highlight the "differenc[es]," physical and behavioral, between these three family members and their innate "scar[iness]," just as the book's illustrations have continued to emphasize discrepancies in size, shape, and action between Frankie and his parents. The subsequent doublespread also shows that grandmother Frances's "surprise" is that she has a literally split identity: two faces, one on either side of her head. Likewise, neither Uncle Franklin nor Great-granddaddy Frank's photographs depict the actions associated with their names. In sum, the family tree reinforces and defamiliarizes the connections between physicality and gendered behavior within the family, making the parents' insistence on Frankie's makeover an affirmation and a departure from the Stein's family his- and her-story.

After viewing the family tree, Frankie decides to remake his identity within the private space of his bedroom, the place par excellence for gendered and monstrous transformations in Egielski's, Sendak's, and Mayer's books. John Stephens delineates the features of the female makeover in adolescent fiction by explaining that this process "is physical and visible." He additionally contends that it "may be a result of others acting on the focused body or an act of self-refashioning" that "metonymically expresses a character's unfolding interiority thereby operating as a metonym of growth." Most important, the makeover "does not impose a new personality but discloses what is already there" (Stephens qtd. in Reynolds 102). Since Reynolds persuasively argues that the makeover narrative can apply to male fictional characters, I wish to extend her discussion to *Frankie Stein*. Frankie initially intends to "be scary" by performing in his parents' footsteps, but despite his rehearsals in the mirror, the faintness of his reflection, combined with the image of the Stein family's resident ghost hovering above his head, reinforce the text: "Frankie tried and tried, but he just couldn't act like his parents." The child's identification with his mother and father is coded as spectral within the illustration; Frankie is merely haunted and ineffable until he "decide[s] on his own kind of scary." Thus, he enacts his own successful makeover that highlights his physicality, making it visible within his home. This transformation is inspired by his parents' continual attempts to reshape his body, but when he refashions his own body, he "discloses what is already there."

To this end, Frankie metamorphosizes into a normative American boy. He emerges from his bedroom smiling, wearing a blue-and-green-plaid shirt, blue jeans, and red shoes, his blond hair neatly combed over to one side. Mr. and Mrs. Stein stare at his transformed body in horror, clutching each other in the recto, parodying reactionary responses to the monster that haunt Frankenstein stories, films, and plays. This is the first doublespread in the book that spatially separates Frankie from his parents, underscoring the difference between his identity and theirs. The child embodies an image of human-monstrousness by hugging and kissing his parents. Although these actions do not reinforce images of normative boyhood, Frankie transforms them into violently affectionate gestures to threaten and scare his parents. Thus, he ascends to canniness in order to perpetuate the monstrous tradition they represent, which enables him, in turn, to act powerfully in and on his domestic world.[34] Frankie's own staging of normative boyhood still reveals that masculinity is a social construct, but his performance also deviates from the children's in the other three picturebooks since he does not gain social or physical power over other monsters (in this case, his parents). Instead, performing conventional masculinity paradoxically enables Frankie to "fit in."

Because Frankie finds his place within his family by performing conventional human boyhood as a new kind of monstrosity, he hangs his photograph at the lowest branch of the family tree. He not only belongs to the Stein family, as this gesture suggests, but additionally, the narrator claims, "From that day forward, Frankie Stein was considered the scariest Stein of all . . ." (ellipses Schaefer's). In her postmodern picturebook study, Allan writes, "Children's literature has traditionally carried a predominantly humanist message about the individual as a unified self with a central core of identity that is unique, rational and established" (74). She further adds that postmodern critics "see identity as constituted in interaction with what is outside of the self and is thus relational or social, rather than individual. Viewed in this way, identity is not fixed but rather *in process* and will never reach completion" (75).³⁵ Frankie's placement of the photograph indicates that he has found his place within his family. However, adding his picture does not preclude his identity from transforming, but rather opens up possibilities for future rifts between representation (what the image shows) and reality (what he does), that is, for his continual growth, like Sendak's Max, Mayer's child, and Egielski's vampire.

By introducing Frankie's sister, the book's final pages anticipate how the performance of gender roles might change within a monstrous family. Here, readers learn that Frankie's status as "the scariest Stein" is contingent: "until Francie Stein came into the world." Foreshadowing the idea that his sister will supplant his title, this female doppelganger baby in a bassinette reproduces Frankie's spatial positioning on the book's first doublespread. Francie is an extension of Frankie, and her visual similarity to her brother implies that gendered and monstrous performances and transformations will be part of her future as well. Notably, the children's parents are absent from this final image. Instead, Frankie bends over the bassinette, standing in the same position as his father in the book's first doublespread. This final image reaffirms that, in contrast to Sendak's, Mayer's, and Egielski's protagonists, the Stein children's identities are shaped not only by their parents but also by each other. Nonetheless, Frankie and Francie, like the sleepless vampire, offer less violently threatening depictions of monstrosity than their picturebook predecessors.

Zombie in Love (2011) differs from *The Sleepless Vampire* and *Frankie Stein* by concentrating on a young adult zombie, Mortimer, a social outsider searching for his ideal romantic mate. Zombies' voracious tendencies have been metaphorically associated with capitalism, colonialism, and social marginalization (to name just a few concepts). As Maria Nikolajeva and Carole Scott explain, consumption structures children's literature: "one of the most central motifs in children's fiction [. . .] [is] the dilemma of eating or being eaten, which is also extremely prominent in *Wild Things*" (183). Writer Kelly DiPucchio and illustrator Scott Campbell replace the zombie's hunger for flesh with his hunger for love.³⁶ Specifically, the disjunctions between DiPucchio's words and Campbell's pictures expose courtship and love's monstrosity by illustrating the psychic turmoil and irrationality attendant to both through Mortimer's decomposition and his voracious appetite for romance. Mortimer ascends into self-empowered adulthood, yet his canniness results in the performance of an ambiguously humanized masculine romantic identity that initially defamiliarizes and eventually affirms heteronormativity.

The book's opening doublespread introduces the zombie within his domestic space, illuminating that his monstrous appearance undermines his desire to fashion a normative masculine identity. Mortimer's skin bears a greenish tinge, and the rings around his eyes suggest decay. Although his entire body is not abject, the monster's face and extremities show signs of disfigurement, including his four-toed feet, his curved ankles, his jutting right ear, and the shadow displacing his nose. The rounded lines of Mortimer's face and his clothing highlight the zombie's physical remnants of humanity, marking him as uncanny.[37] Similar to Frankie Stein's parents, one can read Mortimer as a monster who demonstrates a generalized form of racial or ethnic difference, an association reinforced by zombies' sociocultural origins as enslaved, Haitian field/plantation workers.[38] Yet Mortimer, in contrast to his Caribbean predecessors, lives a life of middle-class leisure, like all the boy characters I investigate in this essay, albeit in a more macabre fashion. He sits in a coffin, surrounded by moribund ephemera, reinforcing the root of his name (mort, death). However, Mortimer's association with death can be read as symbolic of his solitude. Although the opening illustration introduces his ever-present companion, a zombie dog, replete with exposed ribs and loose eyeball, the short sentence "Mortimer was lonely" simultaneously "individuates" the monster by naming him, engenders him as masculine, and also reveals his hordeless existence (Collins and Bond 200).[39] In order to transcend his solitude, the zombie must find a partner, but his visage initially precludes him from attaining this goal.

Although Mortimer is physically other to the humans in the book, many of his actions also do not cohere to the filmic and fictional conventions of zombiehood. Nevertheless, he does embrace movement between public and private spaces, even though his goal is not the consumption of human flesh but romancing human women. In the first of three cliché romantic scenarios, "He gave the girl at the bus stop a fancy box of chocolates"; the adjective "fancy" is visually associated with a box of chocolates in the shape of a coffin, and the lid includes a skull encircled in a heart, thereby merging love, death, and consumption. During Mortimer's second attempt to woo a girl, "He gave the mail carrier a shiny, red heart." The picture contrasts the words by depicting the zombie handing the mail carrier a real human heart and objectifying the corporal wholeness the monster lacks. Likewise, the third picture in this sequence stages equally morbid metaphoric disjunctions when Mortimer offers "the waitress at the diner a stunning diamond ring." Here, the monster surpasses his prior gifts and their connotations, by conflating courtship, romance, and marriage, and by inadvertently emphasizing their deadly undertones, since a finger still occupies the diamond ring. In his discussion of millennial transformations in zombie films, Peter Dendle writes, "Zombie movies in the wake of *Return [of the Living Dead* (1985)] rely less on scenic tension (within a room, for instance) and more on fear of hot pursuit and swift, violent assault" (178). The three pictures show a succession of events where Mortimer's attempts to captivate women represent a form of "hot pursuit." His assault, in turn, becomes violently romantic and utterly comedic rather than violently destructive. Mortimer's attempts to emulate conventional masculine romantic behavior, in short, reveal that, at this point in the narrative, he is more zombie than human.

Mortimer's failed attempts to woo human girls lead him to self-help books, but their kernels of wisdom place the zombie in several scenarios that reinforce his otherness. For example, at the gym, when the monster's decomposed arm is wrenched free during weight lifting, the zombie anxiously stares at his detached appendage. A male gym member in the picture's background objectifies Mortimer's limb, emasculating him with his gaze while demonstrating his own physical prowess (successful weight lifting) and wholeness. As this scenario and others, such as taking dance classes and singing romantic songs on the street corner, show Mortimer's all-consuming pursuit of romance separates him from his domestic environment, forcing him to harness a romantic and social identity within an urban environment, the late twentieth- and early twenty-first-century fictional and filmic zombie narrative setting par excellence. However, this setting ultimately fails to provide him with the physical freedom and sustenance that his filmic and fictional predecessors have achieved by taking over entire cities and voraciously devouring people. He remains consistently hungry for romance, and relentlessly searches for human women, enduring the emasculation that Max, Mayer's child, the little vampire, and Frankie Stein rarely experience. Rather than seeking individuation, such as the sleepless vampire does from other graveyard creatures and Frankie Stein does from his parents, Mortimer searches for a mature and sublimated identity. To this end, his gravitation to a Valentine's Day celebration, the Cupid's Ball, offers him a uniquely romantic opportunity to deploy his knowledge by ascending to the role of the monstrous heteronormative mate.

The doublespread devoted to the Cupid's Ball depicts humans as a horde, exposing their animality on the dance floor, limbs awry, twisting and turning in each other's arms, or gathered round tables, consuming cake and drinking punch. Their colorful clothing and the space's decorative pink banners highlight Mortimer's social isolation; he sits alone at the punch bowl in a ragged black-and-white suit with a cup in his hand. The monster is situated in the right background of the recto, and his gaze is directed at the crowd in the verso. With few exceptions up to this point in the book, the zombie has inhabited the verso in the book's doublespreads and looked toward the recto. Consequently, this jarring shift in his positioning visually underscores his displacement from the ball rather than any lethal and/or violent threat he poses to the humans. Despite the humans' monstrous behavior, though, Mortimer is still physically and spatially distinguished from them, within yet outside the bounds of commodified romantic heteronormativity.

Nonetheless, Mortimer tries to impress human women with new tactics. For instance, the narrator states, "Each time a girl approached the table, Mortimer would smile." His smile, appearing in earlier pages of the book on a smaller scale, finally receives a one-page close-up. Here, readers see his warped teeth, the gaping black holes in his gums, a nose that resembles two holes, and enormous white eyes, with large rings around them. Kyle Bishop has discussed, at some length, zombies' "visual nature," that is, their largely filmic rather than literary origins ("Raising the Dead" 200). This picture, which underscores and freezes a mobile gesture, implies why alongside cinema, graphic novels, and television shows, children's picturebooks may serve as an equally apt genre for representing the zombie. The book maintains these intertextual connections by reinforcing a filmic convention on the next page; Mortimer's expression is so terrifying that "each time [he smiled] the girl would shriek and run away." As Dendle's earlier quotation indicates, in pre-millennial zombie narratives, entrapping indoor spaces are frequently depicted as the most horrific for humans encountering these monsters. The page depicting Mortimer's smile as a close-up implicitly plays upon this convention since the ball takes place in an indoor space and Mortimer's facial expression results in several women fleeing. His smile makes his monstrosity more visible, thereby further defamiliarizing his zombiehood as well as the performance of human masculinity.

After exhausting his wooing efforts, Mortimer is poised to leave the ball, but a thunderous noise announces the arrival of a female zombie. The text above the picture states, "Mortimer turned around. There on the floor was a girl" and thus obscures two vital details: the girl is a zombie, and her detached foot caused her fall. Below the illustration, the text indicates, "Her name was Mildred and she was drop-dead gorgeous. She smiled." Similar to Mortimer's name, Mildred's moniker, by playing upon the word mildew/mold and dread, emphasizes her corporal decay while her detached foot parallels Mortimer's previously detached arm. Moreover, her smile, shown on the next page, matches his in its grotesque otherness. To support their romantic partnership, the zombies face each other on the dance floor, Mortimer toothily grinning as he holds Mildred's calf and foot, in a manner akin to a monstrous Prince Charming. This restaging of a Disney/fairy-tale scenario enables the monsters to stage heteronormative romantic roles even though they are physically othered. Like Frankie Stein, this performance does not grant the monsters power over others, in this case humans, but instead enables them to find their place within and outside of normative society.

To celebrate their romance, Mortimer and Mildred move to a public outdoor setting where monstrosity and romance can converge without the objectification of humanity—a graveyard. Similar to *The Sleepless Little Vampire*, *Zombie in Love* uses a space frequently identified with death to celebrate self-knowledge. Here, the zombies sit in the graveyard on a gruesomely green picnic blanket while Mortimer feeds Mildred a human brain. This scene occurs at night, and parodies romantically bucolic fictional and filmic picnic scenes by substituting conventional human food for conventional zombie food. Bishop writes, in the context of the infamous zombie horde feeding scene in *Night of the Living Dead* (1968), "Romero accomplishes the objectification of the human body by both depicting human flesh to be nothing more than meat [. . .] and by having his zombies act according to the basest of natures—they feed because they are things desiring food, and they show none of the decorum or reservations a living human subject would most likely have" (*American Zombie Gothic* 133). *Zombie in Love* withholds the objectification of the human body as meat until the end when consumption can become literalized in the act of loving each other. Mortimer and Mildred, in contrast to their filmic counterparts in Romero's movie(s), engage in civilized consumption since the brain sits on a plate, and the illustration shows Mortimer's fork poised near Mildred's mouth rather than her jaws and hands tearing human flesh. Thus, the picture merges civilization with one of its taboos: cannibalism. However, the brain is a symbol of enlightenment, and the zombies have become romantically and socially enlightened by finding each other. Their dual ascension into canniness—finally embracing their monstrous natures within this illustration—enables them to act powerfully on the world through their romantic union.

To this end, the book's final picture rewrites conventional heterosexual marriage by showing a hearse, in place of a wedding limo, carrying Mortimer, Mildred, worms, and zombie dog into an implicitly bright future. The human nuclear family, so often idolized in post–*28 Days Later* (2002) zombie films, is displaced by the zombie nuclear family. Due to Mildred and Mortimer's inability to procreate, the ubiquitous worms and zombie dog serve as their surrogate children. Although this picture seems to associate marriage with death, due to the funereal vehicle, it also revises these significations through two visual means. The road the monsters travel is a powerful symbol suggesting forward movement, that is, lively futurity. Furthermore, this illustration shows the zombies and their "children" driving into a heart-shaped moon, the gothicized version of a "happily-ever-after" sunset that culminates romances. Since the picture is also the only one in the book without text and follows a bucolic graveyard romance scene, it implies the achievement of heteronormative, middle-class, narrative closure.[40]

Stephen King discusses the conservative nature of horror in *Danse Macabre*. He writes, horror films "do not love death, as some have suggested; they love life. They do not celebrate deformity but by dwelling on deformity, they sing of health and energy. By showing us the miseries of the damned, they help us to rediscover the smaller (but never petty) joys of our own lives" (210). Despite the inclusion of undead creatures and violent children, the five picturebooks I investigate offer energetic, joyous celebrations of life and health with happy narrative outcomes, in large part because of the younger audiences they are at least implicitly intended for. Yet, quoting King here is apropos in the context of this essay for other reasons. As a child who voraciously consumed monster movies and horror comics, affirming the connections between Cold War boyhood and monstrosity, King's horror fiction has done much to "criti[que]" "traditional forms of masculinity" (Heinecken 119).

Although none of the picturebooks in this essay reproduces King's monstrous "wounded and wounding men" (Heinecken 119), they are all, nonetheless, works that stage fictional challenges to normative masculinity through boys' and monsters' bodies. Mortimer, Frankie Stein, and the Little Vampire offer a range of subject positions for child readers that disassociate violent behavior from physical monstrosity, reframing masculinity by offering alternative roles, behaviors, and bodies. These characters consequently allow younger children—both boys and girls—who may be navigating contemporary constructions of gender a variety of choices for their own emerging identities. Even though Max and Mayer's child act aggressively and violently, they engage in performances that not only reveal masculinity as a social construct, but that also, as other critics have noted, provide catharsis for child readers. The interconnections between masculinity and monstrosity, long since established as a convention in gothic fiction, are consistently rewritten through a variety of contemporary texts, picturebooks included. However, the shift from animalistic hybrid monsters to vampires, Franken-steinian monsters, and zombies attests to transformations in popular adult's and children's culture that ultimately erode the boundaries between them, implying that the picturebook—with its penchant for ingestion and incor-poration—may harbor the potential to be the most productively monstrous cultural text of all.

NOTES

1. Kenneth Kidd, drawing upon Perry Nodelman's analysis, succinctly highlights the importance of Sendak's work: "*Where the Wild Things Are* [. . .] made possible further do-mestications of the monstrous (think Muppets)" (*Freud in Oz* 131). Also, I employ the term *narrative picturebooks* to distinguish the works I discuss from picturebooks that serve as compendiums of various monsters and do not relay extended narratives about them. For instance, the 1960s not only saw the publication of the Sendak and Mayer works I discuss, but also Lois and Louis Darling's *The Sea Serpents Around Us* (1965), a beautiful book about aquatic monsters for child readers, and Georgess McHargue and Frank Bozzo's *The Beasts of Never: A History Natural and Un-Natural of Monsters Mythical and Magic* (1968). The former book includes short anecdotal, as well as historically and socioculturally inflected discussions about each of the monsters it features while the latter book is a child's bestiary. The bestiary, likewise, has maintained its presence within children's picturebooks in the late twentieth and early twenty-first century as Jonathan Hunt's *Bestiary: An Illuminated Alphabet of Medieval Beasts* (1998) and Jim Arnosky's *Monster Hunt* (2011) duly attest. Finally, I use the phrase "American-authored" to refer to the fact that the writers I feature (who are more often than not also the illustrators) were, to the best of my knowledge, born in America and identify themselves as American.

2. Judith Viorst's (writer) and Kay Chorao's (illustrator) book *My Mama Says There Aren't Any Zombies, Ghosts, Vampires, Creatures, Demons, Monsters, Fiends, Goblins, or Things* (1973) is one of the first American narrative picturebooks where literary and filmic monsters appear. A few slightly earlier ones include the Hallmark Play-time Book *Lamont, The Lonely Monster* (1970) and Bill Martin Jr., Albert John Pucci, and Ray Barber's *A Spooky Story* (1970). An illustrated children's poetry collection titled *Nightmares: Poems to Trouble Your Sleep* (1976) written by Jack Prelutsky and illustrated by Arnold Lobel also features pop-culturally familiar creatures such as vampires and werewolves alongside witches, trolls, and ogres. A werewolf does appear in Robin Palmer and Don Bolognese's *Dragons, Unicorns and other Magical Beasts* (1966), but this combination "dictionary" and compendium of "old tales and verses" aligns the monster with other folkloric and fairy-tale creatures.

3. Spooner does not discuss children's literature in her study, although she does exam-ine teen "goth" culture. She indicates that "millennial anxiety is one of the most common" clichés for comprehending the contemporary gothic (8). For clarification, Allan discusses

the postmodern picturebook rather than the monstrous picturebook; however, I feel that her contention about the postmodern picturebook applies to the monstrous picturebook.

4. Halberstam, like Spooner, does not discuss children's literature in her study.

5. I acknowledge a debt to Perry Nodelman here. Of "Sendak's Wild Things," he writes, they "are comfortably round; the only sharp, jagged things about them, their claws and their horns, are actually rounded crescent shapes" (127).

6. Nodelman uses the phrase "normative masculinity" in "Making Boys Appear" (1, 10, 11). What I refer to as "normative masculinity" and later "conventional masculinity" generally accords with "hegemonic masculinity." John Stephens claims, "Although this was not [R. W.] Connell's intention, the phrase is often encountered as a shorthand reference to versions of traditional, macho masculinity characterized by toughness, courage, and muscularity, but also by aggressivity, violence, misogyny, homophobia, and other qualities marked as negative in the discourses of other masculinities and feminisms" (Kindle 141–48). The books I discuss, due to their implied audiences, only rarely represent misogyny and homophobia.

7. I utilize Anna Jackson's formulation of the word "canny," and I unpack this word's definition in the vampire section of my essay.

8. Martin Salisbury and Morag Styles also draw attention to the "furore" the book "caused [...] when it was published, with many critics anxious that it would be too terrifying for children" (38). One very plausible reason why Sendak's book, to my knowledge, has not been explicitly examined in relation to "Monster Culture" is that the book is aimed at younger children whereas Monster Culture's audience was typically made up of teenagers and even adults.

9. This phenomenon, as Skal explains, began with Shock Theater, "a package of fifty-two vintage Universal horror films just sold to television stations across the country" (265). The release of late 1950s and early 1960s horror films, including *The Blob* (1958), *The Horror of Dracula* (1958), *The Curse of Frankenstein* (1957), *The Curse of the Werewolf* (1961), *Blood of Dracula* (1957), and *How to Make a Monster* (1958), reinforces the idea that Monster Culture was not just confined to televisions in living rooms and children reading monster magazines. Other aspects of Monster Culture, aside from those I discuss in this section of the essay, include horror comics (*Tales from the Crypt*, *Chilling Tales*, *Dark Mysteries*) and the other contemporaneous gothic ephemera Skal also discusses, including monster toys (which flooded the children's toy market in 1964) and gothic television shows (*The Munsters* [1964] and *The Addams Family* [1964]) (284).

10. *Famous Monsters* issues from 1963 and 1964 foreground visuals, although 1967, 1968, and 1970 editions of the magazine downplay text a little more than the earlier sixties issues. *Famous Monsters* enabled readers to relish and domesticate monsters' visual ghastliness in a plethora of ways, by, for instance, going behind the scenes of Don Post Studios (July vol. 45 1967) and interviewing Boris Karloff (June vol. 5 1963).

11. In the context of American children's picturebooks from the period, the Wild Things vastly differ from Dr. Seuss's Grinch in *The Grinch Who Stole Christmas* (1957), and Seuss's imaginative creatures in books like *One Fish Two Fish* (1959) and *Hop on Pop* (1963), although Katherine E. Shryock-Hood makes a fairly compelling argument in her dissertation *On Beyond Boo!: Horror Literature for Children* that the Cat in the Hat can be read as a kind

of horror figure (85–126). Furthermore, Ellen Handler Spitz remarks that Mercer Mayer's *There's a Nightmare in My Closet* may remind children of "the lands where Dr. Seuss's fanciful hybrid creatures roam" (65).

12. In his analysis of the moon's symbolism in *Where the Wild Things Are*, Nodelman discusses the "moon's traditional stature as a symbol of behavior beyond the pale of normalcy" (*Words* 143) and states that the moon implies "freedom from restriction" (*Words* 148). Kenneth Kidd examines Max as a "wolf-boy," indicating that instead of reading the book as an example of imperialist fiction, as Jennifer Shaddock does, that "It might be more productive to see in Sendak's book the cultural ascendance of ego psychology, for instance, or at least faith in psychology more generally" as well as for "its gentle domesticity." Notably, Kidd follows his discussion of Sendak's book with a section on "Teen Wolves" in *Thriller* (1983) and *Teen Wolf* (1985) (*Making American Boys* 156). In short, even moreso than Nodelman, he implies that Max could be a werewolf, but doesn't employ the term. Moreover, much of Kidd's analysis relies upon reading Sendak's book as a reworking of Freud's Wolf-man tale.

13. *Horrific*, no. 8, November 1953, and *Menace*, no. 3, May 1953, both feature werewolf stories (Trombetta 102, 106).

14. The ideas in this paragraph respond to one of Kidd's statements: "While Sendak neither romanticizes the child nor minimizes the child's experiences with trauma, his makeover of monstrosity amounts to a kind of gentling of the child rather than a celebration of childhood's radical alterity" (*Freud in Oz* 131). As I hope to demonstrate, I believe Sendak's work, and the other works in this paper, are equally attuned to celebrating alterity. This paragraph also seeks to expand Nodelman's discussion of *Where the Wild Things Are* in "Making Boys Appear."

15. As Paul G. Arakelian shows, *Nightmare* bears visual and verbal similarities to *Where the Wild Things Are* due to the author's extensive use of cross-hatching, an opened window depicting a moon (in various stages), and a child protagonist who defeats a hybrid monster (122–27). However, *Nightmare* and Mayer's oeuvre have been derided by picturebook critics and/or occluded by picturebook criticism. For example, Maria Nikolajeva and Carole Scott claim, "*There's a Nightmare in My Closet* (1968), by Mercer Mayer, is a banal story, obviously inspired by Sendak's *Where the Wild Things Are*" (156). Nodelman also briefly discusses the derivative nature of Mayer's book (*Words about Pictures* 78). Barbara Bader only mentions Mayer's wordless picturebook *A Boy, a Dog, and a Frog* (1967) in passing while devoting a full chapter to Sendak's works (540). Spitz's discussion of *Nightmare* in *Inside Picture Books* and Arakelian's essay are notable exceptions.

16. Ogata discusses the postwar suburban house. She also very briefly comments on "The creative possibilities of being alone in one's room" in *Where the Wild Things Are*, but she does not discuss Mayer's book (139).

17. Considering the closet's symbolic significance within gay and lesbian culture and the child's behavioral rather than physical gender-fluidity in this picturebook, it might be productive to suggest that there's a queer reading in Mayer's book that has been overlooked in academic criticism. Kidd discusses queer readings of *Where the Wild Things Are* in *Freud in Oz* (123–28). I address queerness in monstrous picturebooks more extensively in the vampire section of my essay.

18. I am indebted to historian Edward Westermann for graciously helping with the analysis of military imagery in Mayer's book; I am equally indebted to him for listening to me ramble about picturebooks in his office doorway from February 2013 to May 2013.

19. I am echoing a remark from Marina Warner's analysis of Sendak's book here, as well as trying to complicate one of her claims throughout my essay: "Sendak's brilliant and poignant work may reflect an inherent empathy children have with feral creatures [. . .]. But his classic is also a classic of its time: it reflects adult perception of children today; it forgoes the usual combat tale between hero and ogre in favour of a reciprocal recognition of resemblance, of doubling, of twinship. The ogre—the wild things—no longer appals, like the cannibal giant in the classical myth, or in Beowulf, or in Jack the giant-killer tales, but has become much more clearly the little boy's *alter ego*" (150).

20. Jackson specifically focuses on canniness in the context of the YA ghost novel—Margaret Mahy's *The Haunting*, Penelope Farmer's *Charlotte Sometimes*, and Diana Wynne Jones's *The Time of the Ghost*—yet I find that her formulation works equally well within the context of these picturebooks. Notably, Jackson's use of canny is nongender distinguished, but for this essay, canniness becomes explicitly linked to masculinity.

21. Carrington's article is more concerned with the empirical rather than the fictional gothic child. She analyzes twenty-first-century gothic toys and draws out the implications of Steven Bruhm's "self-possessed" child for twenty-first-century notions of childhood and literacy education.

22. For other child vampires in King's oeuvre, see *Salem's Lot* (1975).

23. As Anne Rice pithily puts the matter, "Vampires transcend gender" (qtd. in Wisker 123). Gina Wisker's essay "Devouring Desires: Lesbian Gothic Horror" is one of several outstanding works that discusses the vampire's queerness.

24. I use the pronoun "it" and "its" in reference to the vampire throughout this section because two doublespreads depict the child as feminine looking—when the werewolf and blue witch are introduced—while the remainder either depict the child as somewhat masculine or gender ambiguous.

25. For the graveyard as a site of educational and social empowerment in children's literature, see also Neil Gaiman and Dave McKean's *The Graveyard Book* (2008).

26. This imagery was not only codified in the first wave of gothic fiction (roughly from *Castle of Otranto* [1764] to *Melmoth the Wanderer* [1820]), but has also been deployed in Victorian gothic fiction and twentieth- and twenty-first-century gothic fiction and horror film, and harkens back to the gothic's Shakespearean and medieval literary predecessors.

27. David Lewis's brilliant analysis of the picturebook's origins, referenced earlier, implies that the genre has distinctively gothic undertones. Per his formulation, the picturebook's very nature illuminates two key features of the gothic that Spooner addresses: "lack of respect for genre boundaries" and "a greater degree of self-consciousness about its nature [than other modes], cannibalistically consuming the dead body of its own tradition" (Spooner 10).

28. Excessive thanks to Paul Anthony Johnson for pointing out the "Dancing Skeletons" connection. The resonance with the danse macabre became clearer after repeated readings of *The Graveyard Book* and Bruhm's exceptional essay "Michael Jackson's queer funk" in *Queering the Gothic*.

29. This statement has been uttered many times within the context of gothic criticism, perhaps most famously by Franco Moretti in his Marxist literary study, *Signs Taken for Wonders* (1983).

30. See, for instance, Elizabeth Young's discussion of James Whale's Frankenstein films in *Black Frankenstein* (177–87) and Rigby's essay "'Do you share my madness?': Frankenstein's queer Gothic," both of which are indebted to Eve Kosofsky Sedgwick's discussion of "the nineteenth-century 'paranoid Gothic'" (Rigby 37).

31. Ken Gelder explains one of several connections between the vampire and the silver screen by writing, "Cinema may be a suitably nomadic home for the vampire: it, too, eventually goes everywhere it has become an internationalised medium" (87).

32. The comic book character Frankie Stein who appeared in *Whoopee* and *Monster Fun* does not physically resemble Schaefer and Atteberry's character; there is also a female Frankie Stein doll on the *Monster High* doll line who bears no resemblance to Frankie or Francie Stein.

33. Peter Hutchings, drawing upon David Punter and other critics, makes a similar remark about Shelley's monster as a tabula rasa in his discussion of Hammer's *Frankenstein* films (100).

34. As readers see in *Frankie Stein Starts School* (2010), the child's performative normative achievements are reversed when he has the opportunity to show his witch, vampire, and skeleton classmates that he can be a scarier monster than they are.

35. Allan links these concerns to postmodernism. They are, likewise, prominent within a contemporary gothic context as Carrington's article affirms by discussing the importance of children's identity construction within the twenty-first century. Most of the contemporary picturebooks examined in this study could easily be called postmodern gothic works for a variety of reasons, such as their emphasis on intertextuality, parody, and self-referentiality, although spatial limitations have prevented me from elaborating this point further.

36. Robert McCammon may have been one of the first horror writers to link zombies, sex, and consumption in his story "Eat Me." More recently, Amelia Beamer's *The Loving Dead* (2010), S. G. Browne's *Breathers* (2009), and Isaac Marion's *Warm Bodies* (2010), as well as its film adaptation (2013), have helped humorously establish the zombie romance subgenre.

37. My use of the term *uncanny* is Freudian in nature and is inspired by Kim Paffenroth's analysis of the zombie's formerly human features in *Gospel of the Living Dead* (9–11).

38. Zombies' "histories" have been extensively discussed in several studies. See, for instance, Kyle Bishop's seminal *American Zombie Gothic: The Rise and Fall (and Rise) of the Walking Dead in Popular Culture*.

39. In their essay "New Millenial Zombies," Margo Collins and Elson Bond claim, "Interestingly, as the humans in zombie stories—whether online, in books, or in film—become more uniform in thought and action, we're beginning to see some individuation of zombies" (200). They do not discuss *Zombie in Love*.

40. In the sequel to *Zombie in Love*, *Zombie in Love 2 + 1* (2015), Mildred and Mortimer wrestle with the joys of raising a human child who is left on their doorstep. The sequel, in short, affirms their inability to procreate, but nicely expands their heteronormative, implicitly middle-class narrative.

WORKS CITED

Allan, Cherie. *Playing with Picturebooks: Postmodernism and the Postmodernesque.* Basingstoke: Palgrave Macmillan, 2012. Print.

Arakelian, Paul G. "Text and Illustration: A Stylistic Analysis of Books by Sendak and Mayer." *Children's Literature Association Quarterly* 10.3 (1985): 122–27. *Project Muse.* Web. 2 March 2013.

Bader, Barbara. *American Picturebooks from Noah's Ark to The Beast Within.* New York: Macmillan Publishing, 1976. Print.

Ball, John Clement. "Max's Colonial Fantasy: Rereading Sendak's 'Where the Wild Things Are.'" *ARIEL: A Review of International English Literature* 28.1 (1997): 167–79. *MLA International Bibliography.* Web. 8 February 2013.

Bishop, Kyle William. *American Zombie Gothic: The Rise and Fall (and Rise) of the Walking Dead in Popular Culture.* Jefferson: McFarland, 2010. Print.

———. "Raising the Dead: Unearthing the Non-literary Origins of Zombie Cinema." *Journal of Popular Film and Television* 33.4 (2006): 196–205. *Modern Language International Bibliography.* Web. 11 November 2010.

Bruhm, Steven. "Michael Jackson's Queer Funk." *Queering the Gothic.* Ed. William Hughes and Andrew Smith. Manchester: Manchester UP, 2009. 158–76. Print.

Bruhm, Steven, and Natasha Hurley. "Curiouser: On the Queerness of Children." *Curiouser: On the Queerness of Children.* Ed. Steven Bruhm and Natasha Hurley. Minneapolis: U of Minnesota P, 2004. ix–xxxviii. Print.

Carrington, Victoria. "The Contemporary Gothic: Literacy and Childhood in Unsettled Times." *Journal of Early Childhood Literacy* 12.3 (2011): 293–310. *Academic Search Complete.* Web. 2 March 2013.

Claridge, Laura F. "Parent-Child Tensions in *Frankenstein*: The Search for Communion." *Studies in the Novel* 17.1 (1985): 14–26. *Academic Search Complete.* Web. 15 January 2013.

Collins, Margo, and Elson Bond. "'Off the Page and into Your Brains!': New Millennium Zombies and the Scourge of Hopeful Apocalypses." *Better Off Dead: The Evolution of the Zombie as Post-Human.* Ed. Deborah Christie and Sarah Julie Lauro. New York: Fordham UP, 2011. 187–204. Print.

Crisp, Thomas, and Brittany Hiller. "'Is This a Boy or a Girl?': Rethinking Sex-Role Representation in Caldecott Medal-Winning Picturebooks, 1938–2011." *Children's Literature in Education* 42 (2011): 196–212. *Academic Search Complete.* Web. 3 February 2014.

Dendle, Peter. "Zombie Movies and the 'Millennial Generation.'" *Better Off Dead: The Evolution of the Zombie as Post-Human.* Ed. Deborah Christie and Sarah Julie Lauro. New York: Fordham UP, 2011. 175–86. Print.

DiPucchio, Kelly. *Zombie in Love.* Illust. Scott Campbell. New York: Atheneum Books for Young Readers, 2011. Print.

Dyer, Richard. *White.* London: Routlege, 1999. Print.

Egielski, Richard. *The Sleepless Little Vampire.* New York: Arthur A. Levine Books, 2011. Print.

Gelder, Ken. *Reading the Vampire.* London: Routledge, 1994. Print.

Halberstam, Judith. *Skin Shows: Gothic Horror and the Technology of Monsters*. Durham, NC: Duke UP, 1995. Print.

Heinecken, Dawn. "Haunting Masculinity and Frightening Femininity: The Novels of John Bellairs." *Children's Literature in Education* 42 (2011): 118–31. *Academic Search Complete*. Web. 5 February 2014.

Hood, Katherine E. Shryock. *Oh Beyond Boo!: Horror Literature for Children*. U of Michigan: ProQuest LLC, 2008. Web. 8 November 2013.

Hughes, William, and Andrew Smith. "Introduction: Queering the Gothic." *Queering the Gothic*. Ed. William Hughes and Andrew Smith. Manchester: Manchester UP, 2009. 1–10. Print.

Hutchings, Peter. *Hammer and Beyond: The British Horror Film*. Manchester: Manchester UP, 1993. Print.

Jackson, Anna. "Uncanny Hauntings, Canny Children." *The Gothic in Children's Literature: Haunting the Borders*. New York: Routledge, 2008. 157–76. Print.

Kidd, Kenneth B. *Freud in Oz: At the Intersections of Psychoanalysis and Children's Literature*. Minneapolis: U of Minnesota P, 2011. Print.

———. *Making American Boys: Boyology and the Feral Tale*. Minneapolis: U of Minnesota P, 2004. Print.

King, Stephen. *Danse Macabre*. New York: Gallery Books, 2010. Print.

Lewis, David. "Pop-ups and Fingle-Fangles: The History of the Picture Book." *Talking Pictures: Pictorial Texts and Young Readers*. Ed. Victor Watson and Morag Styles. London: Hodder & Stoughton, 1996. 5–22. Print.

Mallan, Kerry. "Picturing the Male: Representations of Masculinity in Picture Books." *Ways of Being Male: Representing Masculinities in Children's Literature and Film*. Ed. John Stephens. New York: Routledge, 2002. 14–35. Kindle.

Mayer, Mercer. *There's Something There!: Three Bedtime Classics*. New York: Dial Books, 2005. Print.

McMahon-Coleman, Kimberley, and Roslyn Weaver. *Werewolves and Other Shapeshifters in Popular Culture: A Thematic Analysis of Recent Depictions*. Jefferson: McFarland, 2012. Print.

Mintz, Steven. *Huck's Raft: A History of American Childhood*. Cambridge, MA: Harvard UP, 2006. Print.

———. "The Changing Face of Children's Culture." *Reinventing Childhood after World War II*. Ed. Paula S. Fass and Michael Grossberg. Philadelphia: U of Pennsylvania P, 2012. 38–50. Print.

Nikolajeva, Maria, and Carole Scott. *How Picturebooks Work*. New York: Routledge, 2006. Print.

Nodelman, Perry. *The Hidden Adult: Defining Children's Literature*. Baltimore: Johns Hopkins UP, 2008. Print.

———. "Making Boys Appear: The Masculinity of Children's Fiction." *Ways of Being Male: Representing Masculinities in Children's Literature and Film*. Ed. John Stephens. New York: Routledge, 2002. 1–13. Kindle.

———. *Words about Pictures: The Narrative Art of Children's Picture Books*. Athens: U of Georgia P, 1988. Print.

O'Flinn, Paul. "Production and Reproduction: The Case of *Frankenstein*." *Popular Fictions: Essays in Literature and History*. Ed. Peter Humm, Paul Stignant, and Peter Widdowson. London: Methuen, 1986. 197–221. Print.

Ogata, Amy. "Building Imagination in Postwar American Children's Rooms." *Studies in the Decorative Arts* 16.1 (2008): 126–42. Web. 8 February 2013.

Paffenroth, Kim. *Gospel of the Living Dead: George Romero's Visions of Hell on Earth*. Waco, TX: Baylor UP, 2006. Print.

Reynolds, Kimberley. "Come Lads and Ladettes: Gendering Bodies and Gendering Behaviors." *Ways of Being Male: Representing Masculinities in Children's Literature and Film*. Ed. John Stephens. New York: Routledge, 2002. 95–114. Kindle.

Rigby, Mair. "'Do You Share My Madness?': *Frankenstein's* Queer Gothic." *Queering the Gothic*. Ed. William Hughes and Andrew Smith. Manchester: Manchester UP, 2009. 36–51. Print.

Salisbury, Martin, and Morag Styles. *Children's Picturebooks: The Art of Visual Storytelling*. London: Laurence King Publishing, 2012. Print.

Schaefer, Lola M. *Frankie Stein*. Illust. Kevan Atteberry. Tarrytown: Marshall Cavendish, 2007. Print.

Sendak, Maurice. *Where the Wild Things Are*. New York: Harper & Row, 1963. Print.

Skal, David J. *The Monster Show: A Cultural History of Horror*. New York: Penguin, 1993. Print.

Spitz, Ellen Handler. *Inside Picture Books*. New Haven, CT: Yale UP, 1999. Print.

Spooner, Catherine. *Contemporary Gothic*. London: Reaktion Books, 2006. Print.

Stephens, John. "Preface." *Ways of Being Male: Representing Masculinities in Children's Literature and Film*. Ed. John Stephens. New York: Routledge, 2002. Kindle.

Trombetta, Jim. *The Horror! The Horror!: Comic Books the Government Didn't Want You to Read!* New York: Abrams ComicArts, 2010. Print.

Warner, Marina. *Monsters of Our Own Making: The Peculiar Pleasures of Fear*. Lexington: U of Kentucky P, 2007. Print.

Wisker, Gina. "Devouring Desires: Lesbian Gothic Horror." *Queering the Gothic*. Ed. William Hughes and Andrew Smith. Manchester: Manchester UP, 2009. 123–41. Print.

Young, Elizabeth. *Black Frankenstein: The Making of an American Metaphor*. New York: New York UP, 2008. Print.

"In the Darkest Zones"

The Allure of Horror in Contemporary Revisionist Fairy-Tale Novels for Children

JESSICA R. McCORT

THE FAIRY TALE, TRADITIONALLY, IS A FORBIDDING GENRE THAT OFTEN depends upon terror to achieve its effects. Although fairy tales do generally conclude with a happily-ever-after ending, the landscape in which they have unfolded over the last several centuries is a violent and bloody one. The tales told by the Grimms, in particular, are overwhelmingly dark: children and adolescents are abandoned, devoured, dismembered, threatened with cannibalism, beaten, starved, put into comas, maimed, imprisoned, transformed into animals, enslaved, seduced, and decapitated.[1] More often than not, the main characters are gleefully tormented by vengeful adult antagonists, with wicked (step)mothers, (step)fathers, (step)sisters, suitors, husbands, and witches wreaking havoc on the young protagonists' bodies and psyches. In many of these stories, happily-ever-after comes at a high price, and torment serves as a test or trial, the violence serving to underscore some moral or lesson.[2] As the protagonists overcome the terrors they are forced to encounter, they generally earn the returns of a better life, while those who transgress are punished (sometimes even the protagonists themselves, as part of the lesson they must learn). While many contemporary collections and film versions of traditional fairy tales have indeed sought to sanitize them, ridding the stories of any frightful elements or "negative" influences,[3] many others, however, have endeavored to maintain and in some cases amplify the darker aesthetic of this grim tradition, using the fairy tale's frightening aspects to explore new themes.[4]

Inspired by both the traditional stories and the darker revisions of those tales that emerged during the mid- to late twentieth century, today's literary fairy tales rely heavily upon the powers of horror. These millennial reimaginings, even those intended for young children, often seek to expose the traditional stories' grotesque underbellies, complicating their villains and reenvisioning their victims as (dis)empowered individuals on a quest for identity, all in an effort to emphasize, analyze, and revise the original stories' lessons. In this, they echo the reformative efforts of writers like Anne Sexton and Angela Carter, who employed fairy tales as both a vehicle for social critique and a framework upon which the highly individualized identities of their characters could be woven.[5] Sexton's work in her poetry volume *Transformations*, published in 1971, demonstrates the goals of such feminist fairy-tale revisions. As Vernon Young explained in his contemporary review of *Transformations*, Sexton's work in her poems was castigating: "Anne Sexton is out to *get* the Brothers Grimm, armed with illuminations supplied by Freud [. . . as well as] the wised-up modern's experience of having been victimized by grandmother and recaptured by the pragmatic text" (255). Sexton saw her work in *Transformations* as echoing that of the "black humorists," her retellings at once "funny and horrifying"; she described the quality of her project, in provocative language, as a "rape" of the "old fables" that required the timeworn texts to become very "modern" and "contemporary" (367, 365, 362). According to Sexton, the poems she developed were, like her source material, purposefully "grim," foregrounding horror. Musing that "terror, deformity, madness, and torture were [her] bag," she remarked that the "little universe of Grimm is not that far away" (367). In *Transformations*, Sexton's narrator amplifies and embellishes the earlier stories' horrifying elements to heighten the investigation of a modern woman's experience; regularly using the first-person point of view, the narrator identifies with the persecuted witch, imagines cannibalizing her child, considers a pedophilic father's negative influence upon her identity, criticizes an elderly aunt for sexually abusing her and stealing her youthful energy, and lingers over the victimized female body. What she produces is a series of sinister fairy-tale poems that blur the clearly drawn line between good and evil in the source tales and call attention to the victims' and the villains' motivations.

The menacing work of writers like Sexton and Carter sought to change the legacy of the traditional stories, recuperating their usable parts and sloughing off the residue that the authors saw as decaying or destroying the imagination and agency of female readers in particular. For these authors, the fairy tale was a source of both narrative freedom and oppression. Most importantly, these dark feminist appropriations tended to center on an "intense quest for self" (Zipes *When Dreams Come True* 128–29). As Elizabeth Wanning Harries notes in her study of women writers and the fairy tale, twentieth-century women writers' major contribution to the tradition was their joining of the stories to their own or their characters' self-narratives (139–42). In these feminist revisions, folk and fairy tales increasingly became part of the language through which authors attempted to encode revelations about their own or their characters' private experiences, the tales' forms, motifs, plots, and symbols integral to their blending of cultural narratives drawn from the public domain with either overt or covert autobiography. This knitting of the fairy tale to narrators' or characters' self-narratives made identity development a crucial element in the modern literary fairy tale, individualizing that which had traditionally been thought of as universal or symbolic. In the case of Sexton, for example, she rehashed and twisted easily recognizable fairy tales to illuminate her personal mythology; in *Transformations*, she assumes the roles of the Evil Queen, Rapunzel, Sleeping Beauty, and more as she seeks to come to terms with her own past experience. As Sexton noted in a letter to Kurt Vonnegut, "I think [the *Transformations* poems] end up being as wholly personal as my most intimate poems, in a different language, a different rhythm, but coming strangely, for all their story sound, from as deep a place" (367).[6]

Although they may seem far removed from the magic kingdom of the contemporary child's fairy-tale world, Sexton's and Carter's dark revisionist fairy tales have indeed bled onto the pages of today's fairy-tale revisions for children and young adults, especially the more literary ones. Generally classified as "fractured fairy tales," recent revisions, such as Jon Scieszka's *The Stinky Cheese Man and Other Stories* (1992) or *The True Story of the Three Little Pigs* (1996), Emma Donoghue's *Kissing the Witch: Old Tales in New Skins* (1999), and Francesca Lia Block's 2000 collection *The Rose and the Beast: Fairy Tales Retold*, demonstrate a darker aesthetic that magnifies rather than downplays the untoward elements in earlier stories to concentrate more on the personal journeys of the characters. Scieszka's *The True Story of the Three Little Pigs*, for example, takes us into the world of the Big Bad Wolf, who doesn't see himself as a murderous villain at all (this picture book is targeted toward young readers ages 5–8). Told from the perspective of the Wolf, individualized as Mr. Alexander T. Wolf, the book promises to deliver the "truth" behind the earlier story, which has been hidden from the reader all this time:

> Here is the "real" story of the three little pigs whose houses are huffed and puffed to smithereens . . . from the wolf's perspective. This poor, much maligned wolf has gotten a bad rap. He just happened to be in

the wrong place at the wrong time, with a sneezy cold, innocently trying to borrow a cup of sugar to make his granny a cake. Is it his fault
those ham dinners—rather, pigs—build such flimsy homes? Sheesh.
("The True Story of the Big Bad Wolf")

While Scieszka's book seeks to (somewhat) rehabilitate the Wolf, Block's
story "Wolf" revives Little Red in the modern world, pitting her against a
more realistic, and therefore even more terrifying, version of the Big Bad
Wolf, a stepfather who has been molesting her. The recent film *Maleficent*
(2014) also works in this vein; it operates under the premise that viewers
have their understanding of the Sleeping Beauty story all wrong and concentrates on Maleficent's turn toward revenge after the rape of her wings by
a monomaniacal man only interested in his own social advancement.

These fractured fairy tales, like Sexton's, refuse to cleanse the original
stories of elements that might frighten readers, even when they seek to rehabilitate their villains (again, *Maleficent* offers a good example here; while
the film does seek to transform her from a villain into a heroine, it adds the
gruesome element of Stefan's theft of her wings and lingers over the terrible
pain she suffers to provide her a motive for all that follows). Instead, they
focus on the stories' darkest zones, using these zones to reveal some lesson
about their characters' personal development. In the remainder of this essay,
I will examine two contemporary children's novels that work in the shadows of the fairy-tale texts that are their sources while concentrating heavily
on their protagonists' personal growth, Neil Gaiman's *Coraline* (2002) and
Adam Gidwitz's *A Tale Dark and Grimm* (2010). I will argue that Gaiman
and Gidwitz augment the most terrifying aspects of the traditional stories
by blending them with elements drawn from the gothic horror genre. Instead of shifting attention away from the frightening, Gaiman and Gidwitz
concentrate their readers' focus on the most macabre aspects, centering
their novels on children facing and defeating their worst nightmares. Simultaneously, Gaiman and Gidwitz use the frame of the fairy tale to explore
the identity development of their characters. While the source fairy tales
they draw upon are not particularly invested in the individual identities of
their characters, Gaiman's and Gidwitz's novels are primarily about a quest
for selfhood, echoing the tactics used by authors who revised fairy tales
for adult readers during the mid- to late twentieth century. Furthermore,
these books are deeply invested in the moral fortitude of their protagonists,
fixating on the choices that the boys and girls in question must make, as
well as the consequences of those choices.[7] As I proceed, I will focus on the

following questions: In what ways are the modes and methods of horror central to Gaiman's and Gidwitz's fairy-tale novels? Why do these authors make their modern fairy tales *more* frightening than their predecessors? How is Gaiman's and Gidwitz's use of violence both similar to and different from the application of violence in the traditional fairy tales? How do these newly fanged fairy tales concentrate on the individuation of their protagonists? And finally, are these novels as transgressive as the revisionary work of writers like Sexton and Carter? Do they seek to challenge or reinstate the status quo—or both?

Imagine this scenario. You walk into a decrepit, deserted house, moving cautiously through an empty kitchen, a dirty bathroom with a "dead spider the size of a small cat" in the tub, and down a desolate hallway (Gaiman *Coraline* 127). You enter what used to be a bedroom with a "large metal ring" in the center of the floor, and you realize, grimly, that this ring opens a trapdoor, a door that you have to open to discover what's inside. "Terribly slowly, stiffly, heavily," the trapdoor lifts to reveal a set of stairs leading down into utter darkness, and terribly slowly you make your way down those stairs, into the darkness and stench, which smells of damp soil and rotting bread dough. You feel along the walls and find a light switch, which turns on a naked bulb that sways dimly from the ceiling, revealing crude drawings of eyes on the peeling walls, cardboard boxes filled with molding newspapers, and a pile of curtains—with a foot protruding from underneath. You pull back the curtains, and there, on the floor, is a bloated, swollen doppelganger of your father. The thing turns its head to look at you, and its "mouth open[s] in the mouthless face, strands of pale stuff sticking to the lips, and [in] a voice that no longer even faintly resemble[s your] father's," it whispers your name (129). After a few painful moments, in which you discover that this zombie-grub version of your father now stands between you and the cellar stairs, between you and escape, the "white, and huge, and swollen" thing "lunge[s]" across the cellar toward you, "its toothless mouth open wide" (131). You swiftly realize you're left with two choices: "scream, and try to run away, and be chased around a badly lit cellar by the huge grub-thing" until it catches you and devours you—or draw on your own resources and do "something else" (131).

This seems like a lovely scene right out of the pages of your favorite children's book, right? Though it seems to be drawn more from the latest horror flick haunting the screens, it comes, in fact, from the critically acclaimed children's book *Coraline*, written by Neil Gaiman and published in 2002. In *Coraline*, Gaiman creates an updated, "refreshingly creepy" version of Lewis

Carroll's fantastic *Alice* books blended with the fairy tales "Hansel and Gretel" and "Bluebeard" (Gaiman "Questions and Answers").[8] In the novel, a young girl wanders into an inverse version of her own environs through a magical door, finding on the other side a woman who initially seems like a dream fulfilled, but who, underneath it all, is an ancient, wicked crone with a taste for children. This evil woman, at first, tries to ensnare her intended victim through feigned kindness and delicious foods; she soon turns, however, to the methods of entrapment and aggressive force to get what she wants. After imprisoning the young girl and threatening to take her soul, the crone winds up getting caught in a trap set by the protagonist and is eradicated as a threat to the girl's existence (the strains of "Bluebeard" and "Hansel and Gretel" here should be obvious).

If *Coraline* is indeed a fairy tale for a new generation of readers, as Gaiman himself has suggested ("it is a fairy tale the same way that 'Hansel and Gretel' is a fairy tale"), it is one in which the horror story and the fairy tale meld, with Gaiman drawing on certain motifs, stock characters, and effects that are integral to the horror genre to heighten the suspense and symbolic force of his story. Gaiman's use of the door between the two worlds as a focal point symbolizes this fusion, as it is a recognizable symbol drawn from both children's books and horror novels and films. In the *Alice* books, for example, the small door through which Alice passes into Wonderland serves as a portal to the subconscious dreamscape, a space both invigorating and intimidating. In the fairy tale "Bluebeard," it represents the divide between good and evil, and the portal through which the young girl is introduced to the concept of sin; once she opens the door, she can never return to naïve innocence. In the horror genre, as Clive Bloom demonstrates in "Horror Fiction: In Search of a Definition," the closed door performs a similar function, serving as a divide between the "real" world and the sinister supernatural world lurking on the other side: "The dark passage that leads to the locked door becomes the paradigmatic scene, symbolic of the meeting of two worlds, the journey to the 'other side,' the site of the inexplicable at horror's core" (165).

In *Coraline*, what lies in wait on the other side of the tempting door is much like the demonic presence in the attic in *Insidious* or in room 217 in *The Shining*; she is a "supernatural, demonic, violent and unpredictable" Other Mother who wants to annihilate all the young female protagonist holds dear (Bloom 165). To fashion this being, Gaiman draws on both Bluebeard and the evil witch in "Hansel and Gretel," as well as the stock characters of the zombie, the doppelganger, the bodysnatcher, and the vampire.

Furthermore, Gaiman also uses the motif of revulsion to characterize the Other Mother and her minions, constructing grotesque bodies that are problematically amorphous, replicable, and penetrable. Throughout the novel, Gaiman employs the aesthetics of horror to amplify the salient features of his villains, in turn making the opponents that must be defeated all the more formidable—and the reward for the protagonist at the end of the book all the sweeter. As Coraline moves through this infinitely more terrifying world, she grows increasingly more aware of herself as an individual, learning to assert herself as an important member of her social sphere.[9] As David Rudd has argued, *Coraline* "is centrally concerned with how one negotiates one's place in the world; how one is recognised in one's own right rather than being ignored on the one hand, or stifled on the other" (160). What this assertion of identity looks like, however, is worth questioning.

The mapping of the two worlds in *Coraline* depends heavily on the terrorization of the familiar, or the use of the Freudian uncanny, "that class of the frightening which leads back to what is known of old and long familiar"; as Coraline herself muses, "It was so familiar—that was what made it feel so truly strange" (Freud 195; Gaiman *Coraline* 85). In the novel, the childhood home is turned into a haunted house; it comes alive and turns on its youngest inhabitant as prey: "the house itself seemed to have twisted and stretched. It appeared to Coraline that it was crouching and staring down at her, as if it were not really a house but the idea of a house—and the person who had the idea, she was certain, was not a good person" (125).[10] As Rudd also notes, *Coraline*, like many a hair-raising horror text, "is not concerned with such things as bug-eyed monsters or little green men but things far closer to home, which, as a consequence, are the more disturbing (it is much harder to escape that which is on your doorstep; that which can gain entry into your bedroom)" (161). As in Stephen King's *The Shining*, in which the father, ravaged by alcoholism and his own insecurities, becomes the Overlook's henchman, the mother and father in *Coraline* are twisted into simulacra of their former selves by the powerful evil that resides in the house. These doppelgangers, as subordinates of some larger entity, want to love her or eat her—or both, as the black cat (one of the scary things conversely made friendly in the book) describes.[11] The Other house and its inhabitants suggest latent anxieties about the childhood home and the child's relationship with his or her parents. In the scene in which Coraline must avoid being eaten by her decaying Other Father, for example, there is an undercurrent running throughout the scene that suggests either physical or sexual abuse on the part of the father. In this scene, the father transforms from loving, doting parent into the monster under the bed (his cellar is situated under the outline of a bed in an abandoned bedroom), his transformation marked by his constantly swelling, omniverous whiteness (which distorts his features to such an extent that he is no longer recognizable). Coraline, however, refuses to be a victim; she escapes being consumed by the Other Father because she takes the appropriate action of evasion.

In *Coraline*, the most threatening monster is the Other Mother; not surprisingly, Coraline has been having problems with her real mother on the other side of the wall.[12] The Other Mother, like the Other Father she has created, also wants to devour Coraline, but her voraciousness represents something else entirely. As Karen Coats has argued, "this is the true horror of the Other Mother—for her, love is a regressive desire to consume Coraline" (88). The child skeletons in her closet are proof of her kind of love. She is "La Belle Dame sans Merci," the woman who appears beautiful and loving, but is poison underneath. The vampiric Other Mother wants to draw upon Coraline's life force to continue her own primeval existence; we get the sense, from Gaiman's description of the "very old and very slow" thing stalking Coraline in the corridor between the two houses, that the Other Mother, like Stephen King's spidery It, has been around for a while (Gaiman *Coraline* 55).[13] More important, the Other Mother is everything that Coraline's real mother is not: she cooks delicious meals; she dotes on her daughter and wants to play games with her; she provides everything Coraline wants. But, as Coraline herself notes, "I don't *want* whatever I want. Nobody does. Not really. What kind of fun would it be if I just got everything I ever wanted? Just like that, and it didn't mean anything" (145). The Other Mother's attempts to fulfill all of Coraline's desires rob the girl of her ability to think for herself. The Other Mother is the stereotypically "ideal" mother, the self-sacrificing, doting parent who puts her daughter's needs above her own at all times and, as a result, destroys the girl's ability to construct her own identity. Like Norman Bates's mother in *Psycho*, the Other Mother possesses an overwhelming maternalism that is also portrayed by Gaiman as monstrous; if it is not confronted, as Gaiman makes clear, it will warp and destroy the child. Coraline comes to understand what is valuable in her real mother only by projecting onto the false mother all that she thinks she wants; this ideal mother, she slowly discovers, is the truly terrifying option.[14]

To further construct a sense of foreboding in his readers, Gaiman draws heavily upon the grotesque construction of the human body in horror literature and film and the heroine's revulsion in response to that grotesque body, often relying on what Stephen King refers to as "the gross-out," "that most childish of emotional impulses" (200). Clive Bloom notes that, "for many contemporary critics," "[revulsion] has become the *central motif* of the horror genre: the body, its fluids, passages and surfaces, is the registration for horror's symbolic significance" (164). Gaiman, in *Coraline*, is deeply invested in this motif, the "bad" bodies in his novel repulsive "things" that trigger revulsion and fear in the heroine. In this, Gaiman splinters the threat of the hungry evil witch found in one of his source tales into several grotesque bodies, heightening the fear quotient of his story (there is no rehabilitation of the villain in this novel). The Other Father, for instance, becomes a rotting version of the person he had been formed to imitate: "the thing was pale and swollen like a grub, with thin, sticklike arms and feet. It had almost no features in its face, which had puffed and swollen like risen bread dough" (Gaiman *Coraline* 132). The father's body smells of sour wine and moldy bread; it has what seems like vomit or disintegrating skin sticking to its lips; its face looks like pale clay; its skin is "tacky"; it looks at her vacantly, but hungrily; its voice is "wet"; it "flop[s]" and "writhe[s]" about on the floor; it "slither[s]" like a serpent (132–37). In short, Gaiman pulls out many repulsive horror tropes to turn the Other Father's body into something so disgusting that it must be destroyed. Indeed, Coraline's first reaction to the zombie-like thing on the floor is to "ma[ke] a noise, a sound of revulsion and horror," and to stand frozen to the spot (132–33). Importantly, however, she does not remain petrified. She instead decides to cross the boundary between her body and the Other Father's and to rip off the last of his button eyes, which allows her to escape his clutches.

Coraline's confrontation with the Other Misses Spink and Forcible, also extensions of the Other Mother's evil power, occurs under similar terms. After entering the darkened abandoned theater, dog-bats zooming threateningly overhead, Coraline discovers the pair ensconced together in what seems to be a spider's egg sac attached to the back wall: "Inside the sac was something that looked like a person, but a person with two heads, with twice as many arms and legs as it should have. The creature in the sac seemed horribly unformed and unfinished, as if two Plasticine people had been warmed and rolled together, squashed and pressed into one thing" (121). If we force ourselves to imagine what Coraline sees, the effect is gruesome, as the two seem like a set of deformed twins shoved back into the womb, their bodies melding into one monstrously amorphous form. Coraline again must cross the boundary between her own body and the repulsive bodies before her; she must push her hand into the womblike egg sac and retrieve from one of the many hands the marble that represents the soul of one of the murdered children. This retrieval, which requires skin-on-skin contact between Coraline and the monstrous Other, is depicted in heightened detail, with deliberate slowness:

> She had never been so scared, but still she walked forward until she reached the sac. Then she pushed her hand into the sticky, clinging whiteness of the stuff on the wall. It crackled softly, like a tiny fire, as she pushed, and it clung to her skin and clothes like a spider's web clings, like white candy-floss. She pushed her hand into it, and she reached upward until she touched a cold hand, which was, she could feel, closed around another glass marble. The creature's skin felt slippery, as if it had been covered in jelly. Coraline tugged at the marble. (122)

Like the hand shooting out of the grave at the close of *Carrie*, "one of the creature's hands ma[kes] a grab for Coraline's arm." Coraline, however, refuses to succumb to her fears; she extricates both herself and the marble from the monster's clutches, fleeing with her spoils intact. Despite its triumphant nature, the scene uncomfortably suggests that the egg sac is an extension of the Other Mother's womb, reabsorbing its offspring once it has outlived its usefulness to her, further complicating the novel's depiction of the mother-daughter relationship.

What are scenes this frightening, so sensory and so ghastly, doing in a book most often picked up by tween readers, ages seven to thirteen? Why are such scenes so central to Gaiman's book and his construction of the Other World that Coraline must learn to navigate? Mainly, Gaiman's narrative method suggests that the novel must be truly terrifying in order to get its message across (*Coraline*, like any good fairy tale, has a moral; in fact, it has several). One of the main lessons Coraline must learn is suggested in a story that she tells the black cat just before she reenters the Other Mother's world to retrieve her parents from the evil woman's clutches. She tells the cat about a time when she and her father were exploring the junkyard behind her house and came upon a swarm of ground bees. Her father yelled for her to run and remained behind, getting stung several times, to save Coraline from the swarm. After the event, her father went back to retrieve his glasses, which he had dropped. As Coraline stares into the dark passage she knows she must enter, she tells the cat that her father said he wasn't brave for taking the stings so that she could escape. Instead, "going back again to get his glasses, when he knew the wasps were there, when he was really scared. *That was brave*" (69–70).

The child reading *Coraline* learns that one can only grow up by facing one's fears, being brave when one doesn't want to be brave at all, a lesson that can translate from the haunted corridors of Coraline's home to the schoolyard (the novel ends with Coraline no longer afraid of her first day in a new school). She also learns that she has to rely on her own intelligence to defeat evil. Recalling a television program she had watched on protective coloration, Coraline sets up an elaborate ruse to escape the severed hand of the Other Mother, which has come back to her world to retrieve its key, the only remaining link between the real world and the fantasy world. Here, the female hand becomes a confused symbol of power; the severed hand could represent both the Other Mother and Coraline herself, a former appendage of the mother's body that has broken free. In any event, both key and hand end up in a deep, dark well. Rather than Coraline falling through the rabbit hole back into the Other Mother's clutches, the last remnant of the Other Mother falls into oblivion. The moral? "Be wise. Be brave. Be tricky," as spoken by one of the child ghosts who was not wise nor brave nor tricky enough (175). In this, Gaiman heightens the female protagonist's agency in the fairy tale; instead of recreating a victimized Gretel who has the momentary inspiration to push an old witch into an oven, Gaiman makes Coraline a plotter, a unique figure who resonates with young readers as someone they recognize and admire (and someone they could possibly be).

Discussing the appeal of his novel for children, Gaiman mused that "It was a story, I learned when people began to read it, that children read as an adventure, but which gave adults nightmares" (Gaiman "Questions and Answers"). The horror that appears in *Coraline* in part serves to heighten the delicious intensity of the adventure. As Coraline herself muses after she is told by the real Misses Spink and Forcible that she is in peril, danger can seem intriguing to a bored child: "*In danger?* thought Coraline to herself. It sounded exciting. It didn't sound like a bad thing. Not really" (Gaiman *Coraline* 25). For young readers, who just might also be bored out of their wits, the fantastic elements in the novel make the danger seem somewhat safe. Like adults getting pleasure out of the ax-wielding Jack chasing his son through the maze at the close of Stanley Kubrick's *The Shining*, because they suspect that the little boy will most likely escape (and he does, like Coraline, through his own cunning), children reading *Coraline* know that when they close the book, they close the door to the Other World.[15]

Nonetheless, the lessons to be learned in the novel are transferrable to the real world in which the readers move. By amplifying the elements of terror and exposing a recognizable, but highly individualized character to them, Gaiman suggests that readers, young and old, would do better to confront, rather than run away from, their demons. In confronting her fears, Coraline finds her place in the world. When she returns to reality, she is more accepting of her parents, and values her life for its everyday comforts. In this, *Coraline* echoes the interest in female individuality to be found in the feminist fairy-tale revisions discussed above. However, rather than critiquing Coraline's world and the people in it, the novel asks her to accept things as they are. Unlike many of Angela Carter's heroines, for example, who destroy their confining surroundings or transform themselves (in "The Tiger's Bride," for instance, the young girl decides to become an animal and explore the beastly side of her personality rather than return to an exploitative relationship with her father), Coraline does not want to change her world by the end; she just wants to live in it undisturbed. As a result, the lessons to be learned in *Coraline* can be viewed as both valuable and troublesome. On the one hand, Coraline learns of her resourcefulness and bravery; on the other, she uses it to reinstate the status quo, which previously made her decidedly unhappy. In the end, the lesson learned in *Coraline* is one of resignation. Coraline finds herself resigned to her place in the family and her forced entry into a new school. This makes Gaiman, in my view, a realistic fantasist in this particular book. Children often do not have much control over these aspects of their lives. Why pretend that they do? Nonetheless, the book does give primacy to the power of the imagination, suggesting that it is a valuable escape valve from the mundane world that children often, in reality, cannot escape. It also suggests that they should not rely on others to construct these worlds for them; that they should construct them themselves.

Another troublesome aspect of Gaiman's book, in terms of female identity, is that he centers the book on a rehashing of age-old anxieties about the overbearing mother while also echoing new concerns about the underpresent mother; this book, not surprisingly, emerged alongside a wave of "new momism" that heightened the scrutiny and criticism of maternal parenting.[16] The book damns mothers for being both over- and under-involved, providing, much like the traditional fairy tale, negative models on either end of the maternal spectrum (note also the emphasis on the Other Mother as the most active evil figure; the Other Father is merely her henchman). The novel turns on Coraline's entry into an adolescence haunted by frightening or frustrating adult forms of femininity (Mommy Dearest, absentee parent, spinster, spider-woman, minion, ghost), all of which the young girl finds distasteful. The one she looks up to is her father and his quiet bravery. She merely learns to accept her real mother for the flawed woman she is and to reject all other women as monstrous or weird, a rather unredemptive vision of femininity in a book that is largely about a young girl's identity development.

In *A Tale Dark and Grimm*, Adam Gidwitz relies on the darker zones of the fairy tale to develop his own twisted story, suggesting that his young readers must journey into the Schwartzwald in order to learn life's hardest lessons. Gidwitz begins by deliberately juxtaposing his story against other syrupy, sterile versions of fairy tales found in the popular films and storybooks pushed by mainstream culture. He is very conscious of drawing a distinct line between the "old" versus the "new" fairy tale, stating that he is returning to and rehabilitating the traditional stories. In the novel's first sentence, Gidwitz's narrator boldly states that "Once upon a time, fairy tales were awesome," subsequently acknowledging that his readers may doubt his claim: "I know, I know. You don't believe me. A little while ago, I wouldn't have believed it myself" (i). Moving on to explain how today's fairy tales for children became so "unbelievably, mind-numbingly boring," Gidwitz's narrator places blame directly on parents, who orally hold the power to change the narrative into something they deem acceptable:

> You know how it is with stories. Someone tells a story. Then somebody repeats it and it changes. Someone else repeats it, and it changes again. Then someone's telling it to their kid and taking out all the scary, bloody scenes—in other words, the awesome parts—and the next thing you know, the story's about an adorable little girl in a red cap, skipping through the forest to take cookies to her granny. And you're so bored you've passed out on the floor. (ii)

Gidwitz's account of the fairy tale's evolution here suggests that the parts of the stories children find most exciting are those that are the scariest and the most violent, the very stuff that helicopter parents tend to remove. As Gidwitz's rather sinister narrator goes on to explain, the old tales have power because they force children to travel into "a magical and terrifying world" (ii–iii).

The premise of Gidwitz's book is that the Grimms were covering up a marvelous and gory story; the novel is set up, much like Scieszka's *The True Story of the Three Little Pigs*, as the "true" story underlying the entire Grimm collection: "that's not the real story of Hansel and Gretel. You see, there is another story in *Grimm's Fairy Tales*. A story that winds all throughout that moldy, mysterious tome—like a trail of bread crumbs winding through a forest. [. . . It] is the story of two children striving, and failing, and then not failing. It is the story of two children finding the meaning of things" (iii). As the novel progresses, Gidwitz demonstrates that meaning can only be found by facing the "truth," no matter how grisly. His narrator bluntly states in the first chapter: "This story is like no story you've heard before. You see, Hansel and Gretel don't just *show up* at the end of this story. They show up. And then they get their heads cut off. Just thought you'd like to know" (5). Here, the narrator suggests that he is not afraid to be straight with his readers, intentionally revealing the shocking "ending" as a means of enchantment, hoping that the reader will continue forward to gather the gory details.

Gidwitz's book, at its core, remains true to the aesthetic of the Grimm Brothers' tales, maintaining many of the stylistic elements that make the fairy tale recognizable. The novel preserves the traditional frame of the fairy tale, beginning with "Once Upon a Time" and closing with a happily-ever-after conclusion. It is also presented as a collection of stories, with some titles drawn directly from the Grimm's anthology. Within the collection, Gidwitz uses repetition in the plotting of his tales, typically adhering to the repeating actions and lines in the original stories. Despite these similarities, Gidwitz's novel becomes a creature entirely its own, a Frankensteinian monster of a novel that twists recognizable elements into a foreign, provocative story that provides new fodder for the young reader's imagination. To begin, Gidwitz's narrator often punctures the narrative frame, disrupting the story at key moments to focus his readers' attention on important details, draw them explicitly into the tale, and, sometimes, just to say something that he thinks his audience will find amusing. Gidwitz also deconstructs the source text by consistently expanding the frame, asking the reader to push beyond the expected ending, constantly suggesting that there is always something more to learn and understand. For example, Gidwitz's retelling of "Faithful Johannes," the first tale in the book, has five different endings, each pulling the story up short before we get to the "true" ending, which, as the narrator then tells us, is really "The Beginning. For it is here that the tale of Hansel and Gretel truly begins" (24). Every time we get to the end of one of Gidwitz's tales, we can be sure that it is not truly the end (even after the book is finished, the next installments, *In a Glass Grimmly* and *The Grimm Conclusion*, keep the series evolving). Gidwitz also fractures the Grimm anthology by positioning his novel as an offshoot of the original, knitting his own stories to the Grimm stories that open his narrative. Gidwitz initially begins with the Grimm stories "Faithful Johannes," "Hansel and Gretel," "The Seven Swallows," and "Brother and Sister." In the middle, however, he changes the name of the primary source tale "The Robber Bridegroom" to "A Smile as Red as Blood," a more gruesome title that marks this already horrifying tale as a turning point in the book (it is conspicuously the middle story in the nine tales "collected" in the novel). The last three stories in particular, "Hansel and Gretel and the Broken Kingdom," "Hansel and Gretel and the Dragon," and "Hansel and Gretel and Their Parents," are almost entirely of Gidwitz's own creation.

As these titles suggest, Hansel and Gretel are the key players in Gidwitz's story. First of all, Gidwitz gives Hansel and Gretel more agency, making them the instigators of their journey into the Grimm wilderness. They are not abandoned by their parents, instead running away to find a better home because their father cut off their heads and they overheard their mother telling him that he had done the right thing (their heads are quickly, through the fairy-tale's magic, put back on). Gidwitz also heightens the readers' agency, asking them to analyze Hansel and Gretel's decisions. As Gretel is preparing to enter the Robber Bridegroom's hovel, for example, the narrator stops the story's trajectory, speculating on what his readers would do: "*You* would go home, wouldn't you, dear reader? *You* wouldn't be taken in by such a man as this. You would turn right around and leave. Tell me you would. Say you would" (98). The narrator, however, knows his readers all too well: "Oh no, you wouldn't. Not with such an object of your fascination and adoration there waiting for you—for you alone. Haven't you ever had that enchanting friend—the coolest boy, the older girl—and he or she seemed to like *you*? Of all people, *you*? Imagine that he or she is in that house. Waiting for you. For no one but you. What would you do? What *wouldn't* you do?" (99). Through this, Gidwitz encourages his readers to think about what their responses to the stories' challenges would be and to critique the characters' actions, increasing the readers' engagement with the text.

As he seeks to tell the "truth," Gidwitz revels in the horrific. While the Grimms often present matter-of-fact, symbolic representations of violence, occasionally with a few blood drops, Gidwitz gives us the whole hog in the midst of its slaughter (there were a few moments in this book where I, an avid reader of horror and the gothic, actually cringed). Gidwitz's narrator implies that to give children anything less would be pandering to them, suggesting they are not tough enough to handle it. He winks conspiratorially at his readers, acknowledging their ability to tackle brutal stuff, and promises to deliver by rehabilitating the tales for this new generation. The narrator does offer readers a chance to opt out: "Before I go on, a word of warning: Grimm's stories—the ones that weren't changed for little kids—are violent and bloody. And what you're going to hear now, the one true tale in *The Tales of Grimm*, is as violent and bloody as you can imagine. Really. So if such things bother you, we should probably stop right now" (iii). This aside, however, is designed as a challenge to drive readers deeper into the book's terrain, heightening their sense of interest and investment. Gidwitz has suggested in interviews that this technique was inspired by children's responses to his oral storytelling in the classroom. As Rick Margolis describes in a *Publisher's Weekly* write-up of an interview he conducted with Gidwitz, "He'd chosen to read to his class 'Faithful Johannes,' a Brothers Grimm tale that features the decapitation of two children by their parents. He wasn't worried he'd be fired—he'd gotten the idea to read Grimm from the school's principal. Still, he was tentative, watching the audience closely for signs of the story's effect on them. He needn't have worried. 'I was afraid they'd be shocked and terrified,' he recalls. 'Oh, no. They wanted more'" (19).

The framework Gidwitz sets up for his readers' approach to the novel depends on their ability to recognize brutality as an important component of the fairy tale's magic spell. The method of reading that Gidwitz promotes asks readers to look for scary elements in the text and then to seek out clues that suggest which life lessons these moments are meant to represent for both the characters and themselves. In the book, that which is horrifying typically represents a "truth"; there is always a deeper message that Gidwitz is not afraid to be candid about. One such example of Gidwitz's encoding of gruesome elements is his characterization of the witch in "Hansel and Gretel" as a "regular woman" who developed a taste for children's flesh after playing one too many games of "you're so cute, mommy could eat you up": "as you well know, the baker woman was planning to eat them. But she wasn't a witch. The Brothers Grimm called her a witch, but nothing could be further from the truth. In fact she was just a regular woman who had discovered, sometime around the birth of her second child, that while she liked chicken and she liked beef and she liked pork, what she really, *really* liked was *child*" (Gidwitz 43). Gidwitz makes the mother's interactions with the child's body uncanny and cannibalistic, suggesting that there is some deeper desire in her, as in Coraline's Other Mother, to gobble up her offspring's identity. He also connects the cannibalizing baker woman to both his and the readers' very own mothers, noting that they should be careful: "When I was little, my mother used to say, 'Oh, you're so cute! Look at those little arms! [...] Has your parent ever said something like that to you? Most parents say that kind of thing all the time, you know. It's totally normal. Just be careful not to let them actually *taste* you'" (43–44). Gidwitz's statement here is both funny and cautioning, subtly suggesting that the kids reading really should be worried. The underlying argument is that kids should maintain their personal space, not allowing anyone, even their own mothers, to invade their privacy.

To return to the scene in which Gretel learns the truth about the young man she has become infatuated with, readers must decipher along with Gretel the meaning of the white birds she finds caged on his property. Here, an old woman in the tale does the job for Gidwitz, revealing to Gretel her giant folly in "befriend[ing her] death": "He invites girls to this house, and he reaches down their throats and rips their souls from their bodies, and he traps the souls in the cages in the form of doves, to let them rot under his eaves. Then he hacks the girls' bodies to pieces to make our supper" (101). Here, as in "The Robber Bridegroom," it is not enough for the girl to be told of her mistake, she must witness it, along with the readers. Gretel sees the handsome young man reach "his hand into the girl's mouth until his arm was buried deep in her throat. Slowly, painfully, and with great struggle from the girl, he pulled forth a beautiful white dove" (102). This story, one of the most violent in the book, is one of the most luminous. In it, readers are exposed to one of life's hardest lessons—that the people we love and admire most can sometimes be the most dangerous; they become, in the terms of this story's symbolism, rapists of one's innocence and individuality. Gidwitz's revision suggests that readers may be tempted at some point to sacrifice their selfhood to such undeserving people, suggested here by the girls' loss of their souls. Just as Coraline discovers she must "do something else" in order to avoid becoming a victim, Gretel runs away from the man's house, tells the truth about who he is to the villagers, acquires a useful magical weapon, and frees the old woman and the caged girls.

The ending of *A Tale Dark and Grimm* brings the violence within the novel full circle. As the book draws to its close, Hansel and Gretel discover that the final monster they have to defeat is their very own father. They also learn that they must do the same thing to their father that he did to them in order to do the right thing: to save their father from the monster living within him, they must behead him; this is the only way that the dragon he unwittingly becomes (a la *Dr. Jekyll and Mr. Hyde*) can be stopped from destroying the entire country. The father, like the children after their initial demise, is miraculously brought back to life. The moment his children vocally forgive him, he is revived, the "big, happy, sad, complicated" family unit made whole once again (235). This scene is one of the more troublesome moments in the book, as it raises uncomfortable questions, especially among adult readers, about the place of murder and violence in the children's text. Some readers may in fact be appalled by this turn of events in the plot, fearful of the text's influence on troubled children and the dangers of exposing young readers in general to such violent situations.

In regards to this particular scene, Gidwitz tries to assuage such concerns by deciding to set the novel in a faraway, fantastical land and to have the father transform from a man into a dragon. This is one of the only moments in the book in which Gidwitz dials back the violence, deciding not to describe the event in gory detail. Because Gidwitz detaches the action in the scene from his readers' sense of the possible, the father's beheading serves a similar function to the children's beheadings in the source tale "Faithful Johannes." As scholars like Bruno Bettelheim have argued, the traditional fairy tale maintains some modicum of unreality on purpose: "the unrealistic nature of these tales [. . .] is an important device, because it makes obvious that the fairy tales' concern is not useful information about the external world, but the inner processes taking place in an individual" (I disagree with Bettelheim's last point about internality and externality, however, as I note below) (25). Because the father's beheading is such sensitive material, Gidwitz handles it with kid gloves, resorting to the more standard methods of narration used by the Grimms, where the father's decapitation is swiftly described and figuratively comes to represent the children's coming of age. Despite this move, however, much of Gidwitz's book focuses on articulating in specific detail the useful information in the fairy tale, relating it to his readers' negotiations of the external world. Gidwitz's novel largely works through its dissolution of the boundary between character and reader, mainly through the voice of the intrusive, tricky narrator who spends most of his time focusing the readers' attention on the frightening, this intrusive voice hearkening back to the oral quality of the original tales and storytellers who called listeners' attention to important details through a variety of narrative strategies. Again, as in *Coraline*, the emphasis is on the cultivation of the protagonists' strength and bravery. As the narrator notes in the opening of the second book in the series, *In a Glass Grimmly* (after arguing that fairy tales are "horrible," defining the word thus: "*Horrible (adj.)—causing feelings of horror, dread, unbearable sadness, and nausea; also tending to produce nightmares, whimpering for one's parents, and bed-wetting*"), "buried in these rhymes and tales are true stories, of true children, who fought through

the darkest times, and came out the other end—stronger, braver, and, usually, completely covered in blood" (i, iii). Such a portrayal of the fairy tale
echoes Jack Zipes's argument that "Both the oral and the literary forms of
the fairy tale are grounded in history: they emanate from specific struggles
to humanize bestial and barbaric forces, which have terrorized our minds
and communities in concrete ways, threatening to destroy free will and
human compassion. The fairy tale sets out to conquer this concrete terror
through metaphor" (qtd. in Yolen vi).

As *A Tale Dark and Grimm* draws to its close, Gidwitz's narrator
"interject[s] one last time [. . .] to help [the readers], if [he] can" (237). The
narrator asks why this "patricidal beheading ha[d] to happen": "Why something so awful? So gruesome? So upsetting? What did all of this mean—
these strange, scary, dark, grim tales?" For Gidwitz, such stories must be
told, and told in a frightening fashion, so that readers can gain the moral
fortitude and courage needed to face adversity. As his narrator muses at
the close, "to find the brightest wisdom one must pass through the darkest
zones. And through the darkest zones there can be no guide. No guide, that
is, but courage" (238). In this regard, Gidwitz's novel is as traditional as it
gets. By ratcheting up the novel's unreality at its conclusion and concentrating on a moral, Gidwitz constructs a tale that "depicts in imaginary and
symbolic form the essential steps in growing up and achieving an independent existence" (Bettelheim 73). Gaiman's *Coraline* likewise thrives on the
allegorical relationship between the imaginary world in which the novel
takes place and the inner world of the protagonist, suggesting that the lessons to be learned therein are partly about the cultivation of desirable personal attributes that will help one thrive in the real world—heart, courage,
and bravery. Furthermore, both *Coraline* and *A Tale Dark and Grimm* are, in
the end, hopeful. As Bettelheim also rightly notes, "the fairy tale is optimistic, no matter how terrifyingly serious some features of the story may be"
(37). Neither book ends with the defeat of the protagonists. In fact, Gaiman
and Gidwitz make sure to reassure their readers up front that, by the books'
conclusions, the characters' worst fears will be conquered. In his epigraph
to *Coraline*, drawn from G. K. Chesterton, Gaiman specifically foregrounds
the defeat of the dragon as *the* central message of his book: "Fairy tales are
more than true: not because they tell us that dragons exist, but because they
tell us that dragons can be beaten." Gidwitz likewise assures his readers in
his epigraph that the voyage they are about to undertake will indeed be
worth it in the end: "You see, the land of Grimm can be a harrowing place.
But it is worth exploring. For, in life, it is in the darkest zones one finds the

brightest beauty and the most luminous wisdom" (iii). Unlike many fairy tales, however, both Gaiman and Gidwitz refuse to allow their protagonists to give up or remain passive and assume the role of victim. And both books reward such fortitude. However, while Gaiman's novel restores the status quo, Gidwitz concentrates on the disruption and rehabilitation of a faulty civilization where power has been used for evil ends, the book concluding with the children assuming their rightful positions as king and queen.

As scholars such as Maria Tatar have shown, the Brothers Grimm amplified certain frightening aspects in their source tales to teach particular lessons to their particular culture. Gaiman and Gidwitz in their fairy-tale novels do the same. The lessons to be learned and the methods by which they are taught are merely of a different sort. Trafficking heavily in the horrific, subjecting familiar protagonists to terrifying events, and describing those events in finely wrought, gruesome detail, not to mention continually putting young readers in the terrified protagonists' shoes (even going so far as to ask them "What would *you* do in this situation? What *wouldn't* you do?"), Gaiman and Gidwitz emphasize that the external world is a very real threat to the survival of the individual. In the vein of the twentieth-century literary fairy tale, Gaiman's and Gidwitz's novels are at once individualized and externally oriented, asking readers to constantly negotiate the space between the selfhood of the characters and the rapacious outside world. These novels use the themes and tropes of horror to call attention to the risks the civilizing process presents during one's coming of age. Furthermore, the horror in the novels erupts, in many cases, because the heroes/heroines have refused to respect, reproduce, or continue the progress of a world they deem unsatisfactory. Using horror, Gaiman and Gidwitz willfully disrupt and question the status quo. And in the end, like many a horror novel/film and fairy tale before them, they reinstate some semblance of normality.

Nonetheless, in both books, the protagonists' understanding of the societies to which they return, as well as their positions in those societies, are forever altered. In both *Coraline* and *A Tale Dark and Grimm*, the ultimate wisdom to be gained by encountering the horrific is an enhanced sense of self in relation to the society in which that self must operate. The main characters teeter on the brink of mortal (and moral) destruction, but they eventually emerge from the books stronger people with a better sense of their own strengths and weaknesses. Furthermore, Gaiman's and Gidwitz's willingness to acknowledge coming of age as a terrifying process, one best conveyed through horror and dark fantasy, illuminates dangers that some adults would rather keep in the dark: kidnapping, the loss of innocence, the threat of rape and sexual abuse, the very real possibility of feeling endangered by one's parents, and the perilous consequences that come from poor decisions. In their novels, Gaiman and Gidwitz suggest that the confrontation with horror, and fear, is deeply connected to self-discovery. They suggest, in fact, that in the darkest zones we find ourselves.

Above all, these books unsettle as they settle, mainly because they are up front about the existence of violence in the human experience, whether in a world far removed from the readers or in the flat on the other side of the wall. Many children today are well aware that violence exists in the world around them. They know that it could even erupt in the halls of the schools they find so familiar. Many, unfortunately, live in homes that are haunted by physical, sexual, and verbal violence. As Anna Jackson, Karen Coats, and Roderick McGillis explain, the intrusion of the gothic into children's books often "warns [readers] of the dangers mysteriously close to even the most familiar places. It reminds us that the world is not safe. It challenges the pastoral myths of childhood" (12). The use of gothic horror, through its heightened visceral energy, is perhaps even more disruptive. Even as Gaiman and Gidwitz reassure readers that all can be put right, they disturb. Even as they reinscribe the status quo, they challenge the idyllic myths that still hold sway (and are perhaps gaining ground) in our culture's representations of childhood, myths drawn from the philosophies of theorists who viewed the child as a blank slate, innocent and unaware. Gaiman's and Gidwitz's books arguably resonate with young readers because they attempt to "tell the truth" and they do not belittle their intended audiences. Neither author shies away from revealing the darker themes that some adults would like to keep off limits from their children or their charges; in fact, they revel in them. The popularity of Gaiman's and Gidwitz's novels, part of the turn back toward the dark side of fairy tales in popular culture, suggests that many young readers find this approach invigorating and empowering.[17]

The evolution of the fairy tale in many popular children's books and films has stripped it of the raiments that made it so compelling in the first place. A fairy tale without some violence and strangeness and scariness, without some complexity, is a shadow of its former self. As we should remember from Charles Perrault's old story "Le Petit Chaperon Rouge," tame wolves are sometimes the most dangerous of them all. Dragons do exist. And children must learn how to beat them somewhere. Why not in the pages of a book?

NOTES

1. In *The Hard Facts of Grimm's Fairy Tales*, Maria Tatar examines the role of violence in the stories collected by the Grimms more fully, noting that they are filled with "graphic descriptions of murder, mutilation, cannibalism, infanticide, and incest" (3). For more on the symbolic role of violence in the traditional fairy tale, see also Tatar's *Off with their heads!: Fairy Tales and the Culture of Childhood* or Marina Warner's *No Go the Bogeyman: Scaring, Lulling, and Making Mock*. Bruno Bettelheim's *The Uses of Enchantment: The Meaning and Importance of Fairy Tales* is also useful as a landmark discussion of the importance of violent characters and events in relation to children's moral, social, and psychological development, albeit one that has been called into question more recently. In relation to what I discuss in this essay, for instance, Bettelheim views the story "Hansel and Gretel" as celebrating the children's resourcefulness and their ability to get themselves out of a bad situation when confronted with an adult who wants to cause them harm or consume their identity. "To survive," Bettelheim writes, "they must develop initiative and realize that their only recourse lies in intelligent planning and acting" (162). For Bettelheim, "Hansel and Gretel" resounds with children's perception of their parents, and all elders for that matter, as deceitful, tricky, and selfish beings, as well as their feelings of dispossession in their guardians' hands.

2. It should be noted, as fairy-tale scholar Elizabeth Wanning Harries rightly points out in "The Violence of the Lambs," that violence can also appear arbitrarily in the tales: "Violence in the tales (with its obverse, a system of rewards) often educates and 'disciplines' children in what Tatar calls a 'pedagogy of fear' [. . .]. Punitive or disciplinary violence, however—designed to caution children or to give the world a moral spin—is not the only form of violence we see in fairy tales. In some there is a pervasive, almost random violence: inanimate objects become malicious, animals turn hostile" (54–55).

3. For a discussion of American culture's sanitization of the fairy tale, see such landmark scholarship on the subject as Frances Clarke Sayers's early piece "Walt Disney Accused"; Kay Stone's "Things Walt Disney Never Told Us"; Jack Zipes's *Fairy Tale as Myth, Myth as Fairy Tale*; and Elizabeth Bell, Lynda Haas, and Laura Sells's *From Mouse to Mermaid: The Politics of Film, Gender, and Culture*. In American popular culture today, the most sanitized versions of the fairy tales tend to be those mass marketed to young girls through various commercial product lines, as Joanna Weiss notes in her 2008 article "Fear of Fairy Tales."

4. Contemporary American popular culture, in fact, has become obsessed with the murkier side of fairy tales. The fairy-tale-themed television shows and films that have exploded since the early 2000s point to the increased interest among American audiences in fairy tales' shadowy figures and ominous themes. The television series *Grimm*, a police-drama-turned-modern-fairy-tale that began its run just before Halloween in 2011, turned the Grimm ancestral line into a string of descendants who were gifted at hunting down *Wesen*, frightening creatures such as werewolves, ogres, and trolls drawn from the pages of storybooks and deposited into the modern world. *Once Upon a Time* (2011), also episodic in nature, but with more of an interest in family drama and storytelling, similarly focuses on both the bright and dark characters in the tales of Grimm and beyond, bringing to life such negative fairy-tale figures as Rumplestiltskin and the Evil Queen and complicating

their personal histories in order to create multifaceted characters who breathe new life into the old tales. The list of film adaptations of fairy tales for adults in recent years is long: *Red Riding Hood* (2011), *Beastly* (2011), *Mirror, Mirror* (2012), *Snow White and the Huntsman* (2012), *Jack the Giant Slayer* (2013), *Hansel and Gretel: Witch Hunters* (2013), *Maleficent* (2014), *Into the Woods* (2014), and *Cinderella* (2015), to name a few. Many of these films can be classified as dark fantasy, action, and/or horror, since they focus on the frightening aspects of the earlier tales to construct new versions that strive to invoke terror in and spike the pulses of their viewers. In each of these popular culture renditions of fairy tales for new audiences, the villains and the protagonists battle for the attention and admiration of the viewers.

5. Both Carter and Sexton sought, in their revisions, to attack the portrayal of girls' and women's positions in high art, classic literature, and popular/low forms of culture, such as pornography, advertising, and pulp romance.

6. Working in the same vein as Sexton and Carter, many fairy-tale revisions produced since the 1970s seek to examine the imperiled intersection between life lived and life dreamed. For a full discussion of the concentration on individual identity in contemporary fairy-tale revisions for adults, see Elizabeth Wanning Harries, *Twice Upon a Time*, 135–65. See also my discussion of the individualization of the fairy tale by twentieth-century American women writers in "Getting Out of Wonderland: Elizabeth Bishop, Sylvia Plath, Adrienne Rich, and Anne Sexton."

7. These books, as I will argue, strive to instill the sort of moral consciousness that Vigen Guroian fears is evaporating in the children's literature produced for today's youth. For more on this subject, see especially the introduction to *Tending the Heart of Virtue*, 3–16.

8. Though I am not focusing on Carroll's influence on Gaiman in this particular essay, for a discussion from Gaimain on the importance of Carroll's *Alice* books to *Coraline*, see Neil Gaiman and Ray Olson, "The Booklist Interview: Neil Gaiman."

9. Many have argued that this obsession with identity is a major component of Alice's negotiations of both Wonderland and the Looking-Glass World. See, for example, Judith Little's essay "Liberated Alice: Dodgson's Female Hero as Domestic Rebel," Nina Auerbach's "Alice and Wonderland: A Curious Child," or several of the essays in the more recent volume *Alice Beyond Wonderland: Essays for the Twenty-First Century*.

10. The home the Other Mother produces actually shares many traits with Shirley Jackson's murderous estate in *The Haunting of Hill House* (which is also referred to as a "Mother house" and takes on the traits of its evil designer).

11. When Coraline asks the cat what the Other Mother is, he responds, "She wants something to love, I think [...]. Something that isn't her. She might want something to eat as well. It's hard to tell with creatures like that" (Gaiman *Coraline* 78).

12. Critical scholarship devoted to the "Hansel and Gretel" fairy tale often focuses on the binary of the Good Mother and the Bad Mother as a central motif in the story, a motif which is also exploited in *Coraline*. See, for example, U. C. Knoepflamacher's "The Hansel and Gretel Syndrome: Survivorship Fantasies and Parental Desertion," Bettelheim, 159–66, or Zipes, *Happily Ever After: Fairy Tales, Children, and the Culture Industry*, 58–59.

13. Henry Selick plays up these motifs in his film version of the book, in which the Other Mother has claimed numerous victims over a long period of time and is depicted

as a vampiric spider-woman. She does not eat the same foods that humans eat; the other world is portrayed as a web that she has drawn (not to mention the fact that she actually turns into an arachnid).

14. This is similar to the displacement that Bruno Bettelheim suggests occurs in such tales as "Hansel and Gretel" and "Cinderella." See Bettelheim, *The Uses of Enchantment*, 159–66 and 274–77.

15. In the introduction, I discuss the children's horror text as a "release valve." See, on this subject, M. P. Dunleavy and Sally Lodge's "Children's Writers Plumb the Depths of Fear" and Maria Tatar's *Enchanted Hunters: The Power of Stories in Childhood*.

16. See, for example, Philip Wylie's 1942 book *A Generation of Vipers*, which attacked women for being overly involved in their children's lives, coining the term "momism." On "new momism," see Angela McRobbie's "Post-Feminism and Popular Culture" or Judith Warner's "The New Momism." Janani Subramanian and Jorie Lagerwey also discuss this trend in their essay in this collection.

17. As Maria Tatar argues in her essay "Why Fairy Tales Matter," "Fairy tales help children move from that disempowered state to a condition that may not be emancipation but that marks the beginnings of some form of agency" (64).

WORKS CITED

Auerbach, Nina. "Alice and Wonderland: A Curious Child." *Victorian Studies* 17.1 (September 1973): 31–47. *MLA International Bibliography*. Web. 1 November 2013.

Bell, Elizabeth, Lynda Haas, and Laura Sells. *From Mouse to Mermaid: The Politics of Film, Gender, and Culture*. Hoboken, NJ: Wiley, 1996. Print.

Bettelheim, Bruno. *The Uses of Enchantment: The Meaning and Importance of Fairy Tales*. New York: Alfred A. Knopf, 1991. Print.

Bloom, Clive. "Horror Fiction: In Search of a Definition." *A Companion to the Gothic*. Edited by David Punter. Oxford: Blackwell, 2000: 155–66. Print.

Carroll, Lewis. *The Annotated Alice*. Edited by Martin Gardner. New York: Penguin, 2001. Print.

Coats, Karen. "Between Horror, Humour, and Hope: Neil Gaiman and the Psychic Work of the Gothic." *The Gothic in Children's Literature: Haunting the Borders*. Edited by Anna Jackson, Karen Coats, and Roderick McGillis. New York: Routledge, 2008: 77–92. Print.

Coraline. Directed by Henry Selick. 2009. Universal City, CA: Focus Features, 2009. DVD.

Dunleavy, M. P., and Sally Lodge. "Children's Writers Plumb the Depths of Fear." *Publisher's Weekly*, 27 March 1995: 28. Web. *ProQuest*. 15 May 2013.

Freud, Sigmund. "The Uncanny." *Writings on Art and Literature*. Palo Alto: Stanford UP, 1997: 193–233. Print.

Gaiman, Neil. *Coraline*. New York: HarperTrophy, 2002. Print.

———. "Questions and Answers about *Coraline*." *Coraline*. New York: HarperCollins, 2002. PDF eBook.

Gaiman, Neil, and Ray Olson. "The Booklist Interview: Neil Gaiman." *Booklist* (August 2002): 1949. *Literature Resource Center*. Web. 16 June 2013.

Gidwitz, Adam. *In a Glass Grimmly*. New York: Puffin, 2012. Print.

———. *A Tale Dark and Grimm*. New York: Puffin, 2010. Print.

Guroian, Vigen. *Tending the Heart of Virtue: How Classic Stories Awaken a Child's Moral Imagination*. Oxford: Oxford UP, 1998. ebrary. Web. 5 May 2014.

Harries, Elizabeth Wanning. *Twice Upon a Time: Women Writers and the History of the Fairy Tale*. Princeton: Princeton UP, 2001. Print.

———. "The Violence of the Lambs." *Marvels & Tales* 19.1 (2005): 54+. *Literature Resource Center*. Web. 3 May 2014.

Hollingsworth, Chris, ed. *Alice Beyond Wonderland: Essays for the Twenty-First Century*. Iowa City: U of Iowa P, 2009. Print.

Jackson, Anna, Karen Coats, and Roderick McGillis, eds. *The Gothic in Children's Literature: Haunting the Borders*. New York: Routledge, 2008. Print.

King, Stephen. *Danse Macabre*. New York: Simon and Schuster, 2011. Print.

Knoepflamacher, U. C. "The Hansel and Gretel Syndrome: Survivorship Fantasies and Parental Desertion." *Children's Literature* 33 (2005): 171–84. Print.

Little, Judith. "Liberated Alice: Dodgson's Female Hero as Domestic Rebel." *Women's Studies* 3 (1976): 195–205. Print.

Margolis, Rick. "Bloody Good: Adam Gidwitz's 'A Tale Dark & Grimm' is one of the year's best books." *School Library Journal* (December 2010): 19. *ProQuest*. Web. 16 June 2013.

McCort, Jessica. "Getting Out of Wonderland: Elizabeth Bishop, Sylvia Plath, Adrienne Rich, and Anne Sexton." Dissertation. Washington University in St. Louis. 2009.

McRobbie, Angela. "Post-feminism and Popular Culture." *Feminist Media Studies* 4.3 (2004): 255–64. Print.

Mollet, Tracey. "'With a smile and a song . . .': Walt Disney and the Birth of the American Fairy Tale." *Marvels and Tales* 27.1 (April 2013): 109–24. Web. *MLA International Bibliography*. 1 November 2013.

Nelson, Victoria. *Gothicka: Vampire Heroes, Human Gods, and the New Supernatural*. Cambridge, MA: Harvard UP, 2012. Print.

Rudd, David. "An Eye for an I: Neil Gaiman's *Coraline* and Questions of Identity." *Children's Literature in Education* 39 (2008): 159–68. Print.

Sayers, Frances Clarke. "Walt Disney Accused." *Hornbook Magazine* 40 (December 1965): 602–11. Web. *MLA International Bibliography*. Web. 1 November 2013.

Sexton, Anne. *Anne Sexton: A Self-Portrait in Letters*. Edited by Linda Gray Sexton and Lois Ames. Boston: Houghton Mifflin, 2004. Print.

Stone, Kay. "Things Walt Disney Never Told Us." *Journal of American Folklore* 88.347 (1975): 42–50. Web. *MLA International Bibliography*. 1 November 2013.

Tatar, Maria. *Enchanted Hunters: The Power of Stories in Childhood*. New York: Norton, 2009. Print.

———. *The Hard Facts of Grimm's Fairy Tales*. Princeton: Princeton UP, 2003. Print.

———. *Off with their heads!: Fairy Tales and the Culture of Childhood*. Princeton: Princeton UP, 1992. Print.

———. "Why Fairy Tales Matter: The Performative and Transformative." *Western Folklore* 69.1 (Winter 2010): 55–64. Print.

"The True Story of the Big Bad Wolf." *Amazon*. Web. 3 June 2014.

Warner, Judith. "The New Momism." *New York Times Magazine* (2010): 11. *Academic Search Elite*. Web. 5 June 2014.

Warner, Marina. *No Go the Bogeyman: Scaring, Lulling, and Making Mock*. New York: Random House, 2011. Print.

Weiss, Joanna. "Fear of Fairy Tales: The Glossy, Sanitized New Versions of Fairy Tales Leave Out What Matters—The Scary Parts." *Boston Globe*, 21 September 2008. *ProQuest*. Web. 3 May 2014.

Wylie, Philip. *A Generation of Vipers*. 2nd ed. Chicago: Dalkey, 1996. Print.

Yolen, Jane. *Briar Rose*. New York: Tor, 1992. Print.

Young, Vernon. "Review of *Transformations*." *Anne Sexton: Telling the Tale*. Edited by Steven E. Colburn. Ann Arbor: U of Michigan P, 1988. 255–56. Print.

Zipes, Jack. *Fairy Tale as Myth, Myth as Fairy Tale*. Lexington: U of Kentucky P, 1994. Print.

———. *Happily Ever After: Fairy Tales, Children, and the Culture Industry*. New York: Routledge, 1997. Print.

Didactic Monstrosity and Postmodern Revisionism in Contemporary Children's Films

PETER C. KUNZE

IN *THE SIMPSONS* EPISODE "HOMER THE MOE," MOE SZYSLAK RENOVATES his dive bar into a trendy hangout, complete with flashy digital art of volcanoes, roses, and eyeballs. When Carl inquires about the meaning of this new art, Moe claims it is "postmodern" and "pomo." When the other regulars respond with confusion, Moe relents and admits, "Yeah, alright, weird for the sake of weird." Indeed concepts of postmodern culture often privilege the radical, absurd, inaccessible, and alienating, but such an understanding is limiting and woefully inadequate. Postmodernism challenges boundaries and binaries, including those between high art and low culture. While postmodernism may seem to be a term for "adult culture," evidence exists within children's culture as well.[1] Even *The Simpsons*,[2] in terms of its international production, playful allusiveness, and narrative ingenuity, may be read as a "postmodern" show.[3] Postmodernism has reverberated throughout global culture because it represents a shift not only in form and content, but also in production and consumption.

This essay considers two seemingly disparate entities—postmodern culture and children's cinema—to determine how they intersect in the current cultural moment. Film studies has yet to fully wrestle with the importance of children's cinema, though useful critical work on animation is certainly increasing.[4] This essay situates recent digitally animated children's films within the postmodern tradition—to the extent that such a tradition exists. In particular, my interest lies in an examination of how children's cinema has reappropriated the image of the monster, a staple of the genres of the fairy tale and horror, and revises both its articulation and its function within these narratives. I analyze *Shrek* (Adamson; Jenson 2001) and *Monsters,*

Inc. (Docter 2001) because these films were produced by multinational corporations for film audiences around the world, and, narratively speaking, they demonstrate a revisionist approach toward their genres (the fairy-tale film and the horror film, respectively), as is characteristic of postmodernist poetics. In situating these films within the current critical dialogue about postmodernism in film studies, I hope to further the study of postmodernism in children's culture. I also consider the production of children's culture for the contemporary globalized economy, its mass reception by children, and the possible positive effects of such media—a frequently overlooked concern among reception scholars who often privilege the negative impact of media on this demographic who is (supposedly) most vulnerable to the influence of mass media.[5]

Postmodernism (and its variants: postmodern, postmodernist, postmodernity, pomo) is perhaps the most overused, misunderstood term in contemporary criticism. Nearly every employment of the word (at least, every responsible use of it) is accompanied by an explanation of how that author intends for her or his reader to comprehend it. It can be understood as a historical moment, an ahistorical style, or a style emerging from a specific historical moment. Other times, critics, scholars, and laypeople seem to justify their use of the term in the same fashion as US Supreme Court justice Potter Stewart when famously defining hardcore pornography: "I know it when I see it." No doubt, the difficulty of defining the term stems from the fact that postmodernism paradoxically defies definition. To clarify, postmodernism rejects limits, boundaries, totalization, and even clarification. Here, I offer a brief survey of how literary and film critics utilize "postmodernism" in their analyses, before drawing connections between postmodernism and children's cinema.

Generally speaking, postmodernism refers to a cultural shift resulting from social, political, and even economic concerns following World War II, though some trace its emergence more specifically to the 1960s. Jean François Lyotard's definition may be condensed to his oft-quoted phrase "incredulity towards metanarratives" (xxiv), underscoring the failure of traditional epistemological methods to generate legitimate knowledge. The subtitle of Fredric Jameson's seminal monograph defines postmodernism as the "cultural logic of late capitalism," resulting from a globalized market economy. Linda Hutcheon notes in *Poetics of Postmodernism: History, Theory, and Function* the negative manner in which postmodernism is typically defined: "discontinuity, disruption, dislocation, de-centering, indeterminacy, and antitotalization" (3). Hutcheon rightfully rejects defining postmodernism in

favor of summarizing its poetics; that is, the techniques and stylistic qualities of postmodernist fiction, including fragmentation, nonlinear narration,
grim humor, and reflexivity.

In the spirit of playfulness, my focus in this essay will be on revisionism,
by which I mean the return to traditional genres, character types, and plot-
lines to both revise and reexamine the familiar structures of narratives. If
the contemporary writer, as John Barth states, has sensed "the used-upness
of certain forms or the felt exhaustion of certain possibilities" (64), then
these revisionist texts allow the author to criticize or celebrate certain aesthetic and political qualities of the original material. Revisionism also offers
writers a chance to make the old new again; in the process, they testify to
the enduring legacy and influence of these familiar plots and conventions.
Genres such as horror seem especially ripe for such textual recreation (and
re-creation), because the compositional style, iconography, and plot conventions—low-key lighting, looming figures, screaming victims, hair-raising
surprises—are so familiar and recognizable that they are nearly at the point
of being exhausted. Revising horror not only breathes new life into the
genre, but also reveals the techniques and narrative rules that govern it.

Whether such revision remains reverent or critical of its source text underlies the postmodernist debate over parody. Fredric Jameson asserts that
parody intends "to cast ridicule on the private nature of these stylistic man-
nerisms and their excessiveness and eccentricity with respect to the way
people normally speak or write" (5). In contrast, though it remains imitative,
pastiche is "a neutral practice of such mimicry, without parody's ulterior motive, without the satirical impulse (5). Having "lost its sense of humor" (22),
pastiche lacks an edgy aesthetic and political import. Hutcheon challenges
such an interpretation. Considering parody an ideal form for postmodernism, she contends it "paradoxically brings about a direct confrontation with
the problem of the relation of the aesthetic to a world of significance external to itself, to a discursive world of socially defined meaning systems (past
and present)—in other words, to the political and the historical" (34). While
admitting it can be elitist if the audience cannot understand the codes the
artist uses (34), she remains optimistic that parody can be a political act and
that postmodernism, in fact, can be challenging and politically productive.
While I hesitate to argue that the ideology behind *Shrek* and *Monsters, Inc.*
is entirely progressive, I do hope to show how these texts are political in
their reflection of social power and in their "playing" with how power functions to marginalize and silence the Other. Horror is largely a conservative
genre in its aim to remove the threat of a marginalized outsider and restore

the status quo; children's cinema, embracing the potential for subversiveness in revisionist play, prods at these staid conventions of genre in various ways worthy of further discussion—most importantly, the representation and re-presentation of monstrosity/marginalization.

Both in its positioning within a globalized market economy and its essential dependence on mass reproduction, cinema seems an ideal medium for the postmodern era (assuming, of course, we agree with the assessment that postmodernism is a historically situated movement or cultural moment). While classical Hollywood cinema was generally polished and predictable, more recent Hollywood product blurs the distinction between a variety of binaries identified by Carl Boggs and Tom Pollard, including "low" and "high" culture, realism and formalism, conservatism and progressivism, and between genres (164). Their definition of postmodern cinema seems to align and blend with that of postclassical cinema; that is, the formal and narrative modifications in Hollywood storytelling following the Paramount decision and the subsequent dissolution of the studio system (later reorganized and further complicated by conglomeration).[6] They outline five trends in postmodern cinema, but the interests of my essay lie in only two of these categories: the "blockbuster-spectacle" and "playful cinema where little seems to be valued or sacred" (166). Critics often characterize the former, exemplified by George Lucas and Steven Spielberg, as high-concept, which ironically draws attention to the broadly outlined plot, easily distilled into a few sentences. Action and visual effects take precedent over narrative or character development, and the film gives rise to a commodity culture that may include novelizations, figurines, and other merchandise in addition to sequels that seek to capitalize on the popularity of the premise, the actors and actresses, and the technologically enhanced imagery and action sequences of the film. Perhaps the latter has best been displayed in the films of Mel Brooks and (as Boggs and Pollard suggest) John Waters in their irreverent treatment of social mores, propriety, and the status quo. Of course, it is up for debate whether these films actually succeed in their subversiveness or merely play around, echoing critical discussion regarding the extent of parody's political effect in and on postmodern culture.

Shrek and *Monsters, Inc.* benefit from advances in digital animation as well as their generic classification as (allegedly) children's cinema to embody the aspects of postmodernism discussed here. Of course, as products of multinational conglomerations intended for worldwide audiences, they often waver between sincere and facetious subversive gestures. John Hill identifies three significant strains of postmodernism in contemporary cinema: (1) the fundamental transition away from the mass production of studio-era classical Hollywood toward independent filmmaking and conglomeration that has led to a "'postmodern' blurring of boundaries between (or 'de-differentiation' of) industrial practices, technologies, and cultural forms"; (2) the narrative content of film that reflects the themes of postmodernist culture; and (3) the formal aspects of films that parallel artistic decisions seen in other media and forms associated with postmodernism (100). In the discussion that follows, I will draw from all three of these categories, as well as the earlier-mentioned debates about parody, to illuminate not only how *Shrek* and *Monsters, Inc.* are postmodernist films in their digital production, but also in their narrative content.

The question of audience underlies the study of children's literature. At the outset of her seminal, albeit heavily contested, study of children's literature, *The Case of Peter Pan, or The Impossibility of Children's Fiction*, Jacqueline Rose observes, "Children's fiction rests on the idea that there is a child who is simply there to be addressed and that speaking to it might be simple" (1). Rose concludes that children's fiction is "impossible" because it depends on one group (adults) writing for another group (children), yet "neither of them enters the space in between" (1–2). Children's literature (and in that we can include other cultural productions for children, including film) stands alone as a genre because its definition (at least initially) depended not on its form (melodrama, comedy) or its content (western, romance, gangster), but on its presumed audience. Ian Wojcik-Andrews complicates Rose's notion, since children view (and often embrace) films not intended solely or primarily for them (7), while Marah Gubar has recently argued that "insisting that children's literature is a genre characterized by recurrent traits is damaging to the field, obscuring rather than advancing our knowledge of this richly heterogeneous group of texts" (210).

Shrek and *Monsters, Inc.* take the audience-driven definition in another direction. Based upon the films' marketing, plot, and visual style, the general audience might expect the films to be primarily targeted at children. In many ways, these films succeed in appealing to such a demographic: they are light-hearted, brightly colored, relatively inoffensive, void of adult situations, and appropriately humorous (for the *most* part, for the majority of adult viewers). Yet the production and presentation of these films reveal a larger target audience for these films: these are children's films, but they are intended for general audiences, and, consequently, they are designed to appeal not only to children, but also to adults.

This effort can be understood in the context of the film's "voice," an issue within children's literature that has long been a matter of discussion. In his analysis of *Peter Pan*, Michael Egan notes James M. Barrie's use of "the Double Address." Egan defines this voice thusly:

> On the one hand the author speaks directly to this principal audience, his voice and manner serious and gentle, even conspiratorial. From time to time, however, he glances sidelong at the adults listening in and winks. Naturally, his jokes and references on these occasions are not meant to be understood by the children. And thus he is permitted a privileged discourse, unique to the genre, in which he is able simultaneously to quarry to his own unconscious while denying, with a smile, that he is doing so. (46–47)

Egan identifies two distinct audiences: a naïve-child audience and a knowing-adult audience. Understandably, other scholars of children's literature find such an address patronizing toward its younger audience members. Barbara Wall develops this taxonomy further, adding the single address and the dual address. The former "show[s] no consciousness that adults too might read the work" (35), while dual address is more varied in its audience and therefore more difficult for an author to manage. It either does not distinguish between child and adult readers, employing the same "tone of seriousness," or it "confidentially shar[es] the story in a way that allows adult narrator and child narratee a conjunction of interests" (Wall 35). Despite the concerns Wall identifies, however, double address dominates both *Shrek* and *Monsters, Inc.* not because DreamWorks and Pixar, respectively, want to talk down to their implied audience of children, but because, as producers of a commodity in a global market economy, they realize the danger of targeting only one audience and the consequential necessity of appealing to as many demographics as possible. To this end, in contemporary cinema, one could argue that no such thing as the genre of children's movies exists.

Now, admittedly, *Shrek* and *Monsters, Inc.* do not have narrators in the sense that children's fiction does. *Shrek* frames its filmic narrative as a fairy tale being read by Shrek himself from an illuminated manuscript, but soon mocks this convention and discards that narration in favor of implied omniscience. *Monsters, Inc.* includes no narration whatsoever, spoken or written. Nevertheless, both films include various strategies for addressing and appealing to an adult audience, namely through voice talent and humor.

One of the most surprising aspects of these films is their investment in recognizable talent, especially considering that these individuals are unseen and most of these actors are not generally considered to be children's entertainers. Comedian Mike Myers, who voices Shrek, made his film career in movies that clearly target teenage audiences and older, including *Wayne's World* (Spheeris 1992) and the Austin Powers franchise. While Eddie Murphy's more recent films are children's fare, Cameron Diaz and John Lithgow's primary successes have been in adult-themed dramas and comedies: Cameron Diaz's breakout role was in the raunchy comedy *There's Something about Mary* (Farrelly and Farrelly 1996), while John Lithgow's career took off in the early 1980s following Oscar-nominated dramatic performances in *The World According to Garp* (Hill 1982) and *Terms of Endearment* (Brooks 1983). John Goodman and Billy Crystal gained fame as comic actors, though again, not in entertainment directed toward children. Since children would presumably not recognize the voices of these actors, they serve to draw in the audience who buys the tickets: not children, but adults (and, perhaps, teenagers). As such, their employment reveals the considerable financial investment made in the films as well as the expectation that the films will fare well among a range of age groups and countries.

Unsurprisingly, the primary modes of humor in these children's films are slapstick and scatological, since these are among the least intellectually rigorous forms. Their employment in children's films reveals a slightly patronizing attitude toward children, or at least the misguided implication that children cannot perceive wit. The opening sequence of *Monsters, Inc.* features an anxious monster falling over himself,[7] while *Shrek* begins with the title character bathing in mud, his flatulence bubbling up. Later, Donkey proudly admits, "And then one time I ate some rotten berries. Man, there were some strong gases seepin' outta my butt that day!" These farcical elements construct a broad general audience, simple in its tastes and "low" in its orientation. Though their humor is often cheeky, the films, for obvious commercial reasons, seek to exclude no one by amusing everyone (at least as many as possible).

Other modes of humor appeal to older viewers, particularly innuendo and allusions, revealing the creators' understanding of their varied viewers, who have different frames of reference and expectations of a film narrative. In *Shrek*, this aspect of the film's humor is apparent in the sequence in which Magic Mirror informs Lord Farquaad of potential love interests. Using the format of *The Dating Game* (1965–1986), a television show familiar only to older audience members, Magic Mirror quips that Snow White "lives with seven other men, [but] she's not easy!" Such sexual innuendo targets the adult members of the audience, temporarily disregarding the interests and understanding of the implied child viewer, who is supposedly innocent of such adult knowledge. In the same vein, *Shrek's* soundtrack features a range of pop music covers, including The Monkees' "I'm a Believer," Otis Redding's "Try a Little Tenderness," and Joan Jett's "Bad Reputation"; all three of these songs were at least twenty years old at the time of the film's release in 2001. Of course, in the postmodern era, songs are no longer historically situated, as mass reproduction makes such commodities easily available and distributable. Teenagers in 2013 may see the music of Bob Marley, the films of Woody Allen, and the novels of Ayn Rand as central to their identity and culture, despite the disparity between their original contexts and the current moment. Finally, the visual homages (the monsters' entrance in the style of *The Right Stuff* [Kaufman 1983]), the sonic homages (the screeching strings of *Psycho* [Hitchcock 1960]), and Pixar's self-referential tendencies, alluding to its past projects (*Toy Story*) and those in development (*Finding Nemo*) imply a viewer who has a considerable knowledge of popular Hollywood cinema. These qualities are only funny if the audience can make the connections; otherwise, they exhibit the obscurity and elitism Hutcheon warns about. Recognition of these cues creates delight in the adult viewer, not only because he or she "caught" the coded messages, but also because the supposedly ignorant child did not. Therefore, the pleasures to be had by children and by adults watching the film often diverge. *Shrek* anticipates and satisfies the differing frames of references between its adult and child viewers. This aspect of the film reveals how narratives are constructed in postmodern culture to serve as commercially viable commodities with seemingly countless allusions and jokes to maximize appeal. With a plethora of references to be "detected" by viewers, the film rewards viewers not only for their knowledge of popular culture, but also for their popular consumption of such cultural products. While these experiences are not unavailable to younger audiences, they appear to privilege the older audiences who view the films—and purchase the movie tickets and DVDs.

Postmodern narratives attempt to make the old and exhausted new again; as a result, they often reimagine the very function—culturally and socially—of those narratives to begin with. The monster and monstrosity have been subjected to considerable theorization across various disciplines, including philosophy, anthropology, literature, and film studies; a brief survey of this body of work helps to explain how Shrek and the monsters of

Monsters, Inc. operate as monsters and, more importantly, how these representations revise the cultural and social function of monsters. Most perspectives amount to monstrosity as either the embodiment of fear or the denial and repression of some aspect of the self. In his study of the horror film, Andrew Tudor notes that the most common movie monsters between 1931 and 1984 were psychotics, mad scientists, scientific creations, vampires, and mutations; additional creatures included ghosts, magicians and witches, zombies, demons, and werewolves (20). This analysis indicates that most monsters are human or humanoid, which underscores the emphasis on the self in the creation of the monstrous. The inspiration and function of this monstrosity, however, seems to vary, as studies of the monster suggest.

Isabel Cristina Pinedo places her emphasis on the monster's body as contradictory, involved in "the disruption of categories" (21), while both Judith Halberstam[8] and Harry M. Benshoff connect the monster to queerness. Halberstam builds off of theories regarding the monster as embodied fear, contending it "functions as monster [...] when it is able to condense as many fear-producing traits as possible into one body" (21). Though arguing the monster results as a "mechanism of failed repression" (9), Halberstam warns that viewing the monster as "solely sexual aberrance [...] fail[s] to historicize Gothic embodiments" (21). In line with Halberstam's call for historicization, I consider the "monsters" of *Shrek* and *Monsters, Inc.* as cultural products reflective of the turn of the twenty-first century and the need to revisit and revise stagnant cultural narratives. Benshoff, however, views the monster as a metaphor for the homosexual in American society (4). For example, early twentieth-century-representations of the vampire were connected with homosexuality (Benshoff 20); Halberstam fleshes out the relationship between anti-Semitism and vampirism in chapter 4 of *Skin Shows*. These analyses reveal, as Halberstam has contended, multiple fears can coexist within a representation, and said representation needs to be rigorously historicized to be analyzed and understood.

In line with the deconstructive logic often found within postmodern cultural products, David D. Gilmore notes how monsters and humans cannot be fully separated into two different entities. He observes, "The power of monsters is their ability to fuse opposites, to merge contraries, to subvert rules, to overthrow cognitive barriers, moral distinctions, and ontological categories. Monsters overcome the barrier of time itself. Uniting past and present, demonic and divine, guilt and conscience, predator and prey, parent and child, self and alien, our monsters are our innermost selves" (194). For Gilmore, the monstrous, the bestial, the animal contaminates the self—and vice versa. We cannot define the other outside the context of the other, and stark distinctions are constructed and ultimately artificial. The monster, therefore, embodies something beyond the physical self that ultimately is never completely distinguishable from it. Stephen T. Asma, however, draws attention to how the monster triggers "the breakdown of intelligibility" (10). The non-monster (Asma simply uses "we") fails to comprehend the monster or to "readily relate to the emotional range involved" (10). Like Gilmore, Asma sees monsters as an extension of the self: "If we find monsters in our world, it is sometimes because they are really there and sometimes because we have brought them with us" (14). For both, fear remains the fundamental factor of the monstrous: fear over the lack of control over the other, the unknown, and, ultimately, the self.

In traditional literary and cinematic horror narratives, the monster, therefore, must be conquered as a way of preserving the self and perhaps, in the Freudian sense, reinforcing the concept of the complete, controllable ego. At the very least, the monster must be re-repressed so that the protagonist(s) can return to stasis and some delusional sense of safety. Concentrating on the role of the monster, Andrew Tudor has outlined the classic structure of the horror film into three distinct phases of varying lengths (19). The first part of the horror film shows the audience the order that exists prior to the arrival of the monster, the order that must be protected and eventually restored. Into this serenity enters the monster, triggering fear, panic, and physical and emotional devastation. The middle phase comprises the bulk of the film narrative; here, the monster wreaks havoc upon the community while the hero(es) and/or townspeople make vain attempts to subdue or destroy the monster. Finally, the defeat of the monster symbolically reestablishes relative stability. Regardless of the monster in question, the outcome remains the same: the terrorized must stop the monster, often by destroying it. For example, in the classic Universal horror films, Van Helsing impales Dracula, the townspeople immolate Frankenstein in the windmill, and Sir John Talbot bludgeons the Wolf Man. Though more recent horror films ("postmodern horror" or "paranoid horror," as some critics have deemed them) foster an "unstable, paranoid universe" where good and evil are vague and the ending appears open and unresolved (Pinedo 9), the quest to destroy the other (be it the normal or the monstrous) still organizes the narrative action.

The filmmakers of *Shrek* and *Monsters, Inc.* treat the binary of good and evil with suspicion. The essential function of monstrosity in these films differs considerably from the source material of the fairy tale and, more recently, the horror film. Rather than the monstrous being that which must be vanquished, the monster in these contemporary children's films must be understood, empathized with, and respected. Acceptance of the monster into and peaceful cohabitation with society are the objective. By analyzing the clear didacticism of these monstrous creations, one can see yet another example of how *Shrek* and *Monsters, Inc.* both operate as postmodern products in their active revision of existing cultural narratives.

My initial concern in how monstrosity functions in the children's film lies in the visual construction of the monster itself because it usually precedes narrative action or dialogue involving the monster—that is, we see it before we hear it. Animators face the challenge of creating a character that is clearly monstrous, yet not terrifying or discomforting. Compared to William Stieg's original drawing of Shrek in his children's book, the cinematic Shrek is smoother, with rounded out features and unblemished skin. He clearly is more human-like than his literary predecessor: muscular and paunchy, with recognizably human facial expressions. Though Pawel Jedrzejko suggests Shrek "could be associated with the stereotypical features of a Black African heritage" (35), Jane Caputi proposes a better argument for the racialization of these fantastic characters when she suggests Donkey exhibits the damaging stereotypes of the "coon" figure from early American popular culture (34). Certainly skin tone should be a factor in the discussion of these characters: both Shrek and *Monsters, Inc.*'s Mike Wazowski are a light green, while Sully is a blend of blue and purple fur. Usually movie monsters are shades of dark green, brown, and black; the vivid colors of these monsters not only allow the creatures to stand out on screen, but also signify benevolence or, at the very least, harmlessness, by playing upon the juxtaposition of good and light against evil and dark.

The films also draw connections to the movie monster while sanitizing it for children's entertainment through the creatures' smiles. Movie monsters often have grotesque mouths filled with rotten, dirty, and sharp teeth. In the films under examination here, one may best describe the smiles as goofy. Shrek has large teeth, but they are spaced out to separate his smile from the intimidating bestial sneers or the cheeky tooth-filled grin of figures like the Cheshire Cat. Sully possesses sharp canines, but his tendency to smile contentedly minimizes this concern. And Mike's nervous, almost neurotic enthusiasm counters any impression that this cyclopic alien-like creature has ominous intentions; he is far too self-centered and scatter-brained to be a true threat. These qualities aim to make him endearing, not frightening. While these characters possess monstrous traits—physical abnormalities, enormous size, bestial features—their human-like behavior, emotions, and interests allow the child audience not only to view them as innocuous, but also to identify with them. Therefore, the filmmakers move horror from its adult-oriented designation as R-rated fare into the more kid-friendly realm of G-rated entertainment. In the process, the pursuit to destroy the monster becomes an effort to empathize with not just it, but *him* or *her*. Not only does the monster become a teaching device for the child viewing the film, but the film implicitly challenges the adult viewer to consider the psychological function of the monster for the self. Whether or not the adult viewer heeds this call is hard to tell, but the suggestion nevertheless lingers within the narrative.

Herein lies the key difference between how the monster functions in the children's film versus in the fairy tale and the horror film. Arguably, the fairy tale and the horror film, generically speaking, depend more on the good/evil binary than any other genre. From the outset, fairy tales and horror films establish a point of identification for the viewer in the "normal" hero or heroine, as well as a clear and present danger that must be confronted, defeated, and destroyed. In this manner, both genres can be exceptionally violent, yet it is through this fantastic violence that their protagonists, and, by proxy, their audiences, confront the fears and anxieties that the monster embodies. Jack Zipes argues, in a somewhat problematic universal fashion, that "through fantasy [...] we have always sought to make sense of the world, not through reason" ("Why Fantasy" 78). The fairy tale and the horror film create a safe space filled with pleasure and fear to address and (temporarily) vanquish the undesirable in oneself and one's community. The fairy tale's objectives are didactic, while the horror film's are perhaps purgative and titillating, but both make clear that monsters are inherently worthy of destruction. In contrast, these children's films, despite their relative debt to the fairy tale and the horror film as forebears, invert that formula in an important way that reveals a postmodern sensibility, where time-tested formulas are modified, upended, or discarded completely.

The nature of said sensibility is twofold. One, if we view postmodern cinema as the result of a global economy, then the film must be inoffensive enough to travel, since Hollywood depends not only on its domestic market, but more and more on the profits gleaned from worldwide distribution. To this end, films can curb violence or execute it in a manner that is cartoonish: no one is really hurt, or if they are, it occurs off-screen. Two, these films revisit the conventions of their source materials: not just fairy tales and horror films, but also the monolithic Disney hand-drawn animated features that remain for many the gold standard of American children's cinema. By portraying the monsters as the lead characters, the filmmakers offer a new product, but also draw attention to the social politics of marginalization and monstrosity.

The empathetic monster figure, whom the filmmakers position against the "monstrous" humans, often nurtures this reimagining through a learning moment between the "monster" and a "normal" other. This "teachable moment" reinforces the viewer's affections for the "monster" while underscoring the fundamental inversion taking place within the film. Speaking to the charmingly ignorant Donkey, Shrek tries to explain how society simplifies and others him, despite his claims to being a complex creature:

> SHREK: For your information, there's a lot more to ogres than people think.
> DONKEY: Example?
> SHREK: Example? OK, uhm . . . ogres are like onions!
> [SHREK shows DONKEY an onion]
> DONKEY: They stink?
> SHREK: Yes . . . no!
> DONKEY: Oh, they make you cry?
> SHREK: No!
> DONKEY: Oh, you leave 'em out in the sun, they get all brown, start sprouting little white hairs!
> SHREK: No! Layers. Onions have layers. Ogres have layers. Onions have layers. You get it. We both have layers.

Of course, Donkey, the cheerful simpleton foil to the cranky Shrek, still does not understand, and the sincerity of the scene ultimately yields dismissive laughter. In fact, through most of *Shrek*, we are led to believe Shrek is content in his isolation until he confides in Donkey, "They judge me before they know me. That's why I'm better off alone." As the viewer learns at this moment, Shrek has internalized the fear-based hatred the human characters have directed toward him, favoring solitude over ongoing confrontation with their hostility. To this end, he begins to embody the characteristics they have projected onto him, thereby demonstrating the damaging effects of fear, hatred, and bullying. By saving this revelation for later in the film, the audience has had plenty of time to identify and sympathize with Shrek over the violent, underdeveloped, and idiotic human characters. They also have had plenty of time to view him as nothing more than an amusing curmudgeon with a heart of gold. Yet at this moment, *Shrek* temporarily moves away from what Nadia Crandall calls its "almost recidivist" values (167), and gestures toward what Jack Zipes calls "emancipatory fairy tales" that "bring undesirable social relations into question and force [viewers] to question themselves" ("Potential" 322). Though it is beyond the scope of my study to determine the success of this gesture, the progressive critic cannot but hope that children might begin to question their own complicity in marginalizing, bullying, and oppressing others after viewing such a scene.

Monsters, Inc. portrays marginalization in a different manner, though with a similar resolution. The monsters in this film are fundamentally vampiric in their dependence on children's screams for energy; as Monsters, Inc. chairman Henry J. Waternoose III explains to the young trainees, "Our city is counting on you to collect those screams. Without screams, we have no power. Yes, it's dangerous work, and that's why I need you to be at your best. I need scarers who are confident, tenacious, tough, intimidating." Waternoose's directive explains not only why monsters scare children, but reveals why their society needs screams of terror. These monsters are not malicious, just self-serving, the film asserts. Despite Monsters, Inc.'s exploitative agenda, Sully and Mike remain the child viewer's points of identification in the narrative, against their animated peers and their own interests, since children are toxic to the monsters. The film's children become the monsters, as illustrated by the farcical anarchy inspired by the monsters' realization of Boo's presence in their world. Though the child viewer is more physically similar to Boo than Sully or Mike, he or she is encouraged to identify with the monsters, not the human. As Mike and Sully learn to confront and understand their fear-inspiring "monster," so too are child viewers encouraged to regard the so-called monsters of *Monsters, Inc.* as misrepresented, misunderstood, and worthy of acceptance. This cross-identification initiates the didactic intentions of the storyline by encouraging empathy with the Other. The filmmakers ease the potential difficulty of having children identify with those who traditionally inspire terror by showing the children that their animated counterparts (and by extension they themselves) actually terrify their monsters, as revealed in a number of farcical sequences involving panic, tears, and pratfalls. Boo, whose "monstrosity" to the monsters lies in her hyper-cuteness (pigtails, rosy cheeks, incoherent speech), teaches Sully to understand those whom he preys upon at work. As he begins to learn that those he fears are actually innocent or indifferent, not malevolent, the film encourages children to view monsters as sensitive, needy creatures as well. In fact, in its examination of monstrosity and ultimately artificiality, the film perpetuates the same problem the *true* villain—Mr. Waternoose—laments, "Kids these days. They just don't get scared like they used to." *Monsters, Inc.* hopes to make sure that the children do not become scared, because the film teaches its audience that such fear is not based in realistic concern but irrational conclusions. This sentiment is captured in Sully's rejection of Monsters, Inc.'s operation and his paternal nurturing of Boo, despite initially being terrified of what she supposedly represents. The film attempts to mend the rift between the scarer and the scared by removing truly malevolent beings (Randall and Mr. Waternoose) without killing them and showing how the monsters find greater success (both in obtaining energy and in interacting with the Other) by provoking children's laughter. The emended status quo proposes a better world for monsters and children alike founded on a symbiotic relationship, while suggesting to the child viewer the benefits of confronting the Other, not to destroy it, but to appreciate it and work toward mutual understanding. This narrative decision effectively challenges the conventions of horror, which largely depend on the violent annihilation of any threat, rather than a peaceful compromise that mutually benefits both parties. Admittedly, the conclusion aligns with a popular notion of what is acceptable for children to view, but it also counters the aggression of horror with a spirit of empathy and peaceful conflict resolution.

J. Zornado reads the monster-child relationship in film as a metaphor for corporate power. While such a reading works, I find another of his insights more compelling: monstrous children's films "ask us to reconsider how adult culture uses children and more broadly, how those in power demonize the weak for their own ends" (9). The postmodern revision of the good-destroying-evil plot into the good-understanding-"evil" plot has greater potential for creating positive social change. Clearly, *Monsters, Inc.* and *Shrek* reinforce a rather conservative ideology, one that celebrates heterosexual marriage, workplace complicity, and fairly normative gender roles. This tendency is customary for popular entertainment, though some critics continue to be surprised and frustrated by it. Nevertheless, these original tweakings of standard, worn-out formulas make a small gesture toward a more progressive children's entertainment. While postmodern horror films for adults, like *Scream* (Craven 1996) or *A Cabin in the Woods* (Goddard 2012), playfully upend the familiar plot conventions of horror with humor and excess, postmodern children's films that draw upon elements from the horror film work to reveal (with considerable empathy) the ultimate humanity of the monster—that is, the similarity rather than the alterity. Therefore, postmodern horror films are often pastiches (in Jameson's sense) that fail to interrogate the implications therein, but children's films such as *Shrek* and *Monsters, Inc.* gesture toward a noteworthy reexamination of the self/other binary that organizes this popular genre. A politically energizing postmodern product for children, especially in a market that necessitates an internationally appealing, mass-produced commodity, seems unlikely and unrealistic at this time. Yet the conflicting codes and ideologies that exist within these products provide ample opportunities for scholars of postmodern culture and children's culture alike to consider the social potential of postmodern children's culture to create consumers who are engaged and critically aware of the social and political processes they are interpellated into and complicit within their everyday lives.

NOTES

1. See Allan and Sipe and Pantaleo.

2. See Strum. Though its creators do not gear *The Simpsons* specifically at children, the show has a large youth audience, which, in my opinion, makes it worthy for consideration as "children's culture."

3. See Bybee and Overbeck, Orr, and Steeves.

4. For important works in children's film studies, see Wojcik-Andrews and Brown. What we may call "Disney studies" seems to be its own thriving cottage industry within communications and cultural studies.

5. Janet Staiger has observed, "Perhaps we should pay more attention to the apparent good effects of media, such as teaching young children reading at an early age or marshaling youth to care about civil rights or informing all citizens about political controversies" (3).

6. The Paramount decision refers to the Supreme Court's 1948 decision in *United States v. Paramount Pictures, Inc.*, in which the Court decided studios could not own the theaters where their films were exhibited. Not only did this case undermine vertical integration within Hollywood, but it also spelled the end of the classic Hollywood studio system.

7. It should be noted that I gender the monster because, as I will discuss later, the monster's humanoid nature is essential to its representation, especially in making it sympathetic and likable.

8. Halberstam now (March 2013) identifies as "Jack Halberstam." I use "Judith Halberstam" here because it is the name under which Halberstam published *Skin Shows* in 1995. In line with Halberstam's preference, I respect the refusal to establish preference for "his" or "her."

WORKS CITED

Allan, Cherie. *Playing with Picturebooks: Postmodernism and the Postmodernesque*. New York: Palgrave Macmillan, 2012. Print.

Asma, Stephen T. *On Monsters: An Unnatural History of Our Worst Fears*. New York: Oxford UP, 2009. Print.

Barth, John. "The Literature of Exhaustion." *The Friday Book: Essays and Other Nonfiction*. Baltimore: Johns Hopkins UP, 1984. 62–76. Print.

Benshoff, Harry M. *Monsters in the Closet: Homosexuality and the Horror Film*. Manchester: Manchester UP, 1997. Print.

Boggs, Carl, and Tom Pollard. "Postmodern Cinema and Hollywood Culture in an Age of Corporate Colonization." *Democracy & Nature* 7.1 (2001): 159–81. Print.

Brown, Noel. *The Hollywood Family Film: A History, from Shirley Temple to Harry Potter*. New York: I. B. Tauris, 2012. Print.

Bybee, Carl, and Ashley Overbeck. "Homer Simpson Explains Our Postmodern Identity Crisis, Whether We Like It or Not: Media Literacy After *The Simpsons*." *Studies in Media and Information Literacy Education* 1.1 (2001): 1–12. Print.

Caputi, Jane. "Green Consciousness: Earth-based Myth and Meaning in *Shrek*." *Ethics & the Environment* 12.2 (2007): 23–44. Print.

Crandall, Nadia. "The Fairly Tale in the 21st Century: *Shrek* as Anticipatory Illumination or Coercive Ideology." *Turning the Page: Children's Literature in Performance and the Media*. Edited by Fiona M. Collins and Jeremy Ridgman. Bern: Peter Lang, 2006. 165–83. Print.

Egan, Michael. "The Neverland of Id: Barrie, *Peter Pan*, and Freud." *Children's Literature* 10 (1982): 37–55. Print.

Gilmore, David D. *Monsters: Evil Beings, Mythical Beasts, and All Manner of Imaginary Terrors*. Philadelphia: U of Pennsylvania P, 2003. Print.

Gubar, Marah. "On Not Defining Children's Literature." *PMLA* 126.1 (2011): 209–16. Print.

Halberstam, Judith. *Skin Shows: Gothic Horror and the Technology of Monsters*. Durham, NC: Duke UP, 1995. Print.

Hill, John. "Film and Postmodernism." *The Oxford Guide to Film Studies*. Edited by John Hill and Pamela Church Gibson. New York: Oxford UP, 1998. 96–105. Print.

Hutcheon, Linda. *A Poetics of Postmodernism: History, Theory, Fiction*. New York: Routledge, 1988. Print.

Jameson, Fredric. "Postmodernism and Consumer Society." *The Cultural Turn: Selected Writings on the Postmodern, 1983–1998*. Brooklyn, NY: Verso, 2009. 1–20. Print.

Jedrzejko, Pawel. "Fat, Green and *Schrecklich*: Mistaken Identities, Transhumanity and Fairy-Tale Excuses." *Open Letter* 13.3 (2007): 69–88. Print.

Lyotard, Jean François. *The Post-Modern Condition: A Report on Knowledge*. Translated by Geoff Bennington and Brian Massumi. Minneapolis: U of Minnesota P, 1984. Print.

Orr, Brian. "'I'm Bart Simpson, Who the Hell Are You?' A Study in Postmodern Identity (Re)Construction." *Journal of Popular Culture* 37.1 (2003): 56–82. Print.

Pinedo, Isabel Cristina. *Recreational Terror: Women and the Pleasures of Horror Film Viewing*. Albany: State U of New York P, 1997. Print.

Rose, Jacqueline. *The Case of Peter Pan, or The Impossibility of Children's Fiction*. Philadelphia: U of Pennsyvania P, 1993. Print.

Sipe, Lawrence R., and Sylvia Pantaleo, eds. *Postmodern Picturebooks: Play, Parody, and Self-Referentiality*. New York: Routledge, 2008. Print.

Staiger, Janet. *Media Reception Studies*. New York: New York UP, 2005. Print.

Steeves, H. Peter. "'It's Just a Bunch of Stuff That Happened': The Simpsons and the Possibility of Postmodern Comedy." *The Sitcom Reader: America Viewed and Skewed*. Edited by Mary M. Dalton and Laura R. Linder. Albany: SUNY Press, 2005. 261–72. Print.

Stephens, John, ed. *Subjectivity in Asian Children's Literature and Film: Global Theories and Implications*. New York: Routledge, 2012. Print.

Strum, Charles. "The Simpsons Never Change But the Audience Does." *New York Times*, 26 April 1998. Web. 4 November 2013.

Tudor, Andrew. *Monsters and Mad Scientists: A Cultural History of the Horror Movie*. Cambridge, MA: Basil Blackwell, 1999. Print.

Wall, Barbara. *The Narrator's Voice: The Dilemma of Children's Fiction*. New York: St. Martin's, 1991. Print.

Wojcik-Andrews, Ian. *Children's Films: History, Ideology, Pedagogy, Theory*. New York: Garland, 2000. Print.

Zipes, Jack. "The Potential of Liberating Fairy Tales for Children," *New Literary History* 13.2 (Winter 1982): 309–25. Print.

———. "Why Fantasy Matters Too Much." *Journal of Aesthetic Education* 43.2 (Summer 2009): 77–91. Print.

Zornado, J. "Children's Films as Social Practice." *CLCWeb: Comparative Literature and Culture* 10.2 (2008): 1–10. Print.

Get It Together

Anxieties of Collective Responsibility in Contemporary Young Adult Horror Novels

NICK LEVEY AND HOLLY HARPER

IF THERE'S ONE THING YOU CAN DEPEND UPON DURING THE ZOMBIE apocalypse, it's that you won't have to face it alone. The effort to ward off raving hordes of brain-hungry monsters is rarely a solo one: books and films depicting the sudden arrival in our lives of the zombified, demonic, and vampiric are often also about our ability (and of course inability) to work successfully in groups. This idea of a horror-driven lesson on collective responsibility might at first seem strange, but it's a notion we aim to further explore through the reading of two works of young adult fiction. Two recent and popular horror novels for teens, Charlie Higson's *The Enemy* and Michael Grant's *Gone*, seem especially determined to shift the focus of adolescent literature and learning away from issues of selfhood and individuation that tend to characterize understandings of the genre, toward considerations of group consciousness and democratic dynamics. In the hands of Higson and Grant, horror successfully introduces young readers to complex debates about collective responsibility, altruism, and the management of societies in crisis, and is thus shown to have far more to commend it to young readers than just monsters and gore. The importance of these novels is twofold: not only do they reveal the thematic seriousness of the horror genre, they also prepare adolescent readers for a future that might call on them to adopt political responsibilities.

While Carrie Hintz has suggested that in many utopian young adult novels "political and social awakening is almost always combined with a depiction of the personal problems of adolescence" (255), in the two horror novels we study such "personal problems" are muted, or at least shown to be less pressing than a wider sense of social well-being. If anything, protagonists are encouraged to move past personal issues in order to do what is best for the groups to which they belong. In reading *The Enemy* and *Gone*, we thus build upon aspects of the work of Roberta Seelinger Trites, who suggests that the uniqueness of much young adult literature lies "not so much in how the protagonist grows [. . .] but with the very determined way that young adult novels tend to interrogate social constructions, foregrounding the relationship between the society and the individual rather than focusing on Self and self-discovery" (20). Trites argues that much young adult literature is concerned with managing social repression and domination, rather than personal growth or self-discovery:

> Children's literature often affirms the child's sense of Self and her or his personal power [. . .]. But in the adolescent novel, protagonists must learn about the social forces that have made them what they are. They learn to negotiate the levels of power that exist in the myriad social institutions within which they must function, including family; school; the church; government; social constructions of sexuality, gender, race, class; and cultural mores surrounding death. (3)

The young adult genre is "dedicated to depicting how potentially out-of-control adolescents can learn to exist within institutional structures" (7), and is thus not so much focused on self-delineation as recognition of "what it means if we define people as socially constructed subjects rather than as self-contained individuals bound by their identities" (16). As such, growth in the young adult novel generally occurs to the extent that protagonists learn that some degree of self-compromise is always necessary and indeed preferable to a society ruled by the anarchy of pure self-interest.

But Trites's suggestion that young adult literature tends to have an underlying agenda of indoctrinating adolescents "into a measure of social acceptance" (27) needs to be at least partly modified in order to make her account of young adult fiction a suitable description of the works being studied here. For one, Trites's focus on realist novels means that she isn't able to consider that many contemporary young adult *horror* novels, including *The Enemy* and *Gone*, take place in worlds defined by a sort of power vacuum, involving a collapse or complete dismantling of institutions of social repression and domination. If anything, these books of chaos and destruction involve a quasi-utopian encouragement for adolescents to rebuild society in a more egalitarian fashion, putting into practice what they have learned about the distribution of power in the previous (now destroyed) world, and its necessities, benefits, and shortcomings. In Higson's *The Enemy*, the adults of London (and possibly the entire world) have become zombies, leaving kids to fend for themselves. The young protagonists not only have to rebuild sources of power and protection, but reject older institutions of oppression, such as the monarchy, which others attempt to reinstate. In Grant's *Gone*, a mysterious dome surrounds a town as all people over the age of fifteen start to "blink out" or disappear, with young teens and children left to reorganize society in order to survive. But while the ostensible "state of emergency" seems to call for extraordinary measures in order to secure collective well-being (measures recognizable from our own real-world responses to crisis), the novel asks its readers to decide whether the threat from outside is ever greater than the internal crises that special rules of power create. These novels encourage social re-evaluation rather than conformity, and thus sit somewhat uncomfortably alongside the realist paradigm outlined by Trites.

But the utopian push of these narratives—their encouragement to re-build society in an egalitarian fashion—does not necessarily mean they are able to be slotted neatly into the dystopian/utopian subgenre either. Hintz describes utopian and dystopian young adult fiction as that in which characters encounter a "rigorously planned society" that prioritizes "collective well-being over the fate of the individual" (254). Such narratives "honor dissent and agitation, and action based on a prolonged and combative questioning of the society in which the protagonists find themselves" (255). The position characters begin from in Higson's and Grant's horror novels, however, is not one of conflict with an oppressive or draconian society, but of being thrown unpreparedly into a wholly *ungoverned* world. These works do not necessarily relate problems that adolescents face coming up *against* established social institutions, but in facing a world where there are none. Characters must learn to deal with the absence of institutions of power, a world where there are no Althusserian "Ideological State Apparatuses" pro-gramming them into social docility, and no parents telling them when to go to bed. Of course, to some extent what they learn is just how much they do need some of these structures of power after all, and thus they set about recreating them. But the focus in *The Enemy* and *Gone* tends to be on how to fend off the reintroduction of previous forms of corrupt or inequitable social organization and how to forge more ethical ones for the future.

All this is not to say that the collective or group is a place of great harmony in these works. These are *horror* novels, after all, and things are going to go wrong. For reasons that we will explore throughout, difficulties of collective responsibility are both what these books are about, and what makes them horrific, scary, exciting, and bold. While *The Enemy* and *Gone* are filled with zombies, monsters, and gore, the true wellspring of their horror tends to be found in two places: the situation of premature "adultification" forced upon their young characters, who, recalling those in Golding's *Lord of the Flies*, must adopt collective, self-abnegating, and quasi-political responsibilities that their identification as adolescents or children usually protects them from;[1] and the difficulties of group selection, of choosing *the right* kind of collective to belong to. As we shall see, in the face of crisis and social collapse, both narratives offer their characters a choice between a savvy authoritarian savior able to provide a high level of security, and a less outwardly able, but more egalitarian collective. Selecting which form of social organization will create not only the safest, but also the fairest society for all of its members is a decision of utmost importance, and thus considerable anxiety.

We also need to keep in mind what the horror genre brings to these stories, and understand the means by which it allows for and heightens the stakes of narratives about group functioning and collective responsibility. To begin with, horror emphasizes the themes of collective responsibility by making groups and group dynamics a source of great anxiety and danger, more dangerous than the more typically "horrific" threats within the narrative worlds—the zombies, monsters, aliens, and so forth. While Robin Wood has suggested that it is "the relationship between normality and the Monster [. . .] that constitutes the essential subject of the horror film" (204), in these horror novels the importance of the "monstrous Other" is displaced to something like the narrative periphery. Although both of these books contain classic horror threats, we would label them *external* pressures, whose primary function is to exert pressure on the characters' abilities to evince proper degrees of collective responsibility and group functioning. The narrative of *The Enemy* is caused by the transformation of normal adults into zombies, but while these monsters do present very real dangers for the central characters, the core of the novel is much more interested in the problems of collective behavior that plague the children. The monsters become not much more than generic iconography whose main purpose is to put pressure on the children's functioning as a group. While the external threats are different in *Gone*, the challenges of group belonging are quite similar, suggesting that zombies, monsters, and further representations of the Other are the changeable window dressing of the young adult horror genre. The real source of terror is, in one way or another, the social group.

Charlie Higson's *The Enemy* is set in a contemporary London ravaged by a mysterious illness that has transformed anyone over the age of fourteen into raving, zombie-like creatures hungry for the flesh of the unaffected. As a result, the illness has also turned all children and young teenagers into ad-hoc survivalists. The novel centers on a particular group of survivors called the Waitrose crew, named after the shopping mall they have holed up in for safety and companionship. Higson is here recalling the horror film classic *Dawn of the Dead*, in which a group of characters barricade themselves in a shopping complex in order to escape a similar horde of zombies. Within Waitrose the children have formed a micro-society of sorts, with older members Arran and Maxie taking on leadership duties, fighters like Achilleus defending the young and hunting wild dogs for food, and intelligent characters like Ollie functioning as the community brain-trust. For the teenagers and children in this world, the group becomes like a super-organism, able to supplement individual members' shortcomings through collective power. The focalization of the novel is split between the large ensemble cast of characters that occupy the narrative, and so throughout the book the reader is encouraged to practice his or her own form of group awareness, understanding narrative as a "polyphonic" discourse, a construction of perspectives joined as a whole rather than a world shaped by an individual consciousness. Both for the reader and the children in these books, managing a multitude of viewpoints is the key to successfully approaching the world.

The Enemy begins with two scenes that highlight the importance of group organization, as well as what sacrifices being part of a collective demands. The first is a scene in which not sticking together, not following the laws of the group, puts a character in clear danger. It functions as a warning parable of sorts, the kind of cautionary tale young readers would be familiar with from their own lives. Small Sam, who as his name suggests is a particularly diminutive and vulnerable member of the Waitrose crew, was "playing in the carpark behind Waitrose when the grown-ups took him" (1). The kids aren't supposed to be playing outside without a guard, as it's dangerous for them to be unprotected by the larger group—there's already a transgression of collective responsibility going on here. But what makes it an especially perilous situation for Small Sam is that he is singled out by the grown-ups, who are eventually able to separate him from his peers. While in "the panic of the attack the rest of Sam's gang got back safely inside," Sam was "cut off and the roving pack of grown-ups trapped him in a corner" (1). The vulnerable child in this scene is the one the grown-ups are able to isolate from the group.

Forced to fight on his own, Sam is unprotected; within the group he stands a much greater chance of survival. Simply being in the company of others protects him. The message is clear to the point of being heavy-handed.

What is especially unnerving about this scene for the Waitrose crew, and what is so important about it for Higson's narrative, is that the grown-ups have here started to demonstrate what seems like their own form of collective organization. Previously, the zombies have acted in a disorganized, mob-like fashion, and have thus been relatively easy for the Waitrose crew to defend themselves against, employing the power of collective behavior against the shambling horde. But with Small Sam's abduction, it begins to seem as if the grown-ups themselves are starting to clue in to the benefits of group organization and planned attack.

This suspicion is strengthened soon after when, in search of the Mars bars, crisps, and other snacks that might remain untouched in the vending machines of an old swimming-pool complex, a group of Waitrose children are lured into what seems like a trap laid by the grown-ups. While some of the party are wary of trying to scavenge the vending machine's bounty, one of the characters, Freak, is especially persistent, wading into the murky pool in order to reach a partially submerged machine. A horde of grown-ups rise suddenly out of the water, and more of them appear behind the group, blocking their exit. In the fight that ensues, Deke, Freak's best friend, is killed. It is clear that an inability to resist the lure of personal interest indirectly causes Deke's death:

> "We should have never gone into there in the first place," said Achilleus. "Freak's an idiot."
> "Leave it," said Ollie. "We couldn't have known."
> "All for a bloody vending machine," said Achilleus. "Sweets and chocolates. We're not babies." (33–34)

Higson is literally dangling candy in front of children here. Again, the message is clear: if they are to survive, the sugary, indulgent treats of life need to be resisted. Self-interest is a quick route to death.

The anxiety that grows in the Waitrose crew after Deke's death is that their basic collective behavior isn't going to be able to protect them for much longer. With the grown-ups beginning to organize against them, they will either have to grow stronger, better organized, or seek others like themselves to form an even larger and more effective collective: "It wasn't like

grown-ups—usually they were stupid and slow and confused. Little different from the pack of dogs the gang had dealt with earlier. This bunch had
acted together. Sorted. A team" (32). As Ollie states, "these guys are getting
scary" (24). While only flesh-hungry hordes, they are, we are to assume, not
frightening; when acting as a group, they are terrifying.

As if prompted by this anxiety, a stranger calling himself Jester soon arrives bearing a message: Buckingham Palace has been made habitable by
another group of unaffected children. They've planted crops in the gardens
and have a steady supply of clean water from the lakes. Best of all, the palace
grounds are encircled by spiked walls. Jester also proudly proclaims that
they have children acting as the Queen's Guard: "We got our own guards,
now. We're making a fresh start" (64). But while it presents itself as a com-
munal utopia of sorts, a reclaiming of collective power in the symbolic and
literal seat of monarchic rule, this new Buckingham Palace soon becomes
the site of a different sort of crisis. At this stage in the narrative the threat
of the grown-ups takes a back seat. It is here that Higson forces his characters to learn not just about the importance of group consciousness, but of
choosing the most ethical form of group organization. While collective activity is the focus of *The Enemy*, the Waitrose crew is never allowed to grow
complacent—being in a group has obvious benefits, but entails a constant
series of decisions and responsibilities beyond just working together.

After they arrive at Buckingham Palace (experiencing several tragedies
along the way, including the death of their leader Arran), the Waitrose crew
find things more or less exactly as Jester has described: the grounds are full
of fresh vegetables, clean water, and the fence around the palace provides
a great degree of safety. It's a survivalist paradise, the utopia they've been
promised. The threat of the zombified grown-ups seems pushed into the periphery, and children living in this space actually have the luxury of dreaming about how this collective tragedy might actually mark the rebirth of the
world. As one character puts it:

Things are a lot better all round than they were before . . . Think about
it. The oceans are no longer being polluted, the fish aren't being wiped
out, they're breeding now, multiplying like mad, in a couple of years
there'll be more fish in the seas than there have been for centuries,
and it's not just fish, there's whales, dolphins, turtles, wild animals
everywhere. Think of the forests growing, the trees no longer being
cut down. The world is going back to how it *should* be. (232)

But, of course, this situation is too good to be true. The Waitrose crew soon get to meet the monarch whom Jester serves—David King, the self-appointed leader of the palace. For the other children in his group, David is a savior of sorts, and is treated with the deference his surname claims: "'When we first got here it was chaos,' said Jester. 'We were all over the place. But if you want to survive you have to be organized. If you want to grow food, to drink clean water, to stay warm, to defend yourselves, all those things need organization. David arrived a little after the rest of us. He pulled us all together. He organized us'" (234–35). While David is initially courteous to the Waitrose crew and demands they have a feast to celebrate their arrival, all doesn't sit well for some. Ollie, for one, cannot help but feel that there's something amiss with this palace collective, and he soon senses that its apparent success is dependent on a degree of inequality. During the banquet prepared for them by David's people, Ollie notices how several of the palace kids stand guard unnecessarily in the room, as if on show: "the boys in uniform were sitting by the doors, still clutching their rifles. He didn't like the atmosphere it created . . . The enemy was outside roaming the streets, not in here. What were they trying to prove with this display?" (233). Eventually, growing increasingly perturbed, Ollie slips away from the table and downstairs to the kitchen where the food is being prepared: "The room was packed. One group of kids was sweating away at the stoves, another clattering dishes at the sinks, immersed in clouds of steam and smoke. Yet more kids were crowded around a scrubbed wooden table. There looked to be about twenty of them; some in uniform, some still grubby from working in the garden. They weren't eating anything like what was being served upstairs. They had bowls of some kind of thin stew or soup" (235–36). To Ollie it seems clear that "David and his friends were trying to recreate the days of royalty" (233). The abundance and luxury they are feasting on comes at the expense of others' well-being and sustenance.

While spying on the kitchen, Ollie hears some of the oppressed children talking: "'They're scoffing everything upstairs. We'll starve.' 'We'll make do'" (236). Although this sort of self-sacrifice—the classic British "stiff upper-lip" attitude of "making do" despite harsh circumstances—is elsewhere encouraged in the novel (think of the importance of denying the treats of the vending machine, of going without for the benefit of the group), here it is to be understood as an attitude that allows for exploitation and corruption to continue. The willingness to "make do," to deny one's own interests, is a form of collective *complacency*, the wrong sort of group consciousness. It allows for a system that distributes well-being unequally, and at the expense of others' suffering. It is, in short, a version of the old society that has otherwise disintegrated, of the complacency and self-denial that enabled the monarchy and other forms of privilege and self-interest to perpetuate. In essence, it is not a form of courageous selflessness or stoicism at all that these kitchen-kids practice. In accepting their oppression by adopting a "stiff upper-lip," the children are behaving in a manner that promotes inequality, and encourages others not to rebel against unfairness. They are, in effect, being un-group conscious. It will be the job of Ollie, and others like him, to help them realize this.

The greatest risk David King poses is a return to the old way of organization, of corruption and arbitrary privilege. Eventually, members of the Waitrose crew discover his secret plan—to literally reinstate the monarchy. David has been keeping a group of zombified royals captive in order to use them as symbolic figureheads to legitimate his rule, which he intends to expand across London. After discovering his absurd and dangerous plan, the surviving members of the Waitrose crew decide to leave the safety of Buckingham Palace and make their own way through the world once again. They are once again a small but egalitarian collective.

Michael Grant's *Gone*, the first in a series of horror-dystopian books for teens, is another novel where children are forced to go it alone—but also *together*, teaming up in order to survive in the power vacuum caused by the disappearance of adults. In the fictional town of Perdido Beach, everyone over the age of fifteen suddenly starts to "blink out" or disappear. What's more, a strange dome has surrounded the town, locking the children inside and isolating them from the rest of the world. They exist in a microcosm they dub the FAYZ—Fallout Alley Youth Zone. Again, while the absence of parental figures and institutions of power might seem to enable the indulgence of personal interest, this place is far from a narcissistic utopia. The disappearance of the family unit and other powers-that-be exposes the children to the realities of collective organization that are required to keep society running.

As in *The Enemy*, the narrative periphery of *Gone* is populated by familiar tropes of the horror genre: there are unexplained and haunting occurrences, alien presences, and sentient and mutated animals. But the children also become dangers to one another. Several characters begin to develop strange and unpredictable powers that, far from being beneficial, mostly prove to be burdens and dangers. As in *The Enemy*, a charismatic and domineering leader arrives to play out his fantasies of power. Similar to David King, Caine is a very successful leader, but his tyranny ultimately convinces

those who fall out of his favor, or else refuse to abide by his rules, to organize their own collectives governed by a more altruistic ethics. Once again,
the lessons about collective responsibility are quite complex—the moral
isn't simply to stick together, but rather to choose the most egalitarian and
just power system, a decision often involving an implied rebuke of today's
existing social structure.

The main protagonist of *Gone* is fourteen-year-old Sam Temple. In life
before the FAYZ, Sam liked to keep "a lower profile. He stuck to jeans and
understated T-shirts, nothing that drew attention to himself" (5). By being
deliberately unremarkable, he tries to opt out of the social scene that so
many of his peers thrive in. Being the hero of a narrative is exactly what
Sam *doesn't* want, and he will spend most of *Gone* trying to resist the call to
be a leader, as leadership is too close to some sort of hubristic celebration of
individual power: "I don't want anyone taking orders from me. If I wanted
people taking orders from me, all I had to do was stay in town and start
telling people what to do" (104). While around the character of Sam we can
potentially locate a standard narrative of self-discovery, his progression toward taking leadership of the group of children aligned with him is framed
far more as a battle with the unwanted burdens and pressures of collective
responsibility than a desire for personal heroism. *Gone* is not so much a
story of heroism, then, of a shy boy realizing his leadership potential, but of
the realization that the greater need sometimes necessitates getting over our
own personal discomforts.

After everyone over age fifteen starts to blink out, the main source of
anxiety for Sam and his best friend Quinn is not the absence of parental figures, but the fact that this absence is forcing them to interact with and take
responsibility for a host of other children less able to survive on their own.
Previously, Sam and Quinn had been outcasts and loners, preferring their
own company. They enjoyed being apart from the world because it allowed
them to be largely free of responsibility. And they long for a return to this
state of things: "Quinn huffed. But he was running out of resentment. He
shot a dark look at Edilio, a wary look at Astrid. 'It's just weird, brah. Used
to be it was you and me right? . . . I just want to get our boards and head for
the beach. I want everything to go back to how it was'" (104). In the absence
of adults they are not allowed the simple pleasures of surfing or hanging
out by themselves. As older and capable members of this community, they
are forced to become collectively responsible. And it's a drag, interrupting
their fun: "It was happening a lot. Kids coming to Sam, asking him questions
for which he had no answers. He wished they would stop" (47). For Sam it

"would be a relief to walk out into the night. He wanted to get away from all those frightened faces looking to him, expecting something from him" (51). Sam doesn't want anything even approximating collective responsibility. He wants to disappear—which is of course the irony of the threat posed by "blinking out": when he turns fifteen, Sam finally stands to get what he wishes for.

In the early stages of the novel Sam, Quinn, and a group of other children move from place to place without much purpose. But eventually a new group of kids appear in town from the Coates Academy, a wealthy private school, and things immediately start to change. These children arrive in a motorcade of BMWs and give off an air of political sophistication, as if they've been watching news footage of presidential motorcades. As they step out from the convoy of expensive cars, they assemble in a line, "not quite a drill team in their order and precision, but like they had practised it" (139). The Coates kids are led by Caine, a charismatic leader who is supported by his violent and manipulative cronies Drake and Diana. In comparison to Sam and his gang of misfits, the Coates Academy kids are well organized and quasi-militaristic, not averse to taking charge.

Yet it soon becomes clear that this group is overly centred on the focal point of Caine, who, it is revealed later in the novel, is Sam's unknown fraternal twin. If *The Enemy*'s David King was presented as a monarch, Caine is presented as a modern religious guru or media-savvy politician, and demands the same sort of adoration from his followers: "wearing a bright yellow V-necked sweater instead of his blazer, [Caine] stood up in the convertible. He grinned sheepishly and climbed nimbly from the back seat on to the trunk. He gave a little self-deprecating wave, as if to say he couldn't believe what he was doing" (139). As Sam's friend Astrid points out, it all seems like "a well-rehearsed display" (139).

For many children, especially those traumatized by the absence of their parents (one child cries "I want my mom" during Caine's arrival), Caine and his Coates Academy cronies seem appealing, especially *because* they appear organized as a collective (141). The appearance of group cohesion, while it may all just be appearance, is comforting and appealing for these parentless children. Indeed, the children lap up what seems like the media-spectacle of Caine's arrival as if they are already missing the many facades of power and structure presented to them by television. They are comforted as much by the simulation of power as any real expression of it. As Caine consoles a boy crying for his mum—a perfect photo-op—he assures the crowd gathered around him that they "all have to be strong. We all have to get through this.

If we work together to choose good leaders and do the right thing, we will make it." The platitudes are overly familiar yet milk the crowd, hungry for structure and control.

Caine's rhetoric has an instant effect: "the entire crowd of kids seemed to stand a little taller. There were determined looks on faces that had been weary and frightened" (142). His talk of order and collective organization is just what the anxious children need to rouse their spirits. His plan is basic but appealing: "I think we should organize so that things aren't destroyed, and problems can be handled. I think our goal should be to maintain. So that once the barrier comes down, and once the disappeared people come back, they will find that we've done a pretty darn good job of keeping things together" (147). His goal is to preserve a form of social organization, or at least keep one in place that the adults would approve of if they returned.

Even Sam is "mesmerised by the performance" (142). He is also skeptical—he "distrusted rehearsed displays" and still harbors a dislike of showy heroism. But he recognizes that "if Caine really did have a plan, wouldn't that be a good thing? No one else seemed to have a clue" (142). Initially, Caine's arrival actually proves to be a source of relief for Sam—it takes the weight of collective responsibility from his shoulders. But Caine's presence also enables him to take a less anxious view of group organization, and he grows more accepting of the fact that as an older member of the group he has to take on responsibilities befitting his abilities. During Caine's distribution of group duties, for example, Sam accepts the role of fire chief, "not because he wanted to, but because so many other people seemed to want him to" (169).

Caine's plan to simply "maintain" things is soon shown for what it is, however. He becomes increasingly ruthless, defending a fatal attack on a girl named Bette, punishing all those who are developing powers by encasing their hands in concrete (while keeping his own secret, of course), as well as distributing a set of draconian rules that all are expected to follow, which he uses to justify the attack on Bette. The town is soon placed under something like Caine's version of martial law.

The violence against Bette ultimately inspires an argument between Sam and his best friend Quinn that lies at the core of *Gone*'s attempt to encourage its adolescent readers to consider the complex ethics of collective responsibility. As Sam reads out the list of Caine's rules in order to find out which one Bette has apparently broken, he admits that some indeed seem fair and reasonable, such as that everyone has to help out at the nursery or scavenge for supplies. Toward the end of the list, however, things start to seem a little wrong. Everyone has "to pass on information on any bad be-haviour to Drake"; effectively, they are all "supposed to be informers" (180). Free speech is also drastically limited: "We are in a state of emergency. Dur-ing this crisis no one should criticize, ridicule, or hinder any of the people performing their official duties" (181). The last rule is perhaps the worst: "The sheriff may decide that the above rules are insufficient to cover some emergency situations. In those cases, the sheriff may formulate whatever rules are needed to keep order and keep people safe" (181).

While these rules are ostensibly written with collective well-being in mind, for Sam and a few others there's something inherently wrong with them: "Edilio's worried look mirrored Sam's. 'Yeah, man, this ain't right. That's saying Caine and Drake can do whatever they want, any time they want'" (182). For Quinn, however, such extraordinary measures are reason-able: "This isn't normal times, OK? We're cut off, we have no adults of any kind, no police or teachers or parents" (182). For Quinn there "were always bullies, but the adults were still in charge. Now? Now the bullies rule. Differ-ent game, brother, a whole different game. We play by the bully rules now" (183). In Quinn's opinion, the risks of rebellion outweigh what they stand to gain from obeying the rules.

Of course, this list of rules in response to a "crisis" is eerily similar to the Homeland Security and USA PATRIOT acts passed in the wake of 9/11,[2] and Grant is obviously suggesting a political allegory here. The importance of this allegory is that it is children who are to decide on its ethics, and this novel is then to be seen as an encouragement for younger generations to become aware of the corruption that can occur when rules protecting collective well-being are more truly forms of unjust self-protection or the flexing of individual muscle. The reader has to consider whether or not the rules put in place to protect a society from crisis are actually a source of crisis and danger in themselves.

Rejecting Caine's rule, Sam and a band of misfits head out of town. But while within this group Sam eventually assumes leadership, the individual-istic aspects of his narration are muted in favor of the fair and just spirit of collective well-being that his leadership is able to defend. In this novel, Sam doesn't have to discover his "self" so much as get over it. While this may, of course, simply mark his discovery of a new, more mature self, in this new-found identity Sam is far less concerned with his own personal problems, and much more willing to put his "issues" aside for the benefit of the group.

The climax of the novel sees Sam's gang return to town to lead the rest of the children against Caine: "We'll head back to Perdido Beach. We'll go back, and we'll make things right" (389). Once back in town Sam tries to rally the other kids together to overthrow Caine's tyranny, which has turned the FAYZ into a warzone: "Coates kids, Perdido Beach kids, we're together now. We're together . . . We're brothers and sisters now. Doesn't matter we don't know each other's names, we are brothers and sisters and we're going to survive, and we're going to win, and we're going to find our way to some kind of happiness again" (413). After Sam's rousing speech the group "no longer spread in every direction. They didn't march like an army, but they came as close as a bunch of traumatized kids could. They walked with their heads a little higher" (414). This is a group whose sense of collective well-being is much different from the one proposed by Caine.

As Michael Cart and many others have shown, young adult literature came of age in a time when young adults were first starting to be recognized as a legitimate social demographic (5–12). It was thus natural that stories written for them were grounded in themes of self-assertion and discovery. Today, many works of young adult literature still narrate problems arising when society oppresses or restrains young individuals. Suzanne Collins's blockbuster *Hunger Games* series is perhaps the most recent and prominent example, where a totalitarian government forces citizens to lead highly restrictive lives, and the heroine, Katniss Everdeen, must lead a push for revolution. But when young adults are well represented in the media, the market, and the collective consciousness of society—as they are today—such stories are no longer as pressing to tell. Young people don't have to fight as hard to be heard in the world, and it is fitting that stories written for them expand young adult literature's thematic scope beyond the demographic's struggle for recognition.

The Enemy and *Gone* reflect this proposed shift in the social status of young adults by encouraging young readers to contemplate issues related to the political and collective spheres of life, rather than the personal and individualistic.[3] Both novels contain well-established horror tropes, but the most anxious aspects of their narratives center on burdens of collective responsibility. In these works, the main struggle is not to defend against monstrous Others, or to resolve personal problems, but to achieve a form of collective well-being that doesn't depend upon inequality or violence and which isn't merely a reinstatement of the previous configurations of social control from which their worlds have been, for better or worse, freed.

NOTES

1. As Pamela Craig and Martin Fradley suggest, "teen horror's frequent evacuation of adults" can on one level be seen as encouraging a form of adolescent narcissism, but it "also necessarily allows its audience to vicariously work through collective fears and anxieties" (93). In *The Enemy* and *Gone*, we would argue, these collective fears are of being implicated *in* a collective.

2. As Kevin J. Wetmore explains, "although more known and cited as 'the Patriot Act,' the title is actually an acronym which stands for United [*sic*] and Strengthening America by Providing Appropriate Tools to Intercept and Obstruct Terrorism Act of 2001, the official title of the bill and subsequent law. Ironically, it did not actually unite America as many of its provisions proved quite controversial" (204–5). In *Gone*, Caine's rules have a similar effect.

3. Higson and Grant are of course not alone in writing young adult horror narratives that emphasise collective responsibility. Alexander Gordon Smith's *The Fury*, Rick Yancey's *The 5th Wave*, and Sean Beaudoin's *The Infects* can be cited as other recent examples.

WORKS CITED

Beaudoin, Sean. *The Infects*. Somerville: Candlewick Press, 2012. Print.

Cart, Michael. *Young Adult Literature: From Romance to Realism*. Chicago: American Library Association, 2010. Print.

Collins, Suzanne. *The Hunger Games*. London: Scholastic, 2008. Print.

Craig, Pamela, and Martin Fradley. "Teenage Traumata: Youth, Affective Politics, and the Contemporary American Horror Film." *American Horror Film: The Genre at the Turn of the Millennium*. Edited by Steffen Hantke. Jackson: UP of Mississippi, 2010. 77–102. Print.

Dawn of the Dead. Dir. George Romero. Yonsei Digital Media, 2002. DVD.

Golding, William. *Lord of the Flies: A Novel*. London: Faber and Faber, 1958. Print.

Grant, Michael. *Gone*. London: Egmont, 2009. Print.

Higson, Charlie. *The Enemy*. London: Puffin Books, 2009. Print.

Hintz, Carrie. "Monica Hughes, Lois Lowry, and Young Adult Dystopias." *The Lion and the Unicorn* 26.2 (2002): 254–64. Print.

Smith, Alexander Gordon. *The Fury*. London: Faber and Faber, 2012. Print.

Trites, Roberta Seelinger. *Disturbing the Universe: Power and Repression in Adolescent Literature*. Iowa City: U of Iowa P, 2000. Print.

Wetmore, Kevin J. *Post-9/11 Horror in American Cinema*. New York: Continuum, 2012. Print.

Wood, Robin. "An Introduction to the American Horror Film." *Movies and Methods: An Anthology*. Edited by Bill Nichols. Vol. 2. Berkeley: U of California P, 1985. 195–220. Print.

Yancey, Rick. *The 5th Wave*. New York: G. P. Putnam's Sons, 2013. Print.

Teen Terrors

Race, Gender, and Horrifying Girlhood in *The Vampire Diaries*

JANANI SUBRAMANIAN AND JORIE LAGERWEY

IN 2009, THE CW TELEVISION NETWORK, PARTNERING WITH YOUTH-media giant Alloy Media + Marketing, launched its teenage-vampire melo-drama *The Vampire Diaries* (2009–present). Based on a series of young adult novels by L. J. Smith, *The Vampire Diaries* is set in Mystic Falls, Vir-ginia, a small southern town full of supernatural secrets rooted in its Civil War past. The series' central romance involves Elena Gilbert (Nina Dobrev), a human high-school student, caught in a love triangle between the eter-nally young vampire brothers Stefan (Paul Wesley) and Damon Salvatore (Ian Somerhalder). Caroline Forbes (Candice Accola) and Bonnie Bennett (Katerina Graham), Elena's best friends, round out the central cast, with each girl eventually developing her own supernatural storyline. *The Vam-pire Diaries* demonstrates how the contradictions inherent in mixing the gothic mythology of horror with teen melodrama, and indeed in mixing horror and television in general, are mirrored and reinforced in the raced and gendered contradictions of postfeminist girl culture. Using Caroline and Bonnie as our primary texts, we examine the ways in which the show uses tropes of monstrosity to call attention to these raced and gendered subtexts of coming of age in teenage television melodrama.

Until very recently, horror and television have not been very fruitful partners. Of course there have been shows, some of them relatively suc-cessful, that traded on the generic tropes of horror to tell their stories: the anthology classic *The Twilight Zone* (1959–64), dramas ranging from *Kolchak* (ABC 1974–75) to *The X-Files* (FOX 1993–2002), sitcoms like *The Munsters* (1964–66) and *The Addams Family* (1964–66), and of course *Buffy the Vampire Slayer* (1997–2003) and its spin-off series *Angel* (1999–2004).

These shows, however, often relied on the "monster of the week" format, either reproducing the circular disruption, resolution, repeat structure of a traditional sitcom, or focusing on the procedural elements of discovery and detection. Currently, there is a small but critically adored[1] cycle of "quality-TV"[2] horror spreading across America's cable television landscape. Rather than the episodic procedural format of earlier horror shows, series such as *American Horror Story* (FX 2011–present), *The Walking Dead* (AMC 2010–present), and *True Blood* (HBO 2008–2014) have all adopted the combined high-production value and the demographics of quality dramas with the melodramatic characteristics of serialized narrative arcs that are focused on homes, families, and communities besieged by the supernatural. At the same time, adolescent culture, particularly film and television, has been delving deeply into the tropes and conventions of horror with the massive commercial successes of the *Twilight* and *Hunger Games* multimedia franchises and the spinoffs and imitations they have inspired.[3] It is into this televisual landscape that *The Vampire Diaries* premiered.

The Vampire Diaries (*TVD*), trading on the CW's teen market and proven branding strategies, mixes gloss and melodrama in the attempt to create so-called quality television, "characterized by the use of ensemble casts in an hour-long dramatic format, narratives that replaced the familiar procedural milieu with a focus on the familial relationships that existed between friends and colleagues, a tendency towards liberal humanism, a propensity for self-reflexivity, and the adoption of cinematic techniques and aesthetic" (Wee "Teen Television" 50). This combination of self-reflexive teenaged melodrama, quality TV aesthetics, and supernatural horror creates a generic hybrid that exposes an obsession with embodied physicality, which in turn reveals gendered and raced tensions enacted through the tendency toward excess in teenage life and coming-of-age narratives. In this essay, we examine Caroline Forbes and Bonnie Bennett, two *TVD* characters whose monstrous transitions from high-school girls to vampire and witch highlight different facets of their teen-girl identities; Caroline's vampirism highlights her hyper-blonde whiteness and stereotypical mean-girl femininity, while Bonnie's powers of witchcraft perpetuate links between her African American identity and gothic representations of the American South. *TVD* exploits the generic tensions between horror and melodrama, utilizing tropes of supernatural horror to intensify raced and gendered fears of bodily excess and transformation, while simultaneously using the structures and patterns of melodrama to create affective responses in viewers and to reconcile the otherworldly storylines with mundane life.

Horror has a fraught relationship to television programming; as a genre it is defined by "tension, fear, anxiety, sadism and masochism" (Brophy), yet it must contend with television's seriality, mass audiences, and intimate scale without compromising these traditional effects of the genre. Linda Williams, describing horror and melodrama (alongside pornography) as "body genres," argues that these genres evoke a physical response in the spectator parallel to that displayed on screen: "What seems to bracket these particular genres from others is an apparent lack of proper esthetic distance, a sense of over-involvement in sensation and emotion" (606). Teenagers often experience their bodies and emotions as erratic and unrestrained and are thus the perfect embodiment for horrific melodrama. As Katie Kapurch explains in her analysis of the melodramatic conventions in *Jane Eyre* and *Twilight*, elements such as interiority and introspection, a clash between good and evil, and secrets and secretiveness are the cornerstones of both texts. In addition, both *Jane Eyre* and the *Twilight* franchise rely heavily on different facets of the gothic, and their use of both implied (Jane's plainness) and overt (vampires and werewolves) monstrosity compounds the already intense situations the young female protagonists undergo in the course of each narrative.

Robin Wood argues that cycles of horror achieve a certain cultural saturation in times of cultural tension and crisis. He describes the filmic horror cycles of the 1960s and 1970s, when war in Vietnam, oil shortages, the civil rights movement, and the second-wave feminist movement were among the many social, political, and economic crises that presented a cultural need to express these tensions in vanquishable, monstrous form. In the *TVD* era, the dominant forms of social crisis include the worldwide economic crisis precipitated by the collapse of the US housing market in 2008, wars of attrition in Iraq and Afghanistan, racial upheaval in an allegedly postracial moment, the ongoing trend of economic neoliberalism and social neoconservatism in American public culture, and the tensions inherent in the contradictory discourses of postfeminism. Postfeminism is a contested popular and academic discourse that simultaneously implies that feminism is over because it has accomplished its goals, illustrates empowered femininity primarily through the lens of consumer goods rather than politics and, as evidenced by so-called new momism, often actually encourages a retreat to traditionally feminized reproductive and caretaking roles (McRobbie 2004; Negra 2004 and 2009; Douglas and Michaels 2012). The 2000s have seen extraordinary new attempts to exert control over women's bodies, sexuality, and reproduction—precisely the bodily facets that are perceived as out-of-control and confusing in teenaged subjects going through dramatic physical and emotional changes, and those expressed through the embodied excesses of the bloodiness of horror and the teariness of melodrama. The understanding that feminism has accomplished its goals and is no longer necessary goes hand in hand with a reassertion of outside control over women's bodies. Laurie Ouellette defines neoliberalism "as a troubling worldview that promotes the 'free' market as the best way to organize every dimension of social life" (225), a definition that links neoliberal culture specifically to postfeminism, which, as Angela McRobbie and Diane Negra have illustrated, relies on the rhetoric of choice and the onus on girls and young women to make the "correct" choices about their bodies (McRobbie 2004; Negra 2009).

Both *Twilight* and *The Hunger Games*, two of the most successful media franchises of the twenty-first century, highlight the contradictory demands that postfeminist culture makes on its subjects, as both feature young female protagonists who must fight against those attempting to control their bodies but do so ultimately to preserve the sanctity of their conventional, heterosexual partnerships.[4] In *The Hunger Games* the confluence of media-sponsored and government-sponsored control over the young heroine Katniss Everdeen's body is literalized when she is forced to participate in a government-controlled reality television death match. The *Twilight* franchise enacts control over its heroine Bella's body by enacting precisely the postfeminist disciplines outlined above. Bella is framed as making a choice to give up her human life to become a mother, albeit a choice demanded by her fated love story. Her child then literally consumes her dead body, using the tropes of horror to act out the most extreme version of retreatism or new momism. Bella's sacrifice of her (human) life for her child's directly mirrors contemporary governmental policies restricting women's reproductive rights in favor of protecting fetuses. *Twilight*'s bounded filmic and literary texts end with Bella's happy family, thus framing those choices as correct within the postfeminist discourses of choice and sacrifice. It is in this neoliberal postfeminist environment that the girls in young adult literature, television, and film learn to navigate and eventually to internalize the discipline illustrated by Katniss and Bella and required of their bodies and their selves in order to be integrated, postfeminist adult subjects. Yet the bodily and emotional excess experienced by characters in both melodrama and horror threatens to overwhelm the text and deny social integration, highlighting the contradictions postfeminism generates for its teenaged subjects.[5]

Beginning in 1997, the CW's former brand, the WB, premiered a series of five teen dramas that created a brand identity based on bodily and emotional teenage excess as represented through high quality, edgy melodrama and horror: *Buffy the Vampire Slayer* (1997–2003), *Dawson's Creek* (1998–2003), *Charmed* (1998–2006), *Felicity* (1998–2002), and *Roswell* (1999–2000). Valerie Wee says, "All of these shows share a range of distinct characteristics: they feature a young and highly attractive ensemble cast and they all trace the experiences of youth and growing up with an appealing blend of intelligence, sensitivity, and knowing sarcasm" ("Teen Television" 48). The irony, self-awareness, and tongue-in-cheek humor of these shows and the network as a whole embodies what Wee has called the "hyperpostmodernism" ("Scream Trilogy" 44–61) of teenage culture and also points to the way that television horror balances violence and fear with lighter genres such as domestic melodrama and humor.[6] In contrast to this lighter and often more ironic approach to teenage horror and melodrama, recent texts such as *Twilight*, *The Hunger Games*, and *TVD* use melodrama more earnestly. Kapurch argues that "appreciating melodramatic moments in young adult fiction might help to further a regard for affective responses cited by readers, validating the seriousness of coming-of-age experiences" (166). This is precisely the project the CW has undertaken with its casting of affect-heavy, melodramatic, supernatural storylines in the style of prestige or quality drama. The serious tone of *TVD*, in particular, distinguishes it from its more flip and lighter predecessors, creating the same market distinction that *Buffy* and *Dawson's Creek* did for the WB in the 1990s and fitting into the darker approach to teen literature and media that *Twilight*, with its submissive and clumsy heroine, its emphasis on domineering, potentially violent boyfriends, vampire wars, and gloomy northwestern setting, established in 2005.

The shift in tone and the related use of melodrama, horror, and science fiction in young adult literature reflects, in some part, a constantly changing industrial context—one that carefully orchestrates its products across several media platforms and releases them in controlled cycles. As Amy Pattee says in her study of the *Gossip Girl* young adult novels, "The new association of young adult literature with 'media production,' commerce, and marketing is one that invites closer consideration as our reading and recommendation proclivities confer not just literary approval but commercial sponsorship as well" (155). As Pattee describes, young adult novels such as the *Gossip Girl* and *Pretty Little Liars* series are sold as concepts first and then turned into books, television, or films based on market interest (*Gossip Girl* on the

CW from 2007 to 2013 and *Pretty Little Liars* on ABCFamily from 2007 to present). Alloy Media + Marketing, for example, controls the rights to other multiplatform titles such as *The Sisterhood of the Traveling Pants* (Warner Brothers 2005 and 2008), *The Lying Game* (ABCFamily 2011–present) and *The Vampire Diaries*. While each series varies in terms of narrative and thematic specificities, they all involve intense relationships of teenage girls that are based on secrecy and/or conspicuous consumption, commodifying the emotional work of young female friendship in precisely the mode demanded by postfeminist discourses. Alloy defines "teenage girlhood" in this manner and then spins it off into various market iterations, which perhaps explains the melodramatic shift in tone across several teen texts. Equally important, though, as we explore with *TVD*, is the way marketing companies such as Alloy conceive of "teenage girlhood" within these melodramatic formulas in specifically raced and gendered ways.

In this context of conglomerate- and network-approved visions of teen melodrama, *TVD* unfurls stories of two girls who become supernatural entities and their different paths to mastering, controlling, and containing those internal and external excesses in order to come of age into mature postfeminist subjects. As Wee argues about the WB's teen brand, shows such as *Dawson's Creek, Felicity, The Gilmore Girls* (2002–2007), and *One Tree Hill* (2003–2012), and even more speculative shows such as *Buffy, Charmed*, and *Roswell*, took a serious, morally idealistic approach to friendship, families, and personal growth; with that approach came a brand-conscious definition of feminism and "girl-power" ("Teen Television" 48). Francesca Gamber, using the teen protagonist of *The Gilmore Girls* as a case study, points to the ways the network's female-centered dramas focused on smart, ambitious young women who try on multiple feminisms to find the right, individual "fit." According to Gamber, Rory Gilmore (Alexis Bledel) represents third-wave feminism at its best, as the show in many ways responds to critiques of 1960s and 1970s feminism as monolithic with a more diverse, personalized feminism that takes both difference and play into account. With its three smart and feisty female characters, Elena, Caroline, and Bonnie, plus the adult women present in early seasons of the show: Jenna (Sara Canning), Elena's aunt and guardian, who is a graduate student; Caroline's mother, Elizabeth (Marguerite McIntyre), who is Mystic Falls' town sheriff; and Carol Lockwood (Susan Walters), who will eventually (if briefly) become mayor, *TVD* offers multiple femininities and images of girl power to its viewers. *TVD* fans, whether they relate to Caroline's social dominance, Elena's familial and romantic struggles, or Bonnie's growing mastery of her newfound witchcraft skills, identify with the various modes of power these girls represent, mimicking in a sense Rory Gilmore's trying on of different feminisms. Yet the individuated, personal feminism Gamber extols in *Gilmore Girls* can be easily co-opted into consumer culture, resulting in images of intelligent and independent women who nonetheless conform to normative race, gender, and sexual ideals, a cornerstone of the CW's postfeminist brand. The slender bodies of *TVD*'s heroines are clothed in the latest fashions, and their narrative arcs are marked by edgy pop music; perhaps the epitome of this consumer-oriented postfeminist ethos is the plethora of Internet sources that allow fans to "try on" the various feminine identities of the show by purchasing clothing, accessories, or props featured in various episodes.[7]

As a teenage melodrama, *TVD* features massive and traumatic transitions from girlhood to adulthood that allow characters to express their agency within the boundaries of postfeminism outlined above. Bonnie's and Caroline's monstrous transitions are also part of *TVD*'s use of horror and gothic conventions, which highlight the way the show fits into the CW's brand as well as the way these conventions complicate representations of race and femininity by tapping into the excessive and affective qualities of monstrosity itself. *TVD* as a book and television series is firmly rooted in a gothic literary tradition, specifically with markers such as the name of the town—Mystic Falls—and its hidden antebellum history, along with a series of conflicted heroines and doomed love triangles. Female protagonists in the gothic, as with horror narratives in general, function as active agents of discovery, embodiments of monstrosity, *and* victims of the patriarchal and supernatural forces at work, and the centrality of these female characters is crucial to the genre's manifestations on television, as television in general and TV melodrama in particular confines its drama to domestic spaces and the frequently female-centered relationships therein.[8] Helen Wheatley relates the gothic's appearance across television genres to the "uncanny," a Freudian term that applies to unsettling or disturbing images or circumstances, and television in general often delights in combining the familiar with the unexpected—often, of course, for the sake of attracting viewers and boosting ratings (7–8). Several teen shows invoke some aspects of the gothic, whether through an overt use of speculative genres like fantasy and horror or a more subtle invocation of interiority, secrecy, and melodrama. In *TVD* in particular, the uncanny functions as a way to highlight the frightening and unexpected facets of transitioning into adulthood; at the same time its combination of teen tropes and horror conventions calls attention to more troubling connections between its high-school monsters and the history of its southern setting.

TVD and its southern milieu recall aspects of the Southern Gothic, a subgenre that focuses on the American South and its troubled relationship to history, particularly the raced, gendered and classed facets of that history. Gina Herring describes the qualities of the Southern Gothic, as represented in Don Siegel's 1971 film *The Beguiled*: "a steamy Southern backdrop; a ravaged landscape; an isolated mansion shrouded in mystery and gloom; a ruined plantation inhabited by Southern belles prone to neuroses, secrets, passions, and terrors (Simpson xi); and the most Southern and Gothic of subjects, the Civil War."[9] As a melodrama-horror hybrid, *TVD* delights in twists and turns afforded by the narrative formula of the Southern Gothic, and Mystic Falls' facades and characters hide a complex history of violence and monstrosity. The use of one narrative to cover up a "true" narrative is often characteristic of the way southern history is told and retold, as pointed out by Lisa Nakamura, Laurie Beth Clark, and Michael Peterson in their analysis of *True Blood*'s opening credits. As the authors say of *True Blood*'s attempted use of vampire metaphors to represent the South, "Gothic visuality offers an idea of the 'truth' of the South, revealing the violence, sexuality, and faith that lie behind stereotypically polite Southern facades." In contrast to *True Blood*, which delights in an adult-oriented and explicit representation of vampire-human sexuality and violence, *TVD* does not conform to "Southern Gothic cliché: alligators, catfish, ecstatic spirituality and sexuality, and an atmosphere of decay that bespeaks a possibly inbred mutation" (Nakamura, Clark, and Peterson). While the credit sequence shows dark, misty locales, there is only one main "isolated mansion," occupied by the vampire Salvatore brothers; all the other characters seem to live in typical small-town dwellings, and the main streets of Mystic Falls are quaint and unthreatening. Mystic Falls' secret monsters—which include vampires, werewolves, witches, and doppelgangers—are comparatively tame, well-coiffed, hip high-schoolers, reflecting the network, its brand, and its intended demographic. *TVD* represents a conglomerate-approved vision of the South, yet, as we explore below, the gothic genre, its evocation of monstrous femininity, and the "neuroses, secrets, passions and terrors" of its teenage protagonists often overwhelm the glossy surfaces of the show. The teenage identities and monstrous alter-egos of two of these teen girl monsters, Caroline and Bonnie, reveal the ways that uncontained femininity and unacknowledged connections to American racial history reveal cracks in the show's postfeminist address.

Looking closely at the characters of Caroline Forbes and Bonnie Bennett reveals the way the Southern Gothic plays out in a teenage television context. Caroline begins her journey in *TVD* as a seemingly typical highschool girl; while main character Elena grapples with her parents' recent death, Caroline appears to be a popular queen bee with little on her mind except boys and parties. Her transformation into a vampire occurs in the second season and involves an invocation of a kind of inner monstrosity that ultimately tests her limits as a teenage girl and emphasizes her whiteness amid the show's use of fraught racial metaphors. While it may seem that Caroline displays powerful narrative agency and control—and indeed physical power—through her acquired supernatural abilities, she must subject those powers to a rigorous self-discipline that encapsulates the contradictory demands of young postfeminist subjects who are expected to wield the power awarded them by the feminist movement, but to *choose* to restrict that power as dictated by postfeminist ideology.

Caroline becomes a vampire in the second episode of season 2, "Brave New World." After an accident, she is healed with vampire blood, and when she is subsequently murdered by one of the series' villains, she awakes in the hospital in the middle of the night, steals a blood bag from a patient's bedside, and drinks her first sips as a vampire. At first she is tentative and then revolted as she gags and throws the bag to the floor. She is in clear distress, not understanding the cravings she seems to be having. But as the score swells and strings beat an intensifying rhythm, Caroline climbs to the floor on all fours and takes up the blood bag again. This time, she loses all the human control she exhibited a moment ago, and gorges on the blood bag, licking her hands, writhing and groaning as though in sexual ecstasy when she finally gives in to her mysterious craving and consumes the blood. The camera follows her, not in a smooth unified shot, but cutting rapidly between different angles, the editing finally matching the escalated pace of the score. The sounds and movements Caroline makes, plus the style of this sequence, seem to tie the new vampire's drinking both to animalistic behavior and sexual pleasure. Not only does this sequence highlight the show's use of quality television aesthetics, including film-like editing and camera movement that belong to the CW's brand, but its use of Southern Gothic tropes also highlights the parallel between Caroline's vampiric transformation and an awakening teenage sexuality. Similarly, the bloodiness of Caroline's monstrous awakening recalls the inevitable bloodiness of female puberty, emphasizing the metaphorical work Caroline's transition does to link the transition from innocent girlhood to young adulthood that is at first frightening, powerful, and obsessed with out-of-control consumption until ideological strictures are internalized and self-discipline is imposed to contain the powerful monstrosity, whether of a desire to drink human blood or to act as an autonomous, sexual subject in the world. In other words, this scene, while it replays a common trope of young adult literature, is a moment when the internalization of the contradictory postfeminist demands to be a consuming subject and to discipline one's own consumption is visibly rejected onscreen. Caroline is at first disgusted with herself, but then indulges wildly. While Caroline has already had sex in the show, this is the first moment where she appears to be out of control of her bodily desires as well as the noises her body makes and the fluids it can no longer contain. The key to *TVD*'s postfeminist address, however, is that rather than let this unruly feminine desire run amok, the show acts quickly to show Caroline mastering and controlling; that is, suppressing, her new, inappropriate, desire to consume.

Over the course of the next two episodes, Caroline, like the teenage girls watching her, has to come very quickly to terms with her new body and the heightened emotions that come with vampirism. As a gothic heroine, Caroline undergoes a transformative journey marked by discovery, but as a teenage television heroine, she must ultimately contain and discipline her monstrosity. She feeds on humans three times in these two episodes, and each time, she loses control, has blood streaming down her face and hands, and in one instance kills her victim before she can stop herself. The experience of transformation is painful, confusing, and terrifying, but it is ultimately satisfying for Caroline. When season 4 introduces the specter of a cure for vampirism, Caroline admits that she wouldn't take it. She has fully realized herself as a vampire and enjoys the physical powers she has as well as the confidence and self-control she was forced to learn during her transformation. To get to that point, however, she has to submit to training and internalize the discipline not to feed on humans. Additionally, the person who trains her is the show's male lead, Stefan. In other words, under the guidance of a patriarchal presence, she ignores her new body's physical needs and powers in order to fit human moral standards despite no longer being human. The body discipline that young women usually learn to create slender bodies here applies to containing all the desires and powers that are coded as "unnatural" by their association with the supernatural. Susan Douglas describes a similar containment of supernatural powers in her analysis of *Bewitched* heroine Samantha's witchy powers that were ultimately used for only three purposes, to compete with other women for male attention, to help her husband out of problems usually caused by her magic in the first place, and to complete household chores. Douglas called this "pre-feminism" because it acknowledged women's extraordinary powers, but didn't allow for them to be exercised outside the domestic or romantic settings. Whereas Samantha's husband enforced her containment, and she often caused trouble and evoked laughter by breaking his limiting rules and getting him into embarrassing situations; fifty years later, the same containment of extraordinary female power is completely internalized, enacted by choice and self-control, and now defines a postfeminist supernatural heroine. In perhaps the most egregious example of self-discipline, Caroline, who was raped and abused by Damon Salvatore when she was human, even as a vampire lacks the strength to kill Damon and win revenge, and therefore prioritizes Elena's desire to protect Damon and actually work with him to maintain the vampire community's secrets. Caroline is a "successful" vampire, and therefore, in the context of the show, successfully grows up, because she limits her desire and contains the messiness and excess of her feeding to acceptable, off-screen blood bags and woodland animals, and uses her physical strength and powers of manipulation only in defense of her friends, family, or significant others.

As Caroline goes through her transition, she embodies the contradictions of postfeminism in the horror genre as well as unwittingly enacting the power dynamics of Mystic Falls' dominant but unspoken whiteness. The pale skin, rosy cheeks, and artificially blonde hair of actress Candice Accola emphasize Caroline's whiteness and set her apart from the rest of the cast, a fact which makes her initial vampiric transformation—with bright red blood smeared over her face and hands—even more stark. As Richard Dyer argues, blonde hair in actresses emphasizes an almost extreme version of whiteness. "The most celebrated blondes," Dyer writes, "were not true blondes, but peroxided to within an inch of their lives" (78). Caroline is also the epitome of *southern* whiteness—a blonde beauty queen comfortably ensconced in the town's white power structure by virtue of her social success and her mother's role as town sheriff and member of the secretive vampire-hunting Founders Council. In a Southern Gothic mode that imbues the South with a racialized, exotic sensuality, Caroline is a symbol of white self-restraint and social control, albeit in a high-school context. Even as a vampire, she learns to feed on animals and blood bags secreted from the local hospital rather than killing humans. The only two people Caroline feeds on before she learns control are a black nurse in the hospital on the night of her accident and a young black stranger at a school carnival, both in episode 202, the episode in which she becomes a vampire. As explored below, Caroline's whiteness and her black victims, alongside her black friend Bonnie, highlight the layered meanings created by the show's casting, setting, and use of monstrous metaphors.

Caroline, set against a backdrop of the raced and gendered anxieties evoked by the Southern Gothic, embodies disciplined, contained white femininity in a town that continues to fight against uncontained monstrosities—vampires. The use of black actors as extras, as seen by Caroline's two victims, continues a long history of American film and television where blackness serves as merely a backdrop for white actors, and *TVD* for the most part continues this tradition featuring privileged white teenagers and their white, aristocratic ancestors. Bonnie Bennett, played by the half-black, half-Jewish actress Katerina Graham, stands out in *TVD* (and the CW in general) as the only person of color within the show who has character development and a somewhat fleshed-out subjectivity. In addition, nearly all the black characters in the world of *TVD* are witches, a casting and characterization decision that assumes textual and extratextual significance within the show's Southern Gothic setting and adds a racialized facet to Bonnie's monstrous transformation. Bonnie begins her realization of her true witch identity in the show's pilot episode ("Pilot"); while her journey is marked by "growing pains" similar to Caroline's, her character's horrific and melodramatic excesses manifest in predominantly racial, rather than gendered, ways that are ultimately contained and diffused. Caroline undergoes her teenage transformation via her body's messy and voracious consumption of blood, but Bonnie, while still sensing her changing nature through her body, experiences the traumas of adolescence through a more psychic connection to a turbulent past. Bonnie's character development in the show involves a continuing discovery and cultivation of her witchy powers, and her access to magic, just like Caroline's vampire transition, represents a recognition and acceptance of her empowered teenage girl identity. When we first meet Bonnie, she has picked up best friend Elena on their way to the first day of school. Elena is distracted by the fact that this will be her first day back after her parents' death, while Bonnie chatters on about how her grandmother Sheila (Jasmine Guy) thinks Bonnie is psychic. Upon entering the school, Bonnie also complains about the lack of "male real estate" and proceeds to use her alleged psychic powers to predict whether an incoming male student—Stefan Salvatore—is hot or not. The narrative exposition in the pilot introduces us to the major players in the show, but it also distinguishes main characters like Elena and Stefan from supporting ones such as Bonnie and Caroline. Bonnie has less screen time than Elena, and it is Elena and Stefan who are privileged in several tight close-ups, interior monologues, and shot-reverse-shots indicating their immediate attraction to each other. That said, Bonnie's growing realization that she is different from her peers begins in the first ten minutes of the show, and while we are not granted access to her interiority via voiceover, she and Stefan are immediately aligned as two supernatural entities within a human environment, adding a dimension to her character that goes beyond the generally undeveloped role of the "best friend" in teen texts. Going back to the concept of interiority that Kapurch discusses, the fact that Bonnie (or other supporting characters) is not granted access to conventional, more literary forms of interior monologues (a diary, monologues, first-person point of view) highlights her position as a more "typical" teenage character within melodramatic film and television— viewers must glean her character's changes through dialogue, action, and her relationship to others. We do not get inside Bonnie's head; therefore, her relationships to her friends, family, and ancestors become instrumental in her growth as a character. Her relationships are also what prove to be both intriguing and disappointing in terms of her representation as a young black woman; they highlight her narrative arc, but allude to her racial identity in ways that a consumer-oriented teen text is unable to manage.

The first season sets up Bonnie's personal growth within the context of the town's obsession with its history. In "Family Ties" (1.4), for example, the residents of Mystic Falls prepare themselves for the annual Founder's Day, one of a series of events that celebrates the town's history—a history that the town council remains proud of because of its success at keeping out undesirable monstrous elements. On a narrative level, history is one of the larger forces that haunts and shapes the lives of *TVD*'s teenage characters, and on a stylistic level, it creates opportunities for pageantry and spectacle that mark the CW as a network. Stefan says at one point, "There's a lot of history here," and his words of course carry a double-meaning—there are historical artifacts on display *and* the vampire brothers provide a link between the town's storied past and its seemingly simple present. But the episode also highlights the year 1864, when the Civil War raged on, and bringing up 1864 in a southern context inevitably calls attention to race. "Heritage" and "history" in the show's context are defined in terms of the privileged white lineage of the town's founding families and the battles they fought to keep the town safe from undesirable elements, and Bonnie's growing powers not only represent, like Caroline's, a metaphor for the intensity of her teen girl interiority, but also a disruption in the apparently monolithic, seemingly race-less way that Mystic Falls defines its history. In "Family Ties," Bonnie does not have a date to Founder's Day and attends the party alone, practicing lighting candles using telekinesis. In one scene, she tries to light candles in the empty dining room, gives up and walks away in frustration, only to stop in her tracks as she realizes that her efforts actually worked. The camera slowly reveals hundreds of lit candles, framing Bonnie's astonished face amid them. This scene is powerful because Bonnie is the only character so far who has begun to understand and use her power as a "monster." From the beginning of the series, then, Bonnie goes beyond the "black best friend" or "ethnic sidekick" stereotype that is generally afforded to people of color in ensemble casts and begins, via the metaphor of witchcraft, like Caroline with her newfound vampire powers, to explore her identity and agency.[10] At the same time the lush lighting, cinematic shots, and use of a pop song package Bonnie neatly within the CW's glossy aesthetic, drawing attention away from her troubling racial connection to the history evoked earlier in the episode.

"Family Ties" exemplifies the show's oscillation between invoking/fetishizing the town's ancestry and representing its current teenage residents, but later in the first season the racial ghosts of the past threaten to intrude on Bonnie's seemingly postracial present. As subsequent episodes reveal, Bonnie's development as a witch depends heavily on her recent and more distant past, including the help of her grandmother Sheila and the ghost of her Civil War–era ancestor Emily Bennett (Bianca Lawson). Haunting is a narrative device in gothic texts that allows the past to coexist with the present, and gothic heroines in particular confront the spectral presence of the past to grow, change, and take control of their presents. In terms of Bonnie's character development, the haunting represents the growth of powers that threaten to overwhelm her, much like Caroline's out-of-control vampire behavior in season 2. But the haunting also introduces the troubling connection between the show's invocation of history and the unacknowledged racial violence of that history; the persecuted victims in Mystic Falls' Civil War past are represented as predominantly white vampires rather than the black slaves who experienced the psychic and physical violence of slavery. Bonnie's character development tells yet another story: a black teenager, living in a predominantly white southern town, is haunted by her Civil War–era slave-witch ancestor who asks her to honor and continue her legacy—a potentially compelling way of exploring racial difference and coming-of-age within a Southern Gothic context. In "History Repeating" (1.9), for example, the ghost of Emily Bennett appears in Bonnie's science class, interrupting what looks like a typical high-school scene (students zoning out while the teacher talks) and ultimately forcing Bonnie to confront her role in Mystic Falls' past, present, and future. The scene of a teenage girl being plagued by a nightmare in a classroom setting is of course reminiscent of horror films such as *A Nightmare on Elm Street* (1984), and, at the same time, uncanny on a thematic level as Bonnie's seemingly normal teenage existence, represented in the scene by classrooms, hallways, and lockers, is suddenly disrupted by the presence of a Civil War–era slave. This scene represents the way race appears in narratives of American history, as a series of reveals and secrets that have boiled beneath the surface of dominant narratives,[11] and to make Bonnie Bennett a black witch with a Salem lineage and Civil War connections immediately links her to a history of racial and gendered violence and oppression, particularly to the story of seventeenth-century slave Tituba.[12] In some ways, Bonnie exemplifies what Toni Morrison has called the "dark, abiding, signing Africanist" presence in American literature, or the ways blackness, while often rendered invisible in national and literary discourse, has played an integral part in the construction of American identity and culture (5). Mystic Falls in the present day appears to be a peaceful American small town whose identity crises lie within its history of monsters, but the mere presence of Bonnie and her black witch ancestors, as well as the presence of black actresses among a predominantly white cast, suggest a completely different, racialized disruption of the ways American identity is constructed and envisioned. For example, during the Battle of Willow Creek, a pivotal battle in Mystic Falls' Civil War history that is referenced and represented via flashbacks, vampires are rounded up and executed en masse to keep the town pure. This "ethnic cleansing" of monsters immediately assumes a racial resonance because of the event's Civil War context, yet race is never referred to in relation to Willow Creek or its significance to the town's history. Similarly, Bonnie's witchy identity, in the context of the CW's vision of both teenage girlhood and American history, does not prompt the show to engage explicitly with her ancestry and race; her monstrous adolescent transformation becomes merely a means of furthering the narrative roles of the show's white characters.

Bonnie's personal character arc becomes subsumed in larger narratives about collusion and confrontation between black witches and predominantly white vampires in the course of seasons 1 and 2, and she develops her powers only to be caught in a parallel personal battle between protecting the town and protecting the show's white protagonist, Elena. Bonnie's character is consistently denied the growth promised in the first few episodes of season 1 as she and her ancestors turn into static narrative devices used to aid Elena's struggles against a variety of threats, both supernatural and not. As Jordan St. John says, "The scenario is frustratingly familiar to anyone who has spent a lifetime watching black women serve as snappy voices of reason for white main characters and then . . . become startlingly silent when it comes to speaking up for themselves" ("Why *The Vampire Diaries* treatment of Bonnie Bennett—and her fans—bites"). On Twitter, fans excoriated writer/producer Julie Plec for Bonnie's treatment, highlighting not only the degree to which contemporary television is inextricable from the new media platforms that surround it, but also the ways that "blind casting," the process of casting actors of color for parts that have no explicit race guidelines, occasionally works to illuminate the ways in which race is not as "solved" as it is sometimes purported to be in twenty-first-century America. Discussing color-blind casting, Kristen Warner writes, "In theory, this process is progressive because it allows for a variety of talent, regardless of skin color, to audition for a part. However the problem occurs when actors of color are cast because those roles are typically written as normatively white" ("'It's Tough Being Different'"). The decision to cast predominantly white actors as vampires and black actresses as witches on *TVD* suggests the kind of segregated logic that Morrison argues is at work within the American literary canon as a whole; while race is never explicitly discussed, and blackness often functions as a touch of "local color" that exists on the margins of white-centered narratives,[13] it functions as an integral, structural presence in the "ways that Americans choose to talk about themselves" (15, 17). The show avoids explicit references to race, yet in representing a black teenager being haunted by a Civil War past, race inevitably spills over into the show's extratextual meanings, adding another, albeit unintended, facet to the monstrous and often unmanageable transitions faced by teenage girls in postfeminist culture.

Along with Caroline's, Bonnie's monstrous growing pains reveal cracks in the seemingly postfeminist and un-raced facades of this teen text, recalling the vulnerability of young female bodies as sites for enforcing or remembering dominant cultural norms of race and gender. Bonnie, Caroline, and Elena are representative of the way the CW portrays teenage girls in general: as hyper-skinny and dressed in the latest designer fashions, two qualities that have attracted significant media attention. Alynda Wheat asks of the CW's *90210* (2008–2013) reboot, "Are the Skinny Starlets of *90210* Creating a Bad Example?", yet the number of "as seen on" Websites identifying fashions on teen shows continues to proliferate, suggesting that these skinny starlets successfully sell fashion.[14] The surveillance of young female bodies and their fashion choices, both on and off television, highlights postfeminism's paradoxical celebration of "girl power" and its containment of female bodies, reflected in Caroline's transition from out-of-control to demure and in her continuing status as the show's social (and fashion) queen bee. McRobbie suggests "that by means of the tropes of freedom and choice which are now inextricably connected with the category of 'young women,' feminism is decisively aged and made to seem redundant" (255). This move away from previous generations' feminism—even third-wave movements that demanded racial and ethnic inclusion—goes hand in hand with discourses of girl power and individualism, yet in consumer culture this individualism is often defined as the "right" to indulge in shopping and beauty regimens. Avoiding collectivity in favor of individuality not only serves a market-driven outlook, but it also avoids in-depth explorations of race, gender, and community. The shopping and beauty rituals that postfeminism holds up in the name of individualism and choice are also those which mark teenage cultural texts as marketable; neoliberal postfeminism and the capitalist drive of the entertainment industry seem to dovetail perfectly when creating and addressing the ideal female adolescent.

NOTES

We would like to thank Ali Hoffman-Han, Megan Musgrave, Jessica McCort, and the external reviewers for their helpful feedback on various stages of this essay.

1. For example, the criticism aggregating site Metacritic reports positive popular press reviews of *True Blood* (http://www.metacritic.com/tv/true-blood), *The Walking Dead* (http://www.metacritic.com/tv/the-walking-dead), and *American Horror Story* (http://www.metacritic.com/tv/american-horror-story). All three shows have received academic attention as well. On *The Walking Dead*, see for example Cameron (2012) and McAlister (2010); on *True Blood*, see for example Hudson (2013); on *American Horror Story*, see Keetley (2013) and Subramanian (2013).

2. The label "quality TV" has come to be a shorthand indicator of television with high production values, a distinctive visual style, a serial narrative, complex often morally ambiguous characters, a home on certain prestigious networks like HBO or AMC in the United States, and BBC One in the United Kingdom, and critical acclaim or awards. The term is in fact part of an ongoing debate within television studies dating at least to Jane Feuer, Paul Kerr, and Tise Vahimagi (1984) about MTM, the production house responsible for 1970s hits like *The Mary Tyler Moore Show*. Charlotte Brunsdon (1990) questioned the power relations, class, and taste judgments inherent in the label, and more recently, scholars have questioned the gendered nature of the term, as in Negra (2004).

3. While *Buffy the Vampire Slayer* arguably spearheaded the subgenre of strong female protagonist-driven teen horror, we argue that *The Vampire Diaries* and its multiplatform approach to speculative television is closer in terms of both business practices and postfeminist politics to its contemporaries *Twilight* and *The Hunger Games*.

4. See Petersen for an exploration of the ways the franchise inspires contradictory responses from self-proclaimed feminists.

5. See Willis for an explanation of rewriting melodramatic excess in a late twentieth-century context.

6. As Stacey Abbott discusses regarding *Supernatural* (2005–present), an earlier supernatural horror drama on the CW that paved the way within the network brand identity for *TVD*, humor and horror are linked by their generic push for physical reactions from audiences. The combination of fear, disgust, fascination, and slapstick that can often characterize both genres, along with their general preoccupation with exaggerated plots, character development effects, and the body and its excesses are intended to spark such physical responses.

7. See, for example, http://vampirestylediaries.tumblr.com/.

8. See Herring and Doane for a more in-depth exploration of gothic heroines in film.

9. Herring cites the work of Lewis P. Simpson in *Three by Three: Masterworks of the Southern Gothic*.

10. See Turner for a more in-depth description of the "black best friend" trope.

11. As Jack Halberstam says, "Perhaps because race has been so successfully Gothicized within our recent history, filmmakers and screenplay writers tend not to want to make a monster who is defined by a deviant racial identity" (4).

12. See Kismet Nunez's analysis of Tituba's relevance to the show (2011).

13. The CW is predominantly white in both its casts and crews as well as in the audience address of its programs; the editors of *Teen TV* explain that while Dawn Ostroff, former head of programming at the CW, has stated that the network seeks to expand its appeal to minority audiences, "the majority of teens and young adults slated to be on screen appear to be white" (Ross and Stein 17).

14. See Alloy Entertainment's official *The Vampire Diaries* fashion page: http://vampire diaries.alloyentertainment.com/tag/fashion/.

WORKS CITED

Abbott, Stacey. "Rabbits Feet and Spleen Juice: The Comic Strategies of TV Horror." *TV Goes to Hell: An Unofficial Road Map of Supernatural*. Edited by Stacey Abbott and David Lavery. Toronto: ECW Press, 2011. 3–17. Print.

Alloy Media and Entertainment. "The Vampire Diaries: Fashion." *The Vampire Diaries*. Official Website. Web. 2 February 2014.

A Nightmare on Elm Street. Dir. Wes Craven. New Line Cinema, 1984. Film.

"Brave New World." *The Vampire Diaries*. Broadcast. Written by Brian Young. Directed by John Dahl. 2010. Los Angeles: CW. Television.

Brophy, Phillip. "The Textuality of the Contemporary Horror Film." *Phillip Brophy*. Accessed 3 March 2013. Web. Originally published in *Art & Text* 11 (1983): 85–95.

Brunsdon, Charlotte. "The Problem with Quality." *Screen* 31.1 (Spring 1990): 67–90. Print.

Cameron, Allen. "Zombie Media: Transmission, Reproduction, and the Digital Dead. *Cinema Journal* 52.1 (Fall 2012): 67–89. Print.

Dargis, Manohla. "Tested by a Picturesque Dystopia: *The Hunger Games* Based on the Suzanne Collins Novel." *New York Times*, 22 March 2012. Web. 13 March 2013.

DasGupta, Satyani. "White Vamps, Black Witches: Race Politics and Vampire Pop Culture." *Stories Are Good Medicine*, 18 December 2010. Web. 10 February 2013.

Doane, Mary Ann. *The Desire to Desire: Woman's Films of the 1940s*. Bloomington: Indiana UP, 1987. Print.

Douglas, Susan, and Meredith Michaels. *The Mommy Myth: The Idealization of Motherhood and How It Has Undermined All Women*. New York: Free Press, 2004.

Dyer, Richard. *White*. London: Routledge, 1997. Print.

"Family Ties." *The Vampire Diaries*. Broadcast. Written by Andrew Kreisberg and Brian Young. Directed by Guy Ferland. 2011. Los Angeles: CW. Television.

Feuer, Jane, Paul Kerr, and Tise Vahimagi, eds. *MTM: "Quality Television."* London: British Film Institute, 1984. Print.

Gamber, Francesca. "Riding the Third Wave: The Multiple Feminisms of *Gilmore Girls*." *Teen Television: Essays on Programming and Fandom*. Edited by Sharon Marie Ross and Louisa Stein. Jefferson, NC: McFarland, 2008. 114–31. Print.

Halberstam, Judith. *Skin Shows: Gothic Horror and the Technology of Monsters*. Durham, NC: Duke UP, 1995. Print.

Herring, Gina. "*The Beguiled*: Misogynist Myth or Feminist Fable?" *Literature/Film Quarterly* 26.3 (1998). Web. 3 March 2013. Originally published in *Literature/Film Quarterly* 26.3 (1998): 214–19.

"History Repeating." *The Vampire Diaries*. Broadcast. Written by Bryan M. Holdman and Brian Young. Directed by Marcos Siega. 2011. Los Angeles: CW. Television.

Hudson, Dale. "'Of Course there are Werewolves and Vampires:' *True Blood* and the Right to Rights for Other Species." *American Quarterly* 65.3 (September 2013): 661–87. Print.

James, Kendra, and Jordan St. John. "Why *The Vampire Diaries'* Treatment of Bonnie—And Her Fans—Bites." *Racialicious*, 10 April 2012. Web. 10 February 2013.

Kapurch, Katie. "'Unconditionally and Irrevocably': Theorizing the Melodramatic Impulse in Young Adult Literature through the *Twilight* Saga and *Jane Eyre*." *Children's Literature Association Quarterly* 37.2 (2012): 164–87. Print.

Keetley, Dawn. "Stillborn: The Entropic Gothic of *American Horror Story*." *Gothic Studies* 15.2 (November 2013): 89–107. Print.

McAlister, Elizabeth. "Slaves, Cannibals, and Infected Hyper-Whites: The Race and Religion of Zombies." *Anthropological Quarterly* 85.2 (Spring 2012): 458–83. Print.

McRobbie, Angela. "Post-feminism and Popular Culture." *Feminist Media Studies* 4.3 (2004): 255–64. Print.

Metacritic. Web. 26 January 2014.

Morrison, Toni. *Playing in the Dark: Whiteness and the Literary Imagination*. New York: Vintage Books, 1992. Print.

Moruzi, Kristine. "Postfeminist Fantasies: Sexuality and Femininity in Stephanie Meyer's 'Twilight' Series." *Genre, Reception and Adaptation in the 'Twilight' Series*. Edited by Anne Morey. London: Ashgate, 2012. 47–64. Print.

Nakamura, Lisa, Laurie Beth Clark, and Michael Peterson. "Vampire Politics." *Flow TV* 11.03 (2009). Web. 16 February 2013.

Negra, Diane. "Quality Postfeminism?: Sex and the Single Girl on HBO." *Genders Online Journal* 39 (2004). Web. 26 January 2014.

——. *What a Girl Wants: Fantasizing the Reclamation of the Self in Postfemininsm*. New York: Routledge, 2009. Print.

Nunez, Kismet. "Fandom Matters." *The AntiJemima Life*, 2 December 2011. Web. 12 May 2013.

Ouellette, Laurie. "'Take Responsibility for Yourself': *Judge Judy* and the Neoliberal Citizen." *Reality TV: Remaking Television Culture*, 2nd ed. Edited by Susan Murray and Laurie Ouellette. New York: New York UP, 2009. 223–42. Print.

Pattee, Amy. "Commodities in Literature, Literature as Commodity: A Close Look at the Gossip Girl Series." *Children's Literature Association Quarterly* 31.2 (2006): 154–75. Print.

Petersen, Anne Helen. "That Teenage Feeling: *Twilight*, Fantasy and Feminist Readers." *Feminist Media Studies* 12.1 (2012): 51–67. Print.

"Pilot." *The Vampire Diaries*. Broadcast. Written by Kevin Williamson and Julie Plec. Directed by Marcos Siega. 2009. Los Angeles: CW. Television.

Probyn, Elsbeth. "Television's Unheimlich Home." *The Politics of Everyday Fear*. Edited by B. Massumi. Minneapolis: U of Minnesota P, 1993. 269–84. Print.

Ross, Sharon Marie, and Louisa Stein. "Introduction: Watching Teen TV." *Teen Television: Essays on Programming and Fandom*. Edited by Sharon Marie Ross and Louisa Stein. Jefferson, NC: McFarland, 2008. 3–26. Print.

Simpson, Lewis P. *Three by Three: Masterworks of the Southern Gothic*. Atlanta, GA: Peachtree, 1985. Print.

Subramanian, Janani. "The Monstrous Makeover: *American Horror Story*, Femininity and Special Effects." *Critical Studies in Television* 8.3 (Autumn 2013): 108–23. Print.

"The Sun Also Rises." *The Vampire Diaries*. Broadcast. Written by Caroline Dries and Mike Daniels. Directed by Paul M. Sommers. 2011. Los Angeles: CW. Television.

Turner, Sarah E. "Disney Does Race: Black BFFs in the New Racial Moment." *Networking Knowledge: Journal of the MeCCSA-PGN* 5.1 (2012): 125–40. Print.

"*Vampire Diaries* Style!" *Vampire Style Diaries*. Web. 31 January 2014.

Warner, Kristen. "'It's Tough Being Different': The Pitfalls of Colorblindness in CW's The *Vampire Diaries*." *In Media Res: A Media Commons Project*, 22 March 2011. Web. 10 February 2013.

Wee, Valerie. "The *Scream* Trilogy, 'Hyperpostmodernism,' and the Late-Nineties Teen Slasher Film." *Journal of Film and Video* 57.3 (2005): 44–61. Print.

——. "Teen Television and the WB Television Network." *Teen Television: Essays on Programming and Fandom*. Edited by Sharon Marie Ross and Louisa Stein. Jefferson, NC: MacFarland, 2008. 43–60. Print.

Wheat, Alynda. "Are the Skinny Starlets of *90210* Setting a Bad Example?" *Entertainment Weekly*, 19 September 2008. Web. 13 March 2013.

Wheatley, Helen. *Gothic Television*. Manchester: Manchester UP, 2006. Print.

Williams, Linda. "Film Bodies: Gender, Genre, and Excess." *Film Theory and Criticism*, 7th ed. Edited by Leo Braudy and Marshall Cohen. New York: Oxford UP, 2009. Print.

Willis, Sharon. "The Politics of Disappointment: Todd Haynes Rewrites Douglas Sirk." *Camera Obscura* 18.3 (2003): 130–75. Print.

Wood, Robin. "An Introduction to the American Horror Film." *Movies and Methods Volume II*. Edited by Bill Nichols. Berkeley: U of California P, 1985. 195–220. Originally published in *American Nightmare: Essays on the Horror Film*. Edited by Robin Wood and Richard Lippe. Toronto: Festival of Festivals, 1979. 7–28.

Let the Games Begin

Hybrid Horror in *The Hunger Games* Trilogy

EMILY L. HILTZ

Muttations. No question about it . . . They resemble huge wolves, but what wolf lands and then balances easily on its hind legs? . . . There's something else about them, something that makes the hair rise up on the back of my neck . . . The green eyes glowering at me are unlike any dog or wolf, any canine I've ever seen. They are unmistakably human.

—SUZANNE COLLINS, *THE HUNGER GAMES* (331–33)

IN SUZANNE COLLINS'S WILDLY POPULAR *HUNGER GAMES* TRILOGY, genetically engineered "mutts," such as the eerie half-human, half-wolf monsters the protagonist Katniss describes above, are designed to mortify the contestants both physically and psychologically: "They are meant to damage you. Some take your life . . . others your reason" (Collins *Mockingjay* 311). Designed to hunt and haunt human prey, the diverse mutts created by the government often "incorporate a perverse psychological twist designed to terrify [their victims]." These biologically engineered weapons combine two beings into one body, but some reveal their hybridity more overtly than others. Two types of mutts are created by Collins: monstrous chimeras and covert hybrids, as Jason T. Eberl suggests in his essay "No Mutt Is Good." The difference in these mutts' bodies and actions warrants deeper examination, for hybrid horror is a multifaceted theme Collins uses throughout to question the nature of monstrosity. The mutts act as central metaphors for social disorder and, I suggest, are also central characters in the novels. In this trilogy, there is a war over meaning waged through ambiguous zombie-wolves, lizard-humans, and mockingjays (Olthouse 41). But it is also waged

by the "heroic" protagonists, Katniss and Peeta. All of these mutated characters provoke these central questions: What does it mean to be a monster?
How do we judge monsters—and ourselves—in a time of war and rebellion?

In the *Hunger Games* trilogy, the mutts are prime vehicles for questioning the bodily, psychological, and moral makeup of monstrous behavior,
animal and human alike. Originally, the mutts were created as hybrids designed to enforce Panem's ruling political regime, the authoritarian Capitol. In the most general of terms, the *Oxford English Dictionary* refers to
"hybrid" as "Anything derived from heterogeneous sources, or composed
of different or incongruous elements." Another definition explains that hybrid beings, including animals, plants, and humans, are also "produced by
the inter-breeding of two different species or varieties of animals or plants;
mongrel, cross-bred, half-bred." The majority of the mutts described in
the novels are Capitol products, genetically altered hybrid animals bred as
weapons. "The common term for them was muttations, or sometimes mutts
for short," Katniss tells us (Collins *The Hunger Games* 42). While hybrids are
formed through interspecies mating, chimeras are the products of human
manipulation. Hybrids' cells are composed of DNA from multiple beings,
while chimeras are produced by "grafting cells from one species into the
embryo of another species, resulting in a creature that has some body parts
from one species and some body parts from other species" (Eberl 122). Collins's novels rely on both of these types of mutts. Sometimes their manufactured origins are readily discernible because of their sutured, dehumanized
bodies, as we see with the wolf-mutts, while other mutts hide their monstrous sides. These classifications are most difficult to discern in Collins's
protagonists, Katniss and Peeta, as both become politicized weapons of the
state. Both define themselves, at some point or another, as "mutts"; however,
both are eventually able to resist this control and "evolve" into ethical human beings once again.

In this chapter, mutt identities are examined using the concept of abjection first introduced by Julia Kristeva in *Powers of Horror*. Kristeva describes "the abject" as a being or behavior that "disturbs identity, system,
order. What does not respect borders, positions, rules. The in-between, the
ambiguous, the composite. The traitor, the liar, the criminal with a good
conscience [. . . ,] the killer who claims he is a savior" (4). Abject actions
and characters defy and threaten known categories, such as "human" and
"monster" because they occupy a liminal identity between these labels. The
abject questions such distinctions (Smith Fullerton 8). The monsters in horror are typically abject beings, for they transgress "cultural categories [. . .]

and generally serve to present a chaotic alternative to the place of order and meaning, socially as well as biologically" (Magistrale 7). The abject involves confronting objects or acts that are outside of "normal" and "decent" society and, as a result, are terrifying to behold. Kristeva explains the abject is a "jettisoned object" occupying a "place where I am not" (2–3); however, when viewing the abject, the division between "I" and "not I" collapses because of this partial recognition. Delivering a truth that "reveals something we deny or fear," the abject "is within the self" (Hock-Soon Ng 4–5). The abject beckons to those who have excluded it as a monstrous perversion: "It lies outside, beyond the set, and does not agree to the latter's rules of the game. And yet, from its place of banishment, the abject does not cease challenging its master" (Kristeva 2).

Repulsive matter like corpses, feces, and blood are abject according to Kristeva, for they "show me what I permanently thrust aside in order to live" (5). The abject reminds us that we are inherently linked to these rejected bodies, wastes, fluids, and monstrous actions, "engulfing us" in their threats (4). As a "composite of judgment and affect, of condemnation and yearning" (10), the abject provokes contradiction. "Good" and "normal" society cannot disassociate completely from the abject because it constitutes the very subjects it challenges: "It lies there, quite close, but it cannot be assimilated" (1). Thus the abject is a concept tied to identity formation; Kristeva says it is her cultural primer (2).

This framework, when applied to Collins's monsters, offers three main perspectives for understanding hybrid horror. I suggest mutts terrify because their bodies, intentions, and actions are abject, liminal, and ambiguous. Many muttations throughout Collins's three novels are abject due to their bioengineered makeup and their manufacture as tools used entirely for political ends. The Capitol creates mutts to kill, spy on, and otherwise terrify citizens; however, the mockingjays (as birds and as political symbols) are mutts similarly manufactured for the rebel cause. These hybrids are created to support certain political regimes. Thus, in part, the mutts also demonstrate Kristeva's main contention that abjection dismantles the social order. However, what form of instability is imposed when abject mutts are also used to enforce the status quo, as with the Capitol's mutts? Are Katniss's actions, along with Peeta's, wholly divorced from the Capitol's evil actions? The final section of this work grapples with these questions, suggesting that Collins uses these hybrid monsters to trouble the belief that monsters are always easily discerned as external threats. In these novels, monsters come in many guises. The abjection of Collins's hybrid mutts places audiences in the role of cultural critic, asking readers to question the definitions and actions of human monstrosity.

The monsters created for the *Hunger Games* arena mirror the violence of their creator: the authoritarian government, the Capitol, which rules twelve impoverished districts with an iron fist. Inspired partially by the classic myth of the Minotaur and the labyrinth, the Capitol's ritual of annually sending twenty-three child tributes to their deaths, seventy-five years in the running, sends the following message: "Look how we take your children and sacrifice them and there's nothing you can do" (Fisher 29; Collins *The Hunger Games* 19). The governed are reminded that rebellion only leads to utter destruction. This annual horror takes place in Panem, a postapocalyptic North American state that suffered ecological degradation and civil war until the Capitol established uncompromising order (18). After a period of rebellion against Capitol rule (called the Dark Days), the Games were created as ritualized physical and symbolic punishment. While the Capitol residents, exempt from the Games, treat child torture as an entertaining media spectacular, those from the punished districts are forced to watch their children kill one another as the event unfolds, 24/7, on television: "To make it humiliating as well as torturous, the Capitol requires us to treat the Hunger Games as a festivity, a sporting event pitting every district against the others." After "the Reaping," "everyone is supposed to celebrate. And a lot of people do, out of relief that their children have been spared for another year" (10). However, two children, one girl and one boy aged twelve to eighteen, are chosen from each district and subsequently "imprisoned in a vast outdoor arena that could hold anything from a burning desert to a frozen wasteland" (18), monstrous humans to chimerical beasts.

As Joseph Foy states in "'Safe to Do What?' Morality and the War of All Against All in the Arena," the state-issued horror of the gladiatorial Games demands a "bellum universale" mentality among warriors. This all-against-all ethic assumes self-preservation, rather than compassion or sacrifice, will reign supreme in the arena (211–12). Collins's tale exhibits an unsettling darkness because child warriors not only fight back against animalistic hybrids, but fight one another, in hopes of emerging as the sole survivor, free from the hunger that plagues their districts. Defying the "bellum universale" ethic, Katniss Everdeen, the novels' hero and narrator, originally wins the first Games by threatening suicide; however, her actions do not spell pardon. They instead generate renewed wrath from the Capitol. In retribution for her transgressions, she must face more monsters: genetically engineered mutts, "venomous" politicians,[1] and even herself, as she adapts to her own "mutt" identity as the rebel's Mockingjay in *Catching Fire* and *Mockingjay*, the second and third books in the series.

Katniss derives her rebel name, the Mockingjay, from a hybrid bird whose body illustrates the Capitol's lack of complete control over nature. This hybrid's successful interspecies mating demonstrates that some mutts are able to evolve independently of human control. This is important, given that it is the only fully natural animal hybrid to be found in the trilogy. In book one, the mockingjays are described as the natural offspring of jabberjay fathers and female mockingbirds after the jabberjays were left to fend for themselves in the wild. The jabberjays were unnatural birds created by the Capitol as surveillance tools, devised to record and transmit suspected rebels' speech during the Dark Days. The rebels, however, inverted the jabberjays' power by feeding the birds with lies to misinform the Capitol. The jabberjays were eventually left to die in the wild, but they survived by cross-breeding with natural mockingbirds (Collins *The Hunger Games* 43). The mockingjay's partially natural hybrid development serves as a source of hope for the rebelling districts, as they advertise the mockingjay's natural origins in their propaganda against Capitol control. The mockingjay's evolution is rebellious because free-thinking mutts are virtually nonexistent in Capitol-controlled Panem.

One of the most obvious and memorable muttations devised by the Capitol appears in the last battle in *The Hunger Games*—the zombie-wolves. These predators threaten the very distinctions between inhuman/human, animal/monster, as they are composed of living wolf and dead human parts. Preprogrammed to attack the remaining tributes, these wolves' human features—their eyes and their ability to walk upright—confuse what is considered "normal." Their intentions also confuse Katniss, as she questions whether they are acting in retribution for their deaths in the Games: "Their eyes are the least of my worries. What about their brains? Have they been given any of the real tributes memories? Have they been programmed to hate our faces particularly because we have survived and they were so callously murdered? And the ones we killed . . . do they believe they're avenging their own deaths?" (334). Illustrating how the abject is a "place where meaning collapses" (Kristeva 4), the zombie-wolf muttations horrify Katniss due to their composite ambiguity, which blurs what she knows of the dead tributes as human beings.

In *The Philosophy of Horror: or, Paradoxes of the Heart*, Noël Carroll explains that horror stories necessarily feature monsters that characters find "abnormal," as "extraordinary creatures in an ordinary world": "The

monsters of horror breach the norms of ontological propriety presumed
by the positive human characters in the story" (16). Katniss's reaction to the
zombie-wolf mutts clearly shows these beings transgress her knowledge of
"normal" biological boundaries. Katniss's sense of abnormality is informed
by her everyday life in District 12, which is devoid of the technological ad-
vancements seen in the Capitol. The Capitol is accustomed to manipulating
nature, and thus the zombie-wolves horrify Katniss much more than Capitol residents watching the Games unfold from the comfort of their homes.
Katniss's perspective is likely similar to that of the reading audience, as her
experience of reality in the Seam is quite different from the world thriving
in the Capitol, a place where living and dead beings are easily bioengineered
and combined. As horror is a "genre in which the emotive responses of the
audience ideally run parallel to the emotions of the characters" (Carroll 17),
making Katniss's perspectives and experiences believably align with the
fears of its readers is paramount.

The protagonists' ontologies are certainly ruptured in witnessing the
wolf mutts, but the audience's values are also ruptured. Panem is a familiar, yet strange place for contemporary readers; even though it seems far
removed from current American culture, it is still recognizable. Surveillance, reality television, technology, and war are all aspects of Katniss's life
with which young audiences can identify. The economic divide between
the plush Capitol and the have-not districts, the latter abused and forced
into cutthroat, bestial competition, while the Capitol entertains itself with
never-ending fashions and television likely resonates with contemporary
Generation Y readers. For instance, Mark Fisher explains that *The Hunger
Games*, in both literary and filmic form, "have no doubt resonated so powerfully with its young audience because it has engaged feelings of betrayal
and resentment rising in a generation asked to accept that its quality of life
will be worse than that of its parents" (27). The resentment Fisher refers to,
symbolized through the clear class divisions and disparities of Panem society, likely resonates with young audiences also potentially facing financial
hardship, as the novels were published during the American and European
recessions. Collins also implicates her readers as "watchers" of the Games
broadcasts—media texts familiar to audiences accustomed to consuming
reality television and 24/7 news.

Inasmuch as the series partly critiques its readers for their voyeurism—
aligning them with characters whose consumption of the broadcasts implicitly supports the Games, the familiar yet strange aspects of the story also
function to alienate readers from their world. According to Neil Gerlach,

horror films "plac[e] viewers into an alienated perspective that invites them to reassess power and knowledge in our society" (222). Keeping this in mind, the hybrid horror Collins creates in her mutts, witnessed through Katniss's eyes, challenges the values and boundaries of the reading audience; through their vicarious experience of the mutts, their assumptions about biology and morality are questioned. The existence of mutts in Collins's story inverts assumptions about what is real and what is fiction, as well as what is human, animal, and manufactured—drawing attention to what these entities mean in a postapocalyptic America. Inversion is a key way of alienating characters as well as audiences, as what is known about the world is turned on its head. The mutts are such techniques of inversion that "disrupt our sense of security" (Gerlach 223) and draw attention to the flimsy construction of Panem's as well as readers' realities. As a technique of inversion, the mutts reverse "normal" power relations of animals, women, children, and the lower class, depicting them as menacing and powerful. The convergence of human, animal, and technological parts into chimeric bodies, Collins's mutts invert and thus trouble common-sense knowledge of humanity and heroism. The mutts incite alienation and partial identification, and overall, may provoke audiences to reevaluate what is normal and sacred in modern society.

While the wolf mutts' bodies are transgressive in their conglomeration of the living and dead, their creation also points to the abject behavior of the Capitol. By instrumentalizing the tributes' bodies even in death, their actions cross ethical and moral lines, showing the great extent to which the Capitol rules and dehumanizes Panem's subjects. Kristeva refers to the corpse as "the most sickening of wastes" (3). Similarly, in *The Monstrous Feminine* (which applies the concept of the abject to female monsters in horror film), Barbara Creed states, "[the corpse] signifies one of the most basic forms of pollution—the body without a soul" (10). The zombie-wolves are abject shells designed to terrify their prey. Their partial human appearance suggests that their souls are intact, yet their animalistic behavior suggests otherwise. Their human sides are derived from subjects already victimized: their "second life" as mutts revictimizes their bodies as well as their memory. In sum, these wolf muttations are dually abject: bodily as well as ethically, their creation clearly transgresses Western cultural values concerning the sanctity of death.

For audiences living in modern industrialized societies, zombies are often used to evoke the fear "of losing [one's] individuality and becoming one among 'the many'" (3), a point Shawn McIntosh points out in his chapter,

"The Evolution of the Zombie" in *Zombie Culture*. Collins's use of the zombie-wolves is evocative of this fear, for the dead tributes are grouped into a vicious animal pack serving the Capitol's need to produce a good show. However, these particular mutts also illustrate that they are in part "people who were controlled by someone else to do that person's bidding"—a folkloric conception of zombies that places the onus of villainy on the zombies' evil master, rather than the zombies themselves (McIntosh 13). The "victims of another's evil plans," the zombie-wolves provoke questions of their makeup, their masters, and their consciousness. Although these beings are lethal and fearsome, they are also victimized tools of the state, like Katniss and the remaining tributes. Their liminal bodies also provoke the horrific realization that the Capitol's mutts are not unlike child tributes in the arena, as they too are homicidal pawns. Even as they kill and maim the heroes, the mutts can paradoxically provoke an uncanny identification as ex-tributes, for they are manipulated into what Peeta fears most—being "turn[ed] into some kind of monster that [he's] not" (Collins *The Hunger Games* 141). Through the zombie mutts, Collins conflates the division between heroes and monsters, suggesting they are both victimized by an external political master. Depicting the mutts as both victims and monsters, partly human and dehumanized, Collins develops abject beings that confuse Katniss's and readers' understandings of biology and decency.

Similar to the dehumanized wolf mutts in *The Hunger Games*, in *Mockingjay*, a large pack of part-human, part-lizard mutts assault Katniss's team of rebels. Initially mistaking them as peacekeepers, Katniss describes their hybrid bodies: "A mix of human and lizard and who knows what else. White, tight repitilian skin smeared with gore, clawed hands and feet, their faces a mess of conflicting features" (*Mockingjay* 311). As the Capitol mutilated human corpses by forming the zombie-wolves, the lizards' bodies immediately transgress biological and ethical borders. Hissing Katniss's name, walking upright, and at other times, "fall[ing] to their bellies and skitter[ing] toward us on all fours" (309), they are abject in their simultaneous familiarity (humanness) and difference (monstrousness). Katniss also notes the "evocative" familiar odor they emit that makes her tremble, "the smell of Snow's roses mixed with victims' blood": "It's as if Snow's breathing right in my face, telling me it's time to die" (311, 307, 312). The mutts not only horrify visually, but through a contradictory, abject scent: nature defiled by violence and spilt blood. Katniss is physically sickened by their bodies and smell, "making my heart run wild, my skin turn to ice, my lungs unable to suck air" (311–12). Kristeva explains that the abject elicits physical revulsion that safeguards the onlooker from its threats: "The retching that thrusts me to the side and turns me away from defilement, sewage, and muck" (2). The contradictory natures of the enraged lizard humans are a clear example of abject transgression of biological and moral bounds on behalf of the Capitol.

Although these lizard muttations are not comprised of humans Katniss recognizes, this does not mean they are not real humans being forced to serve the Capitol's wishes. In this sense, they are preprogrammed beings that may be part-human, part-zombie, like the wolves Katniss and Peeta face in *The Hunger Games*. However, unlike the zombie-wolves, the lizards are decidedly more monstrous and other because they are entirely irrational, appearing senseless rather than potentially calculating or revengeful. They lash out at the other mutts around them and even themselves, "driven mad by their need to destroy [Katniss]" (311). They also kill and decapitate human members of the Capitol, people on their own side: "They swarm over the Peacekeepers, living and dead, clamp on their necks with their mouths and rip off the helmeted heads" (309). The indiscriminate killing and mutilation of everyone, even themselves, in the name of reaching the Capitol's target shows they are manufactured puppets of the regime with absolutely no individual, self-interested thoughts. A large part of Katniss's horror in witnessing the zombie-wolves is her lack of knowledge about "their brains" (*Mockingjay* 334), whether they are acting in self-interest. In contrast, the lizards are cast as overtly monstrous, lacking potential consciousness and thus humanity—a point Eberl points out in his reading of the zombie-wolves. He avows that the wolf mutts make Katniss ponder their status as "persons," whether they are conscious of their actions and thus human (130). Despite their human elements, it is clear the tributes are not treated as persons, for law and morals are clearly suspended with the mutts' creation and the operation of the Games. In contrast to the zombie-wolves, Collins's lizards can be said to "scare us from a distance" (Magistrale 17) because they are so unnatural and inhuman(e), despite their partial human form. As a result, one could say that killing them presents less of an ethical quandary than destroying the mutts Katniss recognizes, as she seems to identify partly with the zombie-wolves and their victimization. As Eberl points out, the wolves seem to symbolize how they are "fellow victims of the Gamemakers' cruelty" (130). This is a message that is not mirrored through the monstrous lizards, and for good reason—she never knew the former humans that now comprise the lizard mutts' bodies.

The wolf and lizard muttations are the more overtly monstrous types found in Collins's novels. Their chimeric physiques are designed to elicit an immediate fearful reaction, for they are both familiar and not, a perversion of what is "known" of humanity, nature's biological limits, and the sanctity of life and death. The function of these mutts, beyond scaring characters immediately, is to clearly project the monstrosity of their creator, the Capitol. As part of their abject status, the chimeric lizard and wolf mutts "refuse to participate in the classificatory 'order of things,'" following Jeffrey Jerome Cohen's characterization of monsters in "Monster Culture: (Seven Theses)" (6).

Collins also includes less visible mutts in the trilogy, ones that hide their abject status and trick their prey. Designed to give the appearance of normalcy, these mutts' bodies are specifically designed as disguises and lures. For instance, at first glance, the jabberjays, and other mutts, such as carnivorous squirrels, hostile monkeys, and enhanced bees called trackerjackers, seem like run-of-the-mill animals. In *Catching Fire*, the tributes run across "a welcoming committee" of orange monkeys in the jungle (Collins *Catching Fire* 308). The two groups calmly observe each other, but soon a larger mass of monkeys assemble silently. All of a sudden, "The monkeys explode into a shrieking mass of orange fur and converge on him [...]. Fangs bared, hackles raised, claws shooting out like switchblades. I may be unfamiliar with monkeys, but animals in nature don't act like this. '*Mutts!*'" Katniss screams (308–9). Similar to the jabberjays, which are designed to go unnoticed, the monkeys' exteriors are meant to lure in their prey under false pretenses of normality. This is partly why, in *Catching Fire*, Katniss and Finnick, another Quarter Quell tribute, enter a portion of the jungle that appears safe and normal, but is not. A flock of jabberjays occupy the region, calling out the tortured screams of their loved ones. The jays' original manufacture as recording devices is used for an unexpectedly different, psychologically tormenting purpose in Katniss's second Hunger Games. She wonders if her sister, Prim, has really been tortured, or whether the sounds are a postmodern simulation devoid of an original source. Despite their genetic manipulation, all of these mutts' altered natures are obscured. As a result, tributes often wrongly mistake them as harmless. Upon being drawn in by the false sense of normalcy these more covert and disguised mutts allow, characters are horrified by the subversion of their assumptions about these harmless animals.

The covert mutts flip normal animal behavior on its head, inverting what characters and the audience know about the natural world.[2] This underscores the uncanny quality of these abject mutts, their dual identity as both familiar and strange. According to Freud in "The Uncanny," the dialectic of the "homely" and familiar (*heimlich*) with the foreign and hidden (*unheimlich*) causes a feeling of dread and horror. By reading works of literature psychoanalytically, he suggests bodies brought back to life, for instance, are uncanny and thus frightening because they provoke identification—they are familiar, but also strange. As "the return of the repressed," the uncanny evokes fear because it brings a repressed, once unconscious fear and/or desire to the surface. The abject, as Kristeva outlines, can also be uncanny in how it is both "I" and "not I," confusing the boundary between "us," good and normal society, and "them," the evil others: "The subject [...] attempts to identify with something on the outside, finds the impossible within; when it finds that the impossible constitutes its very being, that is none other than abject" (5). Since the abject's uncanny aspect provokes a contradictory sense of identification and expulsion, this sheds light on Kristeva's point that the abject is both attractive and repulsive: "One thus understands why so many victims of the abject are its fascinated victims—if not its submissive and willing ones" (9). In a similar sense, Cohen suggests in "Monster Culture" that "this simultaneous repulsion and attraction at the core of the monster's composition accounts greatly for its continued cultural popularity, for the fact that the monster seldom can be contained in a simple, binary dialectic" (17). For Collins, the covert mutt further demonstrates that monstrosity comes in many guises, suggesting that the dialectics of abnormal/normal, evil/good are easily ruptured concepts.

Collins's mutts put forth an argument about the nature of monstrosity: monsters reside within "good" and heroic characters as much as in monsters that seem to be external threats. While the covert animal hybrids are uncanny in their familiar appearances, the overt beings are also uncanny and thus horrific because characters partly recognize themselves in these threatening beasts. In particular, the mutts that are in part derived from human DNA, the zombie-wolves and lizard-humans, demand that their prey identify their intelligible, familiar sides. For Katniss, this results in her partial sense of guilt in being alive, faced with the zombie-wolves that are dead agents haunting the living. Although Katniss is forced to fight like the other tributes, and thus is similarly victimized by the Capitol, she becomes conscious of her homicidal actions when she witnesses Glimmer's familiar eyes encased in a wolf's body. In this sense, the zombie identity of the wolf muttations drives home their uncanniness, the humanity they used to inhabit. Staring into Glimmer's eyes, Katniss is reminded she was the direct cause of her demise, dropping a trackerjacker nest[3] on her while she was sleeping. Within the Games, Katniss sometimes played by the rules, trying to survive—her morals were suspended in certain instances. In her conscious realization that these mutts are a horrifying mix of wolf and dead child, Katniss immediately recognizes her own monstrous actions during the Games. Reaffirming the collapsing boundaries between right and wrong, as well as heroism and villainy, these abject beings involve the dual recognition of the Capitol's and Katniss's monstrosity.

The diverse assembly of abject mutts Collins creates in her trilogy make a strong statement about the nature of monstrosity in her postapocalyptic America: "the monster is *us*, on and in us," as Tony Magistrale states in *Abject Terrors* (15). In this sense Collins's monsters challenge the traditional notion that evil and violence are always external to good characters, and thus easily expelled and forgotten. Through the abject hybridity of the mutations, Collins draws attention to the slipperiness of monstrosity—in form and in concept. Evil is sometimes writ on the bodies of the muttations, dehumanizing its human subjects. Other times, their aggressive, ulterior motives are hidden beneath their unethical manufacture. Lastly, monstrosity sometimes resides in the supposedly virtuous human characters, Katniss and Peeta. Overall, the shifting, hybrid form of horror Collins develops through her diverse mutts projects omnipresent monstrosity.

Katniss's experiences in the Games and her later identity as "the Mockingjay" illustrate the transience of monstrosity in the trilogy. At times, Katniss displays moral and heroic sensibilities; at other times, she is "violent. Distrustful. Manipulative. Deadly" (232)—a characterization she gives herself in *Mockingjay*. As a complex and contradictory character, Katniss is a central mutt Collins uses to impart her core theme of ubiquitous monstrosity expressed through varied forms and actions. The abject is embodied in hybrid bodies caught between natures, but the mutts' abjectivity is also alive and well in the protagonists, clearly blurring the lines between goodness and villainy.

Katniss is a character well suited for her later moniker as the Mockingjay, the symbolic leader of the rebellion in book three: "I must now become the actual leader, the face, the voice, the embodiment of the revolution. The person who the districts—most of which are now openly at war with the Capitol—can count on to blaze the path to victory" (*Mockingjay* 10). The hybridity Katniss displays as a mockingjay mutt aptly describes the abject Kristeva theorizes, as "neither good nor evil, subject nor object, but something which threatens the distinctions themselves" (Smith Fullerton 8). Katniss threatens the very distinctions between hero and monster, as she displays the qualities of both, occupying these spaces at different times in the trilogy. For instance, although she plays a large role in crushing the Capitol regime, the new party she helps form at the end of *Mockingjay* also relies on similar violent tactics. Believing that "nothing will ever change," Katniss ironically favors issuing the Hunger Games another time, "a final symbolic Hunger Games, using the children directly related to those who held the most power" (369). The transience of Katniss's identity as hero and mutt illustrates core features of abjection that are also seen in the other mutts. Collins suggests humans can easily slide into—and out of—monstrous hides by naming her main character after the Mockingjay and showing how she breaks assumed boundaries of heroism.

As a tribute in two Hunger Games, at a basic level, Katniss can be viewed as a victimized tool of the state: She was plucked from her home in the Seam and forced into gladiatorial battle for the amusement of the Capitol's citizens. The Games' child warriors certainly subvert the assumption that all children are helpless victims. Instead they are "capable of bravery, moral decision making [. . .] and sometimes [capable in the] brutal and bloody aspects of the warrior," as Rosen and Rosen remark of *The Hunger Games*'s gladiators (311). When not in the arena, Katniss and the other tributes are displayed and paraded around during televised pregame shows that involve lengthy beauty and dress makeovers in the Remake Center (*The Hunger Games* 61). Prior to her second Games, President Snow forces Katniss into a wedding engagement to Peeta, and her wedding dress is even decided upon by the Capitol's inhabitants.

Though she is a pawn in these instances, Katniss defies the Games' cutthroat ethic even before she fights in her first Games. When her sister Prim is chosen to fight in the Games, Katniss "volunteers as tribute" (22). This selflessness already defies the lack of morality the Capitol relies upon in making monsters of the districts' children. As previously mentioned, *The Hunger Games*' ending indicates Katniss may have to play the game, but she does not play by its rules. Threatening suicide, she and Peeta defy the Capitol's stipulation that only one tribute becomes the victor. Cast back into the arena in *Catching Fire*, this time facing several other successful victors, Katniss eventually manages to dismantle the Games from the inside out.[4] This explosion of the Games' arena becomes a symbolic manifestation of rebellion—an incitement that "catches" in the districts. Serving a symbolic, political role in the districts' rebellion, Katniss comes to represent the people, a "child serv[ing] as a collective representation of all that was good, striking to break out of an encrusted social order" (Rosen and Rosen 306).

Partly, Katniss is an agent of change, as she once appears to be created to serve the Capitol, but evolves in order to overthrow it. Are the rebels' tactics devoid of the violent and immoral tactics the Capitol uses? As Mocking-jay, Katniss is still a manufactured entity, and she is well aware of it. For instance, she explains, "What they want is for me to truly take on the role they designed for me ... They have a whole team of people to make me over, dress me, write my speeches, orchestrate my appearances—as if *that* doesn't sound horribly familiar—and all I have to do is play my part" (10–11). The rebels' politicization of the mockingjay illustrates that the two sides of the war are not all that dissimilar in their efforts to instrumentalize nature. Turning the mockingjay into a symbol of hope and defiance, Katniss be-comes the physical embodiment of dissonance, taped for televised "propos" (propaganda segments), equipped with a flashy costume, wielding an en-hanced bow, and fighting in staged fights. While the mockingjay birds have partly natural origins, Katniss's identity as the Mockingjay is highly con-structed and politicized, not unlike the Capitol's DNA-engineered mutts. Initially, Katniss resists adopting the Mockingjay identity, due to her lack of knowledge about the rebels' plan to end the Games and start a war. She states that she and Peeta were "used as pawns" by the rebels (*Mockingjay* 21), just as the Capitol does with its tributes: "It's an awful lot to take in, this elaborate plan in which I was a piece, just as I was meant to be a piece in the Hunger Games. Used without consent, without knowledge. At least in the Hunger Games, I knew I was being played with" (*Catching Fire* 385). Although hybrids appear divorced from human control and involvement, people are certainly involved in using the mockingjay as a symbol, taking it from its natural realm and personifying the mutt for political causes. This shows there is a distinct difference between the mockingjay bird and Kat-niss-as-Mockingjay: politics separates them.

The final book in Collins's trilogy speaks volumes to Katniss's realiza-tion that she disagrees with the rebel regime's lack of morality, despite her support of the rebel cause. Katniss's ruminations on the unethical actions of war—on both sides—suggests that the separation between good and evil is not so distinct. Particularly since she is the face of the rebellion, she can be said to endorse and even carry out the homicide of innocents (*Mockingjay* 211–12). As a result, she likens herself to a monster: "I no longer feel any al-legiance to these monsters called human beings, despite being one myself ... something is wrong with a creature that sacrifices its children's lives to settle its differences" (Collins *Mockingjay* 377). The villain becomes rooted in the cause Katniss believes in—rebelling against Capitol rule. Perhaps this is one of the reasons Katniss becomes more and more attracted to suicide as the trilogy progresses, steadfast in her assertion to die for Peeta in *Catching Fire*, while her desire to "kill [the president], and then die for [her] trouble" in the last book borders on obsession (*Mockingjay* 198). Katniss doubts whether she is a hero, and extends this reflection to her world, questioning whether the rebels are indeed a good force.

Katniss's narration draws attention to the similarities between her cause and the Capitol's—once again suggesting that monstrosity is internalized and omnipresent. During one assault that kills many district citizens, she wonders, "Is my own history making me too sensitive? Aren't we at war? Isn't this just another way to kill our enemies?" (*Mockingjay* 212). In the conclusion of the trilogy, Katniss finds out once and for all that the rebel side is not without its murderous tactics, for the leader of the rebel forces, Alma Coin, orders the murder of its own people—in the name of ending the war. Gale, Katniss's longtime friend and hunting partner, is also involved in the routine assaults on district citizens and is instrumental in Coin's final staged bombing. The "death traps" (203) he devises that "play on human sympathies" (357) are set for human targets, killing innocent children, including Katniss's sister, Prim. Learning once and for all that enemies can lurk in supposedly good places, Katniss executes President Coin in retribution. This aspect of Katniss's journey, her reflections on what is "just" and who is "good," are indicative of her ongoing moral development, progress suggestive of the Mockingjay. The jabberjays' physical evolution into mockingjays allowed them to survive and gain independence from the Capitol, a trajectory similar to Katniss, who escapes the Capitol's intentions for tributes and fosters her own politics, worries, and revolutionary tactics to incite change. The questions Katniss forces herself—and teen readers—to grapple with are not easily answered because her contradictory, abject actions defy the binary logic of "good" and "evil," typically assumed to be separate and fixed entities. Katniss's narration draws attention to the constructedness of this binary, while Collins's diverse monsters threaten the distinctions made between the "evil" Capitol and the "virtuous" rebels. Monsters are evidently found on both sides of this dialectic. In the end, Katniss does not respect either warring side in Panem. The complexity of Katniss's character suggests that she is a hybrid being: At times she is a tool of the Capitol or the rebel movement, and at others, she defies both these regimes by charting her own course.[5]

Another main character, Peeta, occupies a transient identity as both victor and villain when his mind is hijacked by the Capitol. Tortured during his capture, Peeta's memories are manipulated in order to serve the Capitol's interests—to kill Katniss Everdeen. Peeta's outward appearance seems normal. However, his once loving thoughts about Katniss have been inverted, warped to make him believe that Katniss is a dangerous mutt. Since Katniss narrates, readers see Peeta as dangerous and animalistic when he returns to District 13 another weaponized pawn of the Capitol. After almost choking Katniss to death with his bare hands, Peeta is often shackled and monitored closely, much like a dangerous animal in need of containment (*Mockingjay* 177). Although the Capitol intended Peeta to kill Katniss, he is a source of perpetual emotional turmoil for Katniss, not only a physical threat. For one, he is uncanny: he is familiar in appearance, yet he wholeheartedly believes Katniss is a mutt that must be killed. Katniss describes Peeta's unease, saying, "It's like he's waiting for me to transform into a hybrid drooling wolf right before his eyes" (*Mockingjay* 230). Although Peeta eventually has moments of clarity and independent thought, at any moment, his mutt switch is flipped, and he succumbs to his preprogrammed direction to kill Katniss. This internal fight Peeta goes through is partly evocative of the abject seen elsewhere with Collins's mutts, as they are all directed to fulfill their master's orders. At this stage in the storyline, Peeta as hijacked mutt serves as an uncanny reflection of Katniss's friend and lover, dehumanized and manipulated by her opponents.

However, the fact that Peeta is able to resist his mental hijacking and eventually evolves back into an independent human being, suggests he is quite different from the Capitol's other mutts, save for the mockingjay/ Mockingjay, who also evolve. Peeta eventually breaks the Capitol's mental bonds and is virtually free of their manipulation. The fact that Peeta's mind was eventually restored provides hope that freedom and evolution are possible even when subjects are broken into dehumanized, animalistic beings. Such a hijacking draws attention to the moral corruption of the Capitol, how their political ends break boundaries of decency. Peeta's psychic return by the end of *Mockingjay* also suggests that order and freedom can be restored, regardless of Capitol manipulation.

Peeta's evolution from victor to rebel to mutt and back is—in part—an evolution mirrored by Katniss-as-Mockingjay. Although Katniss was never tortured and hijacked like Peeta, from her first time in the Games to the trilogy's close, she also evolves from a tribute pawn into a rebellious subject. However, there are important differences between Katniss's and Peeta's evolution. Katniss's complexity, and at times her contradictory actions—as a savior figure and a vengeful assassin—is not an abjection matched by Peeta, even when he is a hijacked mutt. Katniss's abjection derives from her own decision making, whereas for Peeta, he lacks freedom of choice because the

Capitol manipulated his memories and actions. In this sense, while Peeta can be said to occupy a liminal identity, his abjection is placed onto him by an external force, while Katniss's transient identity is due to her own choices.

Collins's inclusion of characters as mutts foregrounds how monstrosity is free-floating, easily adopted on both sides of the war and sometimes practiced by otherwise good and well-intentioned characters. As a result, the trilogy presents monstrosity in diverse forms: chimeric monsters, hidden hybrids, and liminal lead characters break the biological, psychological, and moral boundaries of characters as well as audiences. The abject offers a lens through which these mutts can be viewed, suggesting they horrify due to their fragmented bodies and actions, their composite parts that test the very limits of what is known and acceptable. Both sides of Panem's war manufacture monsters that take others' lives and confuse what we know of the living, the dead, humanity, and its moral standards. Showing monsters lurk *within* as much as outside of one's door, Collins's novels provoke the horrific realization that monsters are sometimes made in the process of doing good.

NOTES

1. Katniss often refers to the president of the Capitol, President Snow, as a snake.

2. In the case of the Games' arenas, this world is highly unnatural—technological and manipulated according to the Gamemakers' desires.

3. These Capitol muttations are enhanced wasps "spawned in a lab," designed to track and kill their prey. Katniss explains: "Larger than regular wasps, they have a distinctive solid gold body and a sting that raises a lump the size of a plum on contact . . . Some die at once. If you live, the hallucinations brought on by the venom have actually driven people to madness" (Collins *The Hunger Games* 185). These hallucinations are experienced by Katniss in the first Games, while in *Mockingjay*, Peeta also experiences their effects after the Capitol uses trackerjacker venom to hijack his mind.

4. In the second Games, Katniss eventually remembers "who the enemy is"—the Capitol, not the other tributes fighting for their lives. Sending an electrified arrow into "the chink in the armor," the forcefield border of the arena, Katniss causes a major explosion (*Catching Fire* 378). This ends the Games and marks the beginning of the revolution.

5. For example, there are multiple instances in *Mockingjay* that Katniss takes her own action, defying some of the rebels' orders. Most dramatically, she assassinates President Alma Coin, the leader of the rebels and new leader of Panem. In a couple other instances she defies Coin's orders, putting herself in the line of fire during an attack, and organizing her own military mission unbeknown to the rebel leader.

WORKS CITED

Carroll, Noël. *The Philosophy of Horror: or, Paradoxes of the Heart*. New York: Routledge. 1990. Print.

Cohen, Jeffrey Jerome. "Monster Culture: (Seven Theses)." *Monster Theory: Reading Culture*. Edited by Jeffrey Jerome Cohen. Minneapolis: U of Minnesota P, 1996. 3–25. Print.

Collins, Suzanne. *Catching Fire*. New York: Scholastic Press, 2009. Print.

———. *Mockingjay*. New York: Scholastic Press, 2010. Print.

———. *The Hunger Games*. New York: Scholastic Press, 2008. Print.

Creed, Barbara. *The Monstrous-Feminine: Film, Feminism, Psychoanalysis*. London: Routledge, 1993. Print.

Eberl, Jason T. "'No Mutt is Good'—Really? Creating Interspecies Chimeras." The Hunger Games *and Philosophy: A Critique of Pure Treason*. Edited by George A. Dunn and Nicolas Michaud. Hoboken, NJ: Wiley, 2012. 121–32. Print.

Fisher, Mark. "Precarious Dystopias: *The Hunger Games, In Time*, and *Never Let Me Go*." *Film Quarterly* 65.4 (2012): 27–33. Print.

Foy, Joseph J. "'Safe to Do What?' Morality and the War of All Against All in the Arena." The Hunger Games *and Philosophy: A Critique of Pure Treason*. Edited by George A. Dunn and Nicolas Michaud. Hoboken, NJ: Wiley, 2012. 206–21. Print.

Freud, Sigmund. "The Uncanny." *The Standard Edition of the Complete Psychological Works of Sigmund Freud, Volume XVII (1917–1919): An Infantile Neurosis and Other Works*. Edited by James Strachey. London: The Hogarth Press and the Institute of Psychoanalysis, 1955 (1919). 217–56. Print.

Gerlach, Neil. "Narrating Armageddon: Antichrist Films and the Critique of Late Modernity." *Journal of Religion and Popular Culture* 24.2 (2012): 217–29. Print.

Kristeva, Julia. *Powers of Horror: An Essay on Abjection*. Translated by Leon S. Roudiez. New York: Columbia UP, 1982. Print.

Magistrale, Tony. *Abject Terrors: Surveying the Modern and Postmodern Horror Film*. New York: Peter Lang, 2005. Print.

McIntosh, Shawn. "The Evolution of the Zombie: The Monster That Keeps Coming Back." *Zombie Culture: Autopsies of the Living Dead*. Edited by Shawn McIntosh and Marc Leverette. Lanham, MD: Scarecrow, 2008. 1–17. Print.

Ng, Andrew Hock-Soon. *Dimensions of Monstrosity in Contemporary Narratives: Theory, Psychoanalysis, Postmodernism*. New York: Palgrave, 2004. Print.

Olthouse, Jill. "'I Will Be Your Mockingjay': The Power and Paradox of Metaphor in the Hunger Games Trilogy." The Hunger Games *and Philosophy: A Critique of Pure Treason*. Edited by George A. Dunn and Nicolas Michaud. New Jersey: Wiley, 2012. 41–54. Print.

Oxford English Dictionary. "Hybrid, n. and adj." Web. 1 November 2013.

Rosen, Sarah Maya, and David M. Rosen. "Representing Child Soldiers in Fiction and Film." *Peace Review: A Journal of Social Justice* 24.3 (2012): 305–12. Print.

Smith Fullerton, Romayne Chaloner. *Sexing the Fairy Tale: Borrowed Monsters and Postmodern Fantasies*. London: U of Western Ontario P, 1996. Print.

Where Are the Scary Books?

The Place of Scary Books for Children in School and Children's Libraries

KIRSTEN KOWALEWSKI

"WHERE ARE THE SCARY BOOKS?" IT'S A QUESTION FREQUENTLY ASKED of children's and school librarians, and finding them can be a challenge. Most guides to and textbooks on children's literature don't mention the children's horror genre at all. Instead, children's books with a fear factor are often classified as fantasy, science fiction, mystery, or folklore. Esme Codell, in a guide of over five hundred pages, devotes only one page in her chapter on fairy tales and fantasy to stories with "dark humor and a fast moving plot" (272). In *The Reader's Advisory for Children and 'Tweens*, Penny Peck does specifically mention horror and gothic fiction in her chapter on genre fiction for nine- to twelve-year-olds. However, when classifying titles for genre booklists, even she combines horror and gothic fiction with mystery fiction. While there can definitely be some overlap, it is somewhat jarring to see R. L. Stine's lurid *Goosebumps* books on the same booklist with the *Nancy Drew* mysteries (80, 93–94).

The result is that horror fiction, with the exception of middle-grade series fiction, is nearly invisible as a recognized category in the children's collection. Yet, scary books engage readers effectively enough that children continue to demand them. A startling number of people completely lose interest in reading by the time they graduate high school—nearly half of eighteen- to twenty-four-year-olds read no books for pleasure (Gallagher 3). The opportunities for economic success and participation in cultural and civic life available to struggling and disengaged readers are dramatically limited in comparison to those who read independently for pleasure (National Endowment for the Arts 16–18).

Providing children with materials that appeal to them and engage their interests is a major factor in motivating them to read independently for pleasure. Many children struggle with the mechanics of reading; others, who master the skills, learn to dislike and avoid it. To become a reader, a child needs "both the skill and the will" (Layne 6). It is essential for children not just to know how to read, but to do it because they want to, and many children want to read scary books. Librarians who work with children under the age of twelve have a special role in helping children define their reading identity. Choosing to identify, seek out, and share scary books and media with children can take extra effort, but it also gives librarians an opportunity to reach children who might fall by the wayside and encourage them into becoming engaged and even enthusiastic readers. This essay addresses the popularity and diversity of scary books for children and summarizes research that illustrates a relationship between engaged reading and scary books.

"Scary books" are often automatically equated with horror fiction. However, the definition of the horror genre, for the purposes of adult reader's advisory, is fairly narrow. Becky Siegel Spratford, the expert in reader's advisory in the horror genre for librarians, defines horror as "a story in which the author manipulates the reader's emotions by introducing situations in which unexplainable phenomena and unearthly creatures threaten the protagonists and provoke terror in the reader" (Spratford 13). Her definition draws a clear boundary between horror and other related genres, which is helpful in identifying the right kind of book for a particular adult reader.

It's more difficult to draw these boundaries when it comes to children's collections, however, because children's literature is broader and less defined. Katherine Shryock-Hood expands Spratford's narrow definition by including genres and formats as diverse as fairy tales, religious literature, picture books, easy readers, and middle-grade series fiction under the umbrella of horror literature for children. This is a more useful way to approach the search for a "scary book," as it provides not only a criterion for sorting through the diversity of children's literature but also an opportunity to broaden thinking about what a child is really seeking (32).

For the purposes of this essay, scary books for kids include all of these genres and formats, as well as many other titles in genres and topics available throughout library collections, including fiction, nonfiction, and picture books, that take a variety of approaches and are appropriate for children at different stages of reading readiness. Children's collections contain books of all kinds. A child asking for a book on ghosts could be looking for a nonfiction book such as Shirin Yim Bridges's *Horrible Hauntings*, a funny picture book, a Scooby-Doo easy reader, series horror fiction, or a tween novel such as Richard Peck's *Ghosts I Have Been*. Each one of these titles could answer the initial question, and all of them qualify as "scary books."

Children's introduction to horror literature today is almost certain to be nonlinear: it is now nearly impossible to separate a primary text from its multiple interpretations and their manifestations in popular culture. More and more often, reading requires children to connect and interact with books and media instead of approaching them as passive consumers (Dresang 13–14). The mix of visual, print, and interactive media that floods the world today creates what Mitchell and Reid-Walsh refer to as the "cumulative cultural text of popular culture" (qtd. in Sorensen and Mitchell 166). Rather than starting out by reading the original *Frankenstein*, children are more likely to enter from an experience situated in popular culture that presumes or introduces the basics of the story and characters in a mostly nonthreatening way: the movie *Frankenweenie*, the book *Frankenstein Makes a Sandwich*, or an encounter with some kind of media tie-in or product (Sorensen and Mitchell 166). The horror genre thrives on metatexts such as the "Horror Survival Guide from Shocklines" (a humorous list of tips for the person stuck in a horror story) and on intertextual relationships between media and literature.

Librarians able to navigate the resources that fall into the category of scary books can be guides and partners for children interested in further exploration and extension of their knowledge. They have an excellent opportunity to engage children's enthusiasm beyond their entry point into the genre by sharing information that allows children to connect to primary texts and related books and media in a multitude of ways.

Gregory Lamberson, an independent maker of horror movies and a published author in the horror genre, is an example of this multidimensional experience of literacy, through the lens of a variety of media. Although he grew up in the age before VCRs, cable, and the Internet, his introduction to the horror genre included links to diverse kinds of media, including a model kit, the limited horror movies available on his local television station, magazines such as *Famous Monsters of Filmland*, comic books, and books on film history. Some of these immersed him in a fictional world, and some served as metatextual and intertextual sources that informed him about horror films, feeding his interest in horror as both a consumer and creator. As Lamberson's experience makes clear, "scary books for kids" don't necessarily have to be intended to horrify—certainly, not all film history ᴏooks will have that effect—there just needs to be a connection to the horror genre.

Scary books and media provide an opportunity for immediate and compelling emotional engagement (Smith and Wilhelm 11). Once a child's interest is sparked, it can take many directions and dimensions, with the child creating links between related topics and materials, connecting texts and ideas in new ways, and potentially returning to titles and topics of particular interest with new perspectives (Dresang 62).[1] Readers can immerse themselves in a multilayered experience that offers many possibilities for exploration across a wide variety of recognized genres and media (Rose prologue). In the words of Kevin Kelly, the cofounder of *Wired Magazine*, this manner of creating trails and linking "unleashes involvement and interactivity at levels once thought [. . .] impossible. It transforms reading into navigating and enlarges small actions into powerful forces" (qtd. in Rose 1738).

Librarians' role in facilitating engagement and involvement with the horror genre by working with children to build their expertise and engagement is greatly enhanced by knowledge of how titles that fall into the broad category of "scary books" may be related to each other. It's important to take children's interest in nonfiction and nonlinear ways of approaching text seriously if we want to get them to read (Sullivan 23).

There is a historical conflict in librarianship between the belief that libraries should provide what people need or "give 'em what they want" (Rawlinson 2188). That conflict is most visible when it comes to children's books. Children's services in public libraries were largely established in reaction to librarians' realization that, without access to quality children's books, most children were choosing to read dime novels and "sensational literature" (Romalov 118). These books were considered immoral, subliterary, and subversive. Once children were admitted and became library patrons, their reading could be guided. As early as 1906, Anne Carroll Moore, director of the New York Public Library, made it a priority to rid the library of all children's series books. She considered such books "destructive to young people's mental and physical well-being" (Marcus 105). Nonetheless, in a massive 1926 study of children's reading preferences, 98 percent of the respondents cited series fiction titles as their favorites (105). The early prejudice against series fiction meant that some quality series books (such as Laura Ingalls Wilder's *Little House* books) were overlooked by librarians in later years (124). Comic books and pulp magazines, frequently the home to genre storytelling, were also excluded as "trash" (144–45). In 1948, for example, psychiatrist Fredric Wertham successfully crusaded against "violent, immoral comics" (Nel 78). He argued that they contributed to children's maladjustment and delinquency, giving children's librarians additional justification for guiding their patrons away from "'blood and horror' comics" and toward quality literature (qtd. in Nel 78).

Attitudes toward genre fiction began to change in the 1960s, as it became clear that children's interest in reading was declining, and some librarians felt that keeping series books and other popular materials out of the library was a form of censorship (Romalov 124–25). In 1972, the American Library Association (ALA) adopted an interpretation of its "Library Bill of Rights," titled "Free Access to Libraries for Minors," a staunch defense of children's freedom to access libraries and choose their own reading, a sea change from the philosophy of children's librarianship championed by Anne Carroll Moore at the beginnings of the twentieth century (American Library Association, "Free Access"). In the early 1980s, Nora Rawlinson of the Baltimore County Public Library aggressively promoted the idea that libraries should purchase popular fiction based on high demand, a controversial view that gained acceptance as time passed (2188–89). The attitude that popular and genre materials should be provided to library users began to spread throughout the library profession. "Fair service should certainly be provided to patrons who favor bestsellers, mysteries, romances, and other popular literature," wrote John Dessauer (qtd. in Rawlinson 2190). However, negative attitudes toward popular and genre fiction were still evident in the early 1990s when the *Goosebumps* books raised a debate over whether the self-identified horror fiction series for children belonged in libraries, or even in the hands of children at all (Tanner 5).

The rising visibility of quality graphic novels in the same time period and the publication of the massively popular and aggressively marketed *Harry Potter* books starting in 1998 marked the beginning of an overall trend in libraries toward the acceptance of children's genre and series fiction. Today, many libraries have moved beyond acceptance to celebration of series and genre fiction titles. In a reversal of past attitudes by publishers and librarians, it can be actually difficult to find recent books for upper-elementary children and tweens that aren't labeled with a genre or form part of a series (Dresang 97; Marcus 312–15).

There have obviously been changes in general attitudes toward series and "light reading" (Sullivan 52–55). However, some librarians still hold the attitude that many scary books, especially horror fiction series, are "junk food books" (Peck 18). Considerations such as available physical space and finances mean that choices must be made about what is most important to include in a particular collection (Asheim 64). A priority concern of supporting school curriculum needs (common in school libraries) or a limited budget for collection development may determine selections when making purchases that do not satisfy children's preferences for popular "scary books," especially horror fiction series.

Even if a librarian's personal feelings toward scary books and horror fiction series for children may be negative, the culture of librarianship favors a positive approach to selection, in which librarians look for reasons to include a book rather than reasons to exclude it (Asheim 67). Today series books of varying quality (some of them quite good) have a presence in most public and school libraries. Public librarian Barbara Black noted that although she is personally unenthusiastic about series books, choosing to exclude series books also "in a sense, excludes ... readers from the library" (127). From their earliest days, children's library collections have been designed to draw child readers in, and even though ideas about the role of the librarian and the appropriateness of materials for children's collections have altered, that goal remains the same.

The early philosophy of children's library services, accompanied by the activism of influential individuals such as Moore and Wertham, has had long-term impact on perceptions by librarians and other adults about the appropriateness of content and the quality of writing necessary for inclusion in a children's collection (Romalov 125). Even today, although there have been dramatic changes in librarians' attitudes, both series books and reading material for children identified with sensational or gruesome content are approached by some with reservations.

Most children's books, even those with supernatural or frightening content, haven't been specifically identified as belonging to the horror genre in the past. Series books for children that are explicitly identified and marketed as horror are a relatively recent invention of the publishing industry and have had a lot of power in shaping the creation and perception of horror literature and scary books for kids over the past two decades. The *Point Horror* books, first released in the United States in the 1980s and then in Britain in 1991, were among the first to deliberately associate the horror genre with children's literature. The name of the series and even the covers of the books were chosen specifically to market the books as belonging to the horror genre (Wilson 2–3).[2] The result, Michael Wilson reports, was "moral outrage" (2) from parents, librarians, and teachers. In 1992, R. L. Stine's popular *Goosebumps* series, targeted at an even younger audience of middle-graders, had its debut in the United States (Doll). The tremendous popularity of Stine's books with elementary-aged children led to considerable controversy, and the series has appeared on the ALA's lists of the "Top 100 Banned/Challenged Books" for 1990–1999 and 2000–2009. Although the popularity of the series dropped in 1997, the success of its branding cannot be denied, as the various *Goosebumps* series celebrated their twentieth anniversary in 2012, and are still going strong (Doll).

The popularity of Stine's *Goosebumps* books led not only to additional series by Stine, such as the *Give Yourself Goosebumps* choose-your-own adventure books, but almost immediately to other, similar, middle-grade series books that self-identified as horror fiction for children, including Christopher Pike's *Spooksville*, M. T. Coffin's *Spinetinglers*, and Tom B. Stone's *Graveyard School* (Ward "Scaring the Children"). The horror in these books tends to be less realistic and more fantastic, with humor cutting the tension. Doll quotes Stine as saying, "Writing scary stuff for kids is totally the opposite of writing horror for adults . . . I have to be very careful that kids know it's not real, that it's a fantasy and can't happen" (Doll).

These self-identified horror fiction series are worth examining not just as a marketing success but also as a success in getting, and keeping, kids reading. Stephen Krashen, a leading researcher in reading interest and motivation, has done multiple surveys on the topic that name the *Goosebumps* books as a child's first positive reading experience (or "home run" book). In one research study, by Von Sprecken, Kim, and Krashen, fourth graders were asked if they remembered their first pleasurable reading experience and "home run book," and the name of the book. Fifty-three percent (about 66 of the 124 students) remembered their "home run book," and 16 of those 66 students named a "scary book" as their "home run book." Krashen wrote in a summary that 15 of the 16 "scary books" mentioned were by R. L. Stine. Clearly, his books were making an impact (Krashen 82–84). A second survey, by Kim and Krashen, asked the same questions, this time of 103 sixth graders from a low-income school. Seventy-five percent (77 of the 103 students) remembered a home run book. While they reported that many different books were chosen as "home run books," *Goosebumps* is on that list, and two *Goosebumps* titles (*Calling All Creeps* and *Night in Terror Tower*) are individually mentioned (Krashen 83). A third study, conducted by Krashen and Ujiie in 2002, showed that although no specific book claimed a majority of readers, the *Goosebumps* series, which was well past its peak of popularity at that time, was the second most commonly named, behind only the *Harry Potter* books, which also have very dark undertones (37).

Acceptance of the series and enthusiasm for it by educators, librarians, and parents (who may even have been the original readers of the series) has increased as time has passed, and that's a good thing. Fewer and fewer librarians now subscribe to the idea that these books shouldn't be in library collections. In an interview, R. L. Stine said, "I hear from . . . my old readers . . . all the time. And they're now in their twenties and thirties, and it's a wonderful thing . . . Because I hear from these people, and they say, 'You are my inspiration—I wouldn't be a librarian today if it weren't for you'" (qtd. in Gutierrez).

Anecdotal evidence shows that *Goosebumps* has been effective at inspiring increased motivation in reading, especially when paired with encouragement from mentors. One researcher, for example, reported that she was able to boost both the quantity of and enthusiasm for reading in a student by offering her the *Goosebumps* books to build her confidence as a reader (Shin and Krashen 47–48).

With covers and merchandise that scream out to be noticed, the impact of *Goosebumps* and other self-identified children's horror fiction series have made an indelible mark on the way children's horror fiction is identified and defined (Lodge). The altered reception of the books since their initial publication illustrates what a major change there has been in the philosophy of children's librarianship. Now, many librarians not only accept but seek out new horror and horror-related series for children. Unleashing a flood of thrilling, fantastic, scary, gross, and funny series, these titles provide an easy answer when a child asks, "Where are the scary books?"

Goosebumps and similar series books, however, are only a small part of what makes up horror literature for children. Unfortunately, the creation of self-identified adolescent and middle-grade series marketed as horror fiction for children has led to a limited view among adults of what constitutes horror literature, or even more broadly, scary books for children. To merely point a child in the direction of middle-grade children's horror series such as *Goosebumps* may be a disservice to the child. Some children who enjoy books that fall into the genres of horror and suspense are uninterested in *Goosebumps*. McKool recalled an encounter with a student who reported that, while he used to enjoy the *Goosebumps* books, he now found them too formulaic (123). Other children pass over the books entirely. When asked about them in an interview, two sixth graders dismissed the series as "childish" (Worthy 508). In both these cases, they were now reading the more complex and suspenseful works of Stephen King (McKool 123; Worthy 508). Other children may choose to avoid *Goosebumps* because of the way the books are marketed or because they prefer to experience a "scary story" through a different framework. In an e-mail, media specialist Donna Swinford wrote about her own children's experiences with the books, explaining, "My own children . . . had mixed feelings about these when they were that age. My three oldest collected Goosebumps books and loved them. My youngest son claimed he was afraid of the covers on the shelf and never read them, but by Jr. High he was immersed in fantasy books, Harry Potter, Deltora Quest, Robert Jordan . . . which isn't a far cry from the horror and ghost stories of the younger children." With children and tweens seeking out books with more complexity and choosing to read books by authors writing for adult audiences (such as King and Jordan), it is clear that there is a demand for complex horror and suspense stories with more depth and intensity than most horror series can provide and that readers are actively seeking them out. However, it can be a challenge to identify these more complex stories, since most guides to children's literature fail to mention horror as a genre. Although many "scary books" can still be found in booklists of recommended titles in genres such as fantasy, science fiction, adventure, and mystery, it can require some searching to discover them.

Penny Peck does specifically mention horror and gothic fiction in her *Reader's Advisory Guide for Children and 'Tweens,* but she combines it with mystery fiction, as some mysteries have scary or supernatural aspects (93–94). Larson, writing about mystery fiction, also identifies *The Dollhouse Murders* by Betty Ren Wright and *The Westing Game* by Ellen Raskin, both books with supernatural and frightening content, as mysteries. Mysteries without supernatural elements can sometimes be considered "scary books" as well. Swinford mentions "child kidnapping, burglar type . . . and kid detective stories" as popular with children looking for scary books, particularly the books of Peg Kehret, whose mystery and adventure novels include *Horror at the Haunted House* and *The Stranger Next Door.*

The fantasy genre also has its share of dark, supernatural, and gothic stories. In her chapter on fairy tales and fantasy, Codell suggests the gothic tales of John Bellairs and Joan Aiken, as well as Lemony Snicket's *Series of Unfortunate Events,* as read-alikes for the *Harry Potter* books (which are often dark and even terrifying) (272). Tunnell and colleagues include supernatural tales as a subcategory of modern fantasy, naming the ghost story *Wait Till Helen Comes: A Ghost Story* by Mary Downing Hahn as an exemplary title (82–83). Their list of notable authors also includes Bellairs and Wright (91–92). Even though the experts don't recognize these authors and books as part of the horror genre, there are many excellent choices available; the challenge is finding them.

Widening the definition of "scary books" to include nonfiction recognizes the validity of children's reading choices and provides them with new opportunities to connect with multiple formats, both visual and printed. Plenty of girls love nonfiction, but studies show that boys in particular are attracted to nonfiction and nontraditional forms of literacy (Sullivan 23). Kathleen Baxter, a specialist in booktalking nonfiction to boys, described an incident in which a new boy in her neighborhood noticed a copy of the nonfiction book *Encyclopedia Horrifica*, targeted at fourth to eighth graders, out in the open. The cover of the book grabbed his attention, and the colorful illustrations of both mythical and actual creatures and stories that cause fear, horror, and disgust caught him entirely. She wrapped up her anecdote by saying, "Now he wants to borrow the book!" (33).

Children may be drawn from fiction to nonfiction as well because it can provide background knowledge necessary for understanding other stories. Guides to monsters and the fantastic, books about cryptids and the unexplained, myths and legends, folklore, science, short story collections, poetry, books on Halloween, and even cookbooks, all are included in the category of nonfiction, and all of them can provide entry points to engagement and understanding of "scary books."

In school and public libraries most nonfiction collections use the organization scheme of the Dewey Decimal System, which assigns each book a numerical "address" in one of ten numbered categories, based on its primary subject. This "address" then determines the physical location of the book on library shelves. Dewey can be a useful system for organization, but it isn't intuitive, so books on similar topics may be located throughout the collection. For example, a search for nonfiction books on Frankenstein at the Indianapolis Marion County Public Library turned up results as varied as these: *Meet Frankenstein* from Rosen Publishing's series on famous movie monsters, classified in 791 for motion pictures; Steve Parker's *In the Footsteps of Frankenstein*, classified in the 398s under paranormal beings; and Richard Walker's *Dr. Frankenstein's Human Body Book*, classified in 611 under human anatomy. More intuitive and user-centered ways of organizing library collections are under development: the creators of the Metis system consulted children when designing categories, and actually include a category for "scary books" in their schedule of categories (Kaplan et al.).

However, Dewey remains the system of organization used by the majority of libraries. Although it's unlikely that will change soon, it is still possible to implement a user-centered approach in other ways. For instance, bringing related titles together using the lens of "scary books" is a great way to spotlight books physically located in different places that all fall in that category. Bringing the books together physically for a temporary reason such as a display or promotion can be an effective way to attract readers who will look for alternative resources, because they find searching library shelves too time-consuming, complicated, or intimidating (Beers 113).

The youngest children don't usually have the opportunity to choose their own reading material. While there are many scary picture books, adults have much more control over what will be available to young children, and many adults are uncomfortable with providing "scary books," feeling especially responsible for exposing very young children to books that may cause anxiety or fear (Stevenson). Yet, children are often drawn toward monsters, ghosts, and dangerous creatures, and scary picture books offer an opportunity to confront fear in a safe and contained way (Billison).

Most picture books are read by an adult to younger children with limited reading skills, who often absorb much of the story through the illustrations. Ed Emberley's book *Go Away, Big Green Monster* goes so far as to give the child reader physical control over the illustrations, using cutouts so that the child turning the pages first creates the monster and then reverses the process so that it completely disappears (Stevenson). *The Monster at the End of This Book* also gives control to the child, as the terrified "lovable, furry old Grover" (Stone n.p.) unsuccessfully attempts to stop the child from turning the pages and reaching the monster. Darker, more sophisticated picture books, such as Neil Gaiman and Dave McKean's *The Wolves in the Walls*, may have a chaotic look that seems to mix fantasy and reality, but the main character, Lucy, learns to make sense of her world, overcoming her irrational fear of the actually-not-so-scary wolves that have invaded her house and taking charge of the situation (Crawford 40–41).

Scary picture books may be dismissed by librarians and educators as "lurid, terrifying, and wholly inappropriate" (Crawford 39–40). However, those who can overcome personal discomfort, recognize the value of these books to children, and provide access and guidance, can help younger children and the adults who read to them, choose from many options (Stevenson).

Tie-ins between books and other media are so common now, and immerse us so deeply in cultural experiences, that they're often taken for granted (Rose 2–3). The *Goosebumps* books are an early and dramatic example of the power of branding across platforms. A 1995 Halloween special that adapted the book *The Werewolf of Fever Swamp* was so successful that it spawned a television series of the same name, and 1996 saw the debut of *Goosebumps* branded board games, jigsaw puzzles, and trading cards. Book-related merchandise that included bike helmets, boxer shorts, skateboards, sneakers, bed sheets, and even a chocolate Advent calendar all marked with the *Goosebumps* brand, proliferated.[3] Even after the series' popularity dimmed somewhat in 1997, Stine's books have continued to sell and have even continued to inspire media tie-ins. The year 2008 marked the beginning of a new television series, *R. L. Stine's The Haunting Hour*, based on his books, which celebrated their twentieth anniversary in 2012.

Although the visibility of *Goosebumps* as a brand is greater, Universal Studios has done an excellent job of integrating the creatures and villains that star in the Universal Horror movies, produced primarily between 1930 and 1955, into popular culture. These include Dracula, Frankenstein, Frankenstein's bride, the Mummy, the Invisible Man, the Wolf Man, and the Creature from the Black Lagoon. Many of the Universal Horror movies appropriated classic texts such as *Dracula*, *Frankenstein*, and *The Invisible Man* ("Universal Pictures"). While it's unlikely that the average child has either read these works or seen the original movies, most of the monsters are instantly recognizable. A five-year-old can name the creatures from movies like *Mad Monster Party* and *Hotel Transylvania*, pick up the reference to Sesame Street's Count, or recognize Frankenstein on a box of Frankenberry cereal.

Lamberson's early experiences clearly showed that books, magazines, and comics are part of the mix of children's materials as well. The availability of materials has come a long way since Crestwood House published the lone series of books that introduced the children of the 1970s, 1980s, and early 1990s to Universal's monsters (Burrell). Today there are new, high-interest series for children published on the movies and their monsters, as well as series books, individual fiction titles, nonfiction, picture books, graphic novels, television shows, movies, and just about any other media format imaginable, that make a variety of interpretations and uses of these iconic creatures. It's important to note that some of these uses can be problematic: the popular Monster High brand, centered on highly sexualized fashion dolls of "hip, teenage descendants of the world's most famous monsters" (Mattel, Inc.), has been censured for promoting unhealthy attitudes toward appearance and body image for young girls. Nonetheless, awareness of the representation of monsters and horror themes in the mainstream media is an opportunity to showcase the variety and appeal of alternative models (Shewmaker).

Most media tie-ins will be acquired outside school and school libraries. Donalyn Miller argues that, while validating children's reading choices is essential to creating engaged readers, media tie-ins and titles that are situated in current popular culture are too ephemeral and generally lack the quality of writing to justify purchasing them by teachers for their classroom libraries (Miller). Students who develop interest in topics covered by these entry points may have to depend on their own resources to provide them with what they want. Public libraries have a little more latitude, however, and used wisely, media tie-ins can be a powerful draw to reading and learning.

As previously mentioned, Von Sprecken, Kim, and Krashen conducted a research study in 2000, surveying fourth graders to find out what book provided them with their first enjoyable reading experience. In his summary of the results, Krashen noted that, of the students who reported that information, nearly a quarter of them cited a "scary book," with emphasis on the horror fiction series books of R. L. Stine. Even though the popularity of his books had dropped by that point, and many adults still vocally opposed making them available to children, these kids were reading and remembering Stine's books (Krashen 82–84). That is pretty impressive, since only about half of nine-year-olds read for fun regularly; by the time they reach the age of seventeen, less than a quarter of students do so (National Endowment for the Arts 7–8). Miller describes these disengaged readers as "dormant readers" (locations 488–507) who can be awakened with the right book. As Shin discovered, a nine year old who gets hooked on series horror fiction for children is likely to continue reading for pleasure, eventually seeking out more complex and demanding texts (Shin and Krashen 47–48).

Getting children reading early and often is essential and part of that is respecting and validating their reading choices. Not all books written for children speak to them at their own level. Some are written to communicate practical or factual information; some are written to teach manners or morals (Lurie ix–x). Others, like Newbery winners, are chosen by adults as the best of high-quality literature (Perl). Like many other books that appeal to children, though, scary books often express ideas and emotions that make adults uncomfortable, and will be bought, borrowed, or passed from friend to friend, outside a school or other formal environment (Lurie x–xi).

Stephen King has said, "I feel happiest when I see some kid reading one of my books . . . on a schoolbus headed for an away soccer game or flopped out on a beach somewhere during summer vacation" (18). It's more likely than not that this will be the case. King's books won't be found in elementary schools and children's collections, although, as previously stated, tweens and older children do read his books. For instance, Worthy found that her son, described as a disengaged reader by his teachers, was voraciously reading King's books and had been reading horror and suspense books since elementary school (508).

This boy's experience of engaged reading only outside formal learning environments is not unique. Lizzie Skurnick, a voracious reader starting in elementary school, also described herself as disengaged from reading assigned in school. Instead, she either raided her parents' shelves or read books written for her age group, which, while not on adults' literary radar, addressed her and her friends directly (2–5). Worthy identifies readers like her son and Skurnick, who acquired their reading outside recognized channels, using underground, nontraditional avenues, as "renegade readers" (508). Anecdotal accounts aside, research shows that underground reading is not uncommon. In a 2005 study by Clark and Foster, students said they were reading magazines, websites, texts and e-mails, media tie-ins, comics, and newspapers outside of school. In addition, 95 percent of participants said they read fiction outside of school, with adventure, comedy, and horror fiction as their top choices. It's clear that some children are doing a lot of reading, of a variety of materials that are not recognized as "reading" in schools. Unfortunately, renegade readers' underground reading habits can lead to serious misperceptions of children's interests in and attitudes toward reading. In identifying the types of readers in her classroom, Miller specifically mentions the need to identify underground readers, recognize their reading identities, and validate their reading choices (Miller, locations 517, 1206–13). Those choices need to be represented in children's collections, but often aren't. In a 1999 study by Worthy, Moorman, and Turner, sixth graders completed questionnaires about their reading preferences. Their top choices included scary stories (with numerous specific mentions of both Stine and King), comic books, magazines, and other nontraditional reading materials, rather than more literary choices available to them at school. Their preferred reading materials were not easily accessible; while some scary books were available, there weren't enough copies of the most popular titles, and comics were nearly nonexistent. To access what they wanted to read, children who were able to do so purchased their books instead of getting them from the library or classroom. This showed a clear disconnect between what kids wanted to read and what was available in schools and libraries (Worthy, Moorman, and Turner 19–23).

It is still the case that in many places, particularly low-income communities, students do not have print-rich environments available, or the ways or means to purchase their own reading material, and a lack of popular choices means less interest in reading and less time reading. Sadly, these are the children most in need of having their preferences for reading materials met.

Children need to be immersed in all kinds of books and types of reading, including popular, recreational materials, in order to become engaged, literate readers (Gallagher 29–32). Scary books and associated materials are popular with children—sometimes so popular that, even with the best intentions, providing easy access is a challenge—and they should definitely be included in that mix.

"Scary books for kids" may be found throughout the children's collection. Sending children who ask for "scary books" toward middle-grade horror fiction series is a simple way to field a request for a "scary book," but it is a limiting way to approach reader's advisory. One size does not fit all, and there are plenty of other places in the children's collection where "scary books" can be found.

In today's media-saturated world, children are, according to Kate Mc-Clelland, "actively and freely making their own connections, not from right to left, not from beginning to end, but in any order they choose [. . .]. And they have the power to organize their own explorations in any direction" (qtd. in Dresang 62). They intuitively create associations and links to topics and ideas that are unique to them as individuals. They both influence and are influenced by interconnected forms of media and cultural interpretations (Bush; Zipes 58). It is important for librarians to be aware of the connections that can be made between different types of scary books and media, using what is already in their collection. Recognizing that "scary books" can be found in many physical locations and formats in the library, and as part of a variety of genres, gives librarians an opportunity to share books and other media not traditionally identified as "horror" or "scary" with children who identify themselves as readers of horror fiction series or other scary books. A librarian who looks at the collection in terms of what will satisfy children seeking out scary books, in fiction, nonfiction, picture books, and other media, can be more strategic in collection development, and consider new purchases from this cross-disciplinary perspective.

Most libraries, both school and public, do have books for the children seeking their next spooky read. However, without guidance, young readers may still not find what they are looking for, as the number of books and topics can be intimidating. The ability to create a trail of associations doesn't necessarily give children the ability to narrow down their choices or navigate a large collection of materials. Librarians who take advantage of children's interests in "scary books" can better serve children by not just suggesting books when asked, but by offering choices and displaying and promoting them. Bringing together interesting titles from fiction, nonfiction, picture books, and other types of books is a great way to show the variety of what the library has to offer and provides new avenues of exploration for young readers.

Both school and public libraries need to be involved in connecting students with interesting books to take home and read on their own time, essential in developing their skills and engagement with reading (Gallagher 46). Cooperative efforts, thorough knowledge of the existing collection, and an understanding of its limitations are essential in finding the titles that might appeal to children fascinated by the unexplained or thrilled by a good scare and in matching the right book to each reader.

Taking the time to examine the existing collection to discover what treasures it already contains and how it needs to be supplemented to satisfy children's preferences means that the question "Where are the scary books?" can be answered by a librarian who has taken the time to identify them, and can guide children who ask that question, to the book that will engage their interests and satisfy their curiosity, preferences, and needs.

NOTES

1. See Michael W. Smith and Jeffrey D. Wilhelm, *Going with the Flow: How to Engage Boys (and Girls) in Their Literacy Learning*, 11; Dresang, *Radical Change*, 62; Vannevar Bush, "As We May Think." *Atlantic*, 1 July 1945.

2. For specifics, see the American Library Association's lists, "100 Most Frequently Challenged Books: 1990–1999" and "Top 100 Banned/Challenged Books: 2000–2009."

3. See Ward, "Scaring the Children," Tabula Rasa; Doll, "R. L. Stine Has Been Giving Us Goosebumps," *Y.A. for Grownups* (blog); Lodge, "Life after Goosebumps"; and Tanner, "Thrills, Chills, and Controversy."

WORKS CITED

American Library Association. "Free Access to Libraries for Minors: An Interpretation of the Library Bill of Rights." *ALA.org*. American Library Association, n.d. Web. 15 May 2013.

———. "Top 100 Banned/Challenged Books: 2000–2009." *Banned Books Week: Celebrating the Freedom to Read*, 2013. Web. 12 February 2013.

———. "100 Most Frequently Challenged Books: 1990–1999." *Banned Books Week: Celebrating the Freedom to Read*, 2013. Web. 12 February 2013.

Asheim, Lester E. "Not Censorship But Selection." *Wilson Library Bulletin* 28 (1953): 63–67. Print.

Baxter, Kathleen. "Seriously Scary Stuff: Nothing Appeals to Young Readers like Fear, Horror, and Gore." *School Library Journal* 53.9 (2007): 33. Print.

Beers, Kylene G. "Part 2: No Time, No Interest, No Way! The 3 Voices of Aliteracy." *School Library Journal* 42.3 (1996): 110–13. Print.

Billison, Anne. "Fairy Tales or Twilight, Horror and Macabre Fascinate Children." *Telegraph* [London], 2 April 2010. Web. 15 May 2013.

Black, Barbara. "Using Series as Bait in the Public Library." *Rediscovering Nancy Drew*. Edited by Carolyn Stewart Dyer and Nancy Tillman Romalov. Iowa City: U of Iowa P, 1995. 121–23. Print.

Burrell, James. "Cryptic Collectibles: The Creeptastic Crestwood House Monster Series Books!" *Cryptic Collectibles* (blog). 20 September 2010. Web. 15 May 2013.

Bush, Vannevar. "As We May Think." *Atlantic*, July 1945. Web. 13 March 2013.

Clark, Christina, and Amelia Foster. *Children's and Young People's Reading Habits and Preferences: The Who, What, Why, Where, and When*. London: National Literacy Trust, 2005. Qtd. in Christina Clark and Kate Rumbold, *Reading for Pleasure: A Research Overview*. London: National Literacy Trust, 2006, 15. Print.

Clark, Christina, and Kate Rumbold. *Reading for Pleasure: A Research Overview*. London: National Literacy Trust, 2006. Print.

Codell, Esme Raji. *How to Get Children to Love Reading!* Chapel Hill, NC: Algonquin Books of Chapel Hill, 2003. Print.

Crawford, Philip Charles. "Hatching Their Wolfish Schemes: Neil Gaiman's and Dave McKean's *Wolves in the Walls*." *Knowledge Quest* 34.3 (2006): 39–41. Print.

Doll, Jen. "R. L. Stine Has Been Giving Us Goosebumps for 20 Years." *Y.A. for Grownups* (blog). 19 July 2012. Web. 15 May 2013.

Dresang, Eliza T. *Radical Change: Books for Youth in a Digital Age*. New York: H. W. Wilson, 1999. Print.

Foreman, Jack. "Young Adult Novels." *The Essential Guide to Children's Books*. Edited by Anita Silvey. New York: Houghton Mifflin, 2002. 488–92. Print.

Gallagher, Kelly. *Readicide: How Schools Are Killing Reading and What You Can Do About It*. Portland, ME: Stenhouse, 2009. Print.

Gutierrez, Peter. "The R. L. Stine Interview, Part 1: Twenty Years of 'Goosebumps.'" *Connect the Pop: At the Intersection of Pop Culture, Transliteracy, and Critical Thinking* (blog). 2 July 2012. Web. 15 May 2013.

Hood, Robert. "A Playground for Fear: Horror Fiction for Children." 1997. Web. 15 May 2013.

"Humor for Children." *New York Times*, 12 September 1954. Qtd. in Philip Nel, *The Annotated Cat: Under the Hats of Seuss and His Cats*. New York: Random House, 2007, 78. Print.

Indianapolis Marion County Public Library System. "Frankenstein." *SHERLOC: IndyPL's Shockingly Easy Resource Locator*. 19 March 2012. Web. 19 March 2013.

Kaplan, Tali Balas, Andrea K. Dollof, Sue Giffard, and Jennifer Still-Schiff. "Are Dewey's Days Numbered? Libraries Nationwide Are Ditching the Old Classification System." *School Library Journal*. 28 September 2012. Web. 15 May 2013.

Kelly, Kevin. "We Are the Web." *Wired*, August 2005, 95–99. Qtd. in Frank Rose, *The Art of Immersion: How the Digital Generation Is Remaking Hollywood, Madison Avenue, and the Way We Tell Stories*. New York: W. W. Norton, 2011. Kindle edition, chap. 6, location 1738.

Kim, Jiyoung, and Stephen Krashen. "Another Home Run." *California English* 6.2 (2000): 25. Qtd. in Stephen D. Krashen, *The Power of Reading*, 2nd ed. Westport, CT: Libraries Unlimited, 2006, 2. Print.

King, Stephen. "I Want to Be Typhoid Stevie." *Reading Stephen King: Issues of Censorship, Student Choice, and Popular Literature*. Edited by Brenda Miller Power, Jeffrey D. Wilhelm, and Kelly Chandler. Urbana, IL: National Council of Teachers of English, 1997. 13–21. Print.

Krashen, Stephen. *The Power of Reading*. 2nd ed. Westport, CT: Libraries Unlimited, 2004.

Krashen, Stephen, and Joanne Ujiie. "Home Run Books and Reading Enjoyment." *Knowledge Quest* 31.1 (2002): 36–37. Print.

Lamberson, Gregory. "Werewolves, Wolf Men, and Lycans—Oh My!" *Musings of the Monster Librarian* (blog). 15 July 2012. Web. 15 May 2013.

Larson, Jeanette. "The Case of the Missing Books: Getting Kids to Read." *Library Media Connection*, October 2004, 18–21. Print.

Layne, Steven L. *Igniting a Passion for Reading: Successful Strategies for Building Lifetime Readers*. New York: Scholastic, 2012. Print.

Lodge, Sally. "Life after Goosebumps: In the Wake of R. L. Stine's Sizzling Chiller Series, The Kids' Horror Genre Assumes Monstrous Proportions." *Publishers Weekly*, 2 December 1996. Web. 15 May 2013.

Lurie, Alison. *Boys and Girls Forever: Children's Classics from Cinderella to Harry Potter*. New York: Penguin, 2003. Print.

Marcus, Leonard S. *Minders of Make-Believe: Idealists, Entrepreneurs, and the Shaping of American Children's Literature*. New York: Houghton Mifflin, 2008. Print.

Mattel, Inc. "Mattel Unveils New Monster-Themed Franchise." 4 June 2010. News release. 15 May 2013.

McKool, Sharon S. "Factors That Influence the Decision to Read: An Investigation of Fifth Grade Students' Out-of-School Reading Habits." *Reading Improvement* 44.3 (2007): 219–26. Print.

Miller, Donalyn. *The Book Whisperer: Awakening the Reader in Every Child*. New York: Jossey-Bass, 2010. Kindle edition.

Mitchell, Claudia, and Jacqueline Reid-Walsh. "And I Want to Thank You Barbie: Barbie as a Site for Cultural Interrogation." *Review of Education, Pedagogy, & Cultural Studies* 17.2 (April 1995): 143–55. Qtd. in Ingvild Kvale Sorensen and Claudia Mitchell, "Tween-Method and the Politics of Studying Kinderculture." *Kinderculture: The Corporate Construction of Childhood*. Edited by Shirley R. Steinberg, 3rd ed. Boulder, CO: Westview Press, 2011, 166. Print.

National Endowment for the Arts, comp. *To Read or Not to Read: A Matter of National Consequence.* Research report no. 47. Washington, DC: National Endowment for the Arts, 2007. Web. 15 May 2013.

Nel, Philip. *The Annotated Cat: Under the Hats of Seuss and His Cats.* New York: Random House, 2007. Print.

Peck, Penny. *Readers' Advisory for Children and 'Tweens.* Denver, CO: Libraries Unlimited, 2010. Print.

Perl, Erica. "Captain Underpants Doesn't Need a Newbery Medal: In Defense of the Premier Award in Children's Literature." Slate.com. 19 December 2008. Web. 24 November 2012.

Rawlinson, Nora. "Give 'Em What They Want!" *Library Journal,* 15 November 1981, 2188–90.

Romalov, Nancy Tillman. "Children's Series Books and the Rhetoric of Guidance." *Rediscovering Nancy Drew.* Edited by Carolyn Stewart Dyer and Nancy Tillman Romalov. Iowa City: U of Iowa P, 1995. 113–28. Print.

Rose, Frank. *The Art of Immersion: How the Digital Generation Is Remaking Hollywood, Madison Avenue, and the Way We Tell Stories.* New York: W. W. Norton, 2011. Kindle edition.

Shewmaker, Jennifer. "Don't Claim to Be Selling Self-Acceptance to Teens While Selling Sexiness to Six-Year-Olds." *Pigtail Pals and Ballcap Buddies: A Blog That Is Child-Inspired.* 15 June 2012. Web. 15 May 2013.

Shin, Fay, and Stephen Krashen. "Should We Just Tell Them to Read? The Role of Direct Encouragement in Promoting Recreational Reading." Home Run Research. *Knowledge Quest* 32.3 (2004): 47–48. Print.

Shocklines. "Horror Survival Guide from Shocklines." MonsterLibrarian.com. n.d. Web. 19 March 2013. .

Shryock-Hood, Katherine E. "On Beyond Boo! Horror Literature for Children." Diss., Indiana Univ. of Pennsylvania, 2008. Print.

Silvey, Anita, ed. *The Essential Guide to Children's Books.* New York: Houghton Mifflin, 2002. Print.

Skurnick, Lizzie. *Shelf Discovery: Teen Classics We Never Stopped Reading.* New York: Avon, 2009. Print.

Smith, Michael W., and Jeffrey D. Wilhelm. *Going with the Flow: How to Engage Boys (and Girls) in Their Literacy Learning.* Portsmouth, NH: Heinemann, 2006. Print.

Sorenson, Ingvild Kvale, and Claudia Mitchell. "Tween-Method and the Politics of Studying Kinderculture." *Kinderculture: The Corporate Construction of Childhood.* Edited by Shirley R. Steinberg. 3rd ed. Boulder, CO: Westview Press, 2011. 153–72. Print.

Spratford, Becky Siegel. *The Readers' Advisory Guide to Horror.* 2nd ed. ALA Readers' Advisory Series. Chicago: American Library Association, 2012. Print.

Stevenson, Deborah. "Frightening the Children?: Kids, Grown-Ups, and Scary Picture Books." *Horn Book Magazine* 72.3 (1996): 305–14. Web. 15 May 2013.

Stone, Jon. *The Monster at the End of This Book.* Illustrated by Michael Smolin. 2nd ed. New York: Sesame Workshop, 2012. Print.

Sullivan, Michael. *Connecting Boys with Books: What Libraries Can Do.* Chicago: American Library Association, 2003. Print.

Tanner, Nicole. "Thrills, Chills, and Controversy: The Success of R. L. Stine's *Goosebumps*." *Dalhousie Journal of Interdisciplinary Management* 5 (2010): 2–13. Web. 15 May 2013.

Tunnell, Michael O., James S. Jacobs, Terrell A. Young, and Gregory Bryan. *Children's Literature, Briefly*. 5th ed. Columbus, OH: Pearson, 2011. Print.

"Universal Pictures." Horror Film Wiki. n.d. Web. 20 March 2013.

Von Sprecken, Debra, Jiyoung Kim, and Stephen Krashen. "The Home Run Book: Can One Positive Experience Create a Reader?" *California English* 6.2 (2000). Qtd. in Stephen Krashen, *The Power of Reading*, 2nd ed. Westport, CT: Libraries Unlimited, 2006. 82–84.

Ward, Kyla. "Scaring the Children." Tabula Rasa.info. 19 November 2012. Web. 15 May 2013.

Wilson, Michael. "The Point of Horror: The Relationship Between Teenage Popular Horror Fiction and the Oral Repertoire." *Children's Literature in Education* 31.1 (2000): 1–9. Print.

Worthy, Jo. "'On Every Page Someone Gets Killed!' Book Conversations You Don't Hear in School." *Journal of Adolescent and Adult Literacy* 41.7 (1998): 508–17. Web. 15 May 2013.

Worthy, Jo, Megan Moorman, and Margo Turner. "What Johnny Likes to Read Is Hard to Find in School." *Reading Research Quarterly* 34.1 (1999): 12–27. Print.

Zipes, Jack. "Why Children's Literature Does Not Exist." *Sticks and Stones: The Troublesome Success of Children's Literature from Slovenly Peter to Harry Potter*, 39–60. New York: Routledge, 2001. Print.

CHILDREN'S AND YOUNG ADULT WORKS CITED

Bridges, Shirin Yim. *Horrible Hauntings: An Augmented Reality Collection of Ghosts and Ghouls*. Illus. William Maughan. Foster City, CA: Goosebottom Books, 2012. Print.

Coffin, M. T. *Spinetinglers Series*. New York: HarperCollins. Print.

Collins, Suzanne. *Hunger Games Series*. New York: Scholastic. Print.

Emberley, Ed. *Go Away, Big Green Monster!* New York: Little, Brown and Company, 1992. Print.

Frankenweenie. Dir. Tim Burton. Perf. Charlie Tahan and Winona Ryder. Walt Disney Pictures, 2012. Film.

Gaiman, Neil. *The Wolves in the Walls*. Illus. Dave McKean. New York: HarperCollins, 2003. Print.

Gee, Joshua. *Encyclopedia Horrifica: The Terrifying TRUTH! About Vampires, Ghosts, Monsters, and More!* New York: Scholastic, 2008. Print.

Green, Naima. *Meet Frankenstein*. New York: Rosen Publishing Group, 2005. Print.

Hahn, Mary Downing. *Wait Till Helen Comes: A Ghost Story*. New York: Sandpiper (Reissue edition), 2008. Print.

Herman, Gail. *Scooby-Doo Readers Series*. New York: Scholastic. Print.

Hotel Transylvania. Dir. Gennady Tartakovsky. Perf. Adam Sandler and Andy Samberg. Columbia Pictures, 2012. Film.

Keene, Carolyn. *Nancy Drew Series*. New York: Grosset & Dunlap. Print.

Kehret, Peg. *Horror at the Haunted House*. New York: Puffin, 2002. Print.

———. *The Stranger Next Door*. New York: Puffin (Reprint edition), 2008. Print.

Mad Monster Party. Dir. Jules Bass. Perf. Boris Karloff et al. 1969. Starz/ Anchor Bay, 2003. DVD.

Parker, Steve. *In the Footsteps of Frankenstein.* Brookfield, CT: Copper Beech Books. 1995. Print.

Peck, Richard. *Ghosts I Have Been.* New York: Dell Publishing, 1994. Print.

Pike, Christopher. *Spooksville Series.* New York: Aladdin. Print.

Raskin, Ellen. *The Westing Game.* New York: Puffin, 2004. Print.

Rex, Adam. *Frankenstein Makes a Sandwich.* New York: Sandpiper, 2011. Print.

R. L. Stine's The Haunting Hour. Perf. Dan Payne and Bailee Madison. The Hub. 2010. Television.

Rodda, Emily. *Deltora Quest Series.* New York: Scholastic. Print.

Rowling, J. K. *Harry Potter Series.* New York: Scholastic. Print.

Snicket, Lemony. *A Series of Unfortunate Events Series.* Illus. Brett Helquist. New York: HarperCollins. Print.

Stine, R. L. *Goosebumps Series.* New York: Scholastic. Print.

———. *Night in Terror Tower.* New York: Scholastic. Goosebumps 12. Print

———. *Calling All Creeps.* New York: Scholastic. Goosebumps 50. Print.

———. *The Werewolf of Fever Swamp.* New York: Scholastic. Goosebumps 11. Print.

———. *Give Yourself Goosebumps Series.* New York: Scholastic. Print.

Stone, Jon. *The Monster at the End of This Book.* Illus. Michael Smollin. Print.

Stone, Tom B. *Graveyard School Series.*

Thorne, Ian. *Monsters Series.* Mankato, MN: Crestwood House. Print.

Various. *Point Horror Series.* New York: Scholastic. Print.

Wilder, Laura Ingalls. *Little House Series.* New York: HarperCollins. Print.

Walker, Richard. *Dr. Frankenstein's Human Body Book: The Monstrous Truth About How Your Body Works.* London: Dorling Kindersley, 2008. Print.

Wright, Betty Ren. *The Dollhouse Murders.* New York: Holiday House, 2008. Print.

ACKNOWLEDGMENTS

I wish to thank here those whom, without their help, insight, and guidance, this book would not have come to fruition. To the contributors, thank you for your words, your time, and your patience. To the editors, copyeditor, and artists I have worked with at the Press, thank you for your guidance and recommendations throughout. To Katie Keene, thank you for your enthusiasm, advice, and attention to detail. To my husband, thank you, many times over, for giving me the will to finish this book. To my children, who inspired the project, my eternal gratitude. Last, but definitely not least, thanks to my father and my mother for their love and support over the years. And thanks most especially for the Poes.

CONTRIBUTORS

REBECCA A. BROWN holds a PhD in English and teaches at North Seattle College. Her current and forthcoming publications focus on children in horror films, sea monsters in picturebooks, and ghosts in young adult novels. She is also coeditor of the book *Monsters and Monstrosity from the Fin de Siècle to the Millennium: New Essays*.

JUSTINE GIENI holds a PhD in English from the University of Saskatchewan. Her research areas include narratives of sexual trauma, abjection and horror, hysteria, and masculinity studies. Her writing has been published in *MP: Online Feminist Journal, Forum: Postgraduate Journal, Journal of Monsters and the Monstrous*, as well as a forthcoming essay in the collection, *Writing the Last Taboo: Incest in Contemporary Literature*.

HOLLY HARPER is a children's author, bookseller, and independent scholar. Her first two series of books for younger readers are published by Random House Australia. She also maintains the blog *Spinechills*, dedicated to children's and young adult horror writing.

EMILY L. HILTZ is a PhD candidate of communication at Carleton University in Ottawa. Her current research investigates the construction of the notorious woman figure in contemporary visual culture. Broadly, she questions the contours of well-known monsters, how they appear in children's literature texts, and also how they haunt adult audiences in crime television and news. Her work explores how ideas of gender, sexuality, and morality intertwine to produce particular types of monsters and knowledge of villainy. Emily's additional research on fairy tales critiques representations of evil women in literary classics and filmic adaptations such as *Snow White and the Huntsman* and *Once Upon a Time*.

A. ROBIN HOFFMAN is assistant curator in the Department of Exhibitions and Publications at the Yale Center for British Art, which supports her interdisciplinary interests in childhood studies and British print culture of the nineteenth century. Her primary book project derives from doctoral research completed at the University of Pittsburgh, tracing the co-evolution of constructions of literacy and childhood in Victorian alphabet books. Recent publications include the article "George Cruikshank's *Comic Alphabet* (1836) and the Adult Audience 'Á la Mode,'" published in *Nineteenth-Century Contexts*, and entries in the exhibition catalog for *Sculpture Victorious: Art in an Age of Invention, 1837–1901* (2014). Her essay "'How to See the Horror': The Hostile Fetus in *Rosemary's Baby* and *Alien*" was included in *The 'Evil Child' in Literature, Film and Popular Culture*, edited by Karen J. Renner (2013). Other current research focuses on the satirical verses of Hilaire Belloc and the reception history of Roald Dahl.

KIRSTEN KOWALEWSKI is the editor of Monster Librarian, an online resource dedicated to helping librarians in collection development and reader's advisory in the horror genre and in helping readers of all ages find another good book to read. She has a master's degree in library science from Indiana University and is certified to teach school library media. She has worked as a children's librarian in a large public library and as a school library media specialist at the elementary level and has a strong interest in reading engagement. She's had kids of all ages ask her "Where are the scary books?"

PETER C. KUNZE earned his PhD in English from Florida State University and is currently completing his PhD in media studies at the University of Texas at Austin. His research examines the children's culture industry, animation, and sincerity in recent American media. His children's literature criticism has appeared in *Children's Literature Association Quarterly* and *The Lion and the Unicorn*.

JORIE LAGERWEY is a lecturer in television studies at University College Dublin. Her primary research interests are gender, motherhood, branding, religion in popular culture, and television genre. Her current projects include a book titled *Motherhood and Postfeminist Celebrity* and a collection of essays titled *Ex-Pat TV: Television in an Age of Global Mobility*. Her work has appeared in *Cinema Journal, Studies in Popular Culture, Spectator*, Flowtv.org, In Media Res, and Antenna: Responses to Media and Culture.

NICK LEVEY is a postdoctoral researcher at La Trobe University, where he teaches in the English department. He has published on Thomas Pynchon, Don DeLillo, and David Foster Wallace and is currently working on a project devoted to post-press literature. He is the author of *Aldous Huxley's Brave New World* (2011) and various essays and stories.

JESSICA R. MCCORT is an assistant professor at Point Park University in Pittsburgh, Pennsylvania. She received her PhD from Washington University in St. Louis, specializing in American literature and women's writing. McCort's scholarship focuses on two areas: (1) the appropriation of children's literature, particularly Grimm's and Andersen's fairy tales and Lewis Carroll's *Alice* books, by women writers, and (2) gothic horror in literature for children and young adults, particularly in modern fairy-tale revisions. Her work has been published in *Critical Insights: Sylvia Plath* (2013), *Plath Profiles*, and *Inis: The Children's Books Ireland Magazine*, and she has an upcoming piece in the book project *Modernism and Wonderland*.

JANANI SUBRAMANIAN's research interests include the role of science fiction, horror, and fantasy in contemporary culture, as well as race and representation in television and film. Her previous publications include "Monstrous Makeovers: *Fringe, Supernatural,* and Special Effects" in *Critical Studies in Television* and "Alienating Identification: Black Identity from *A Brother from Another Planet* and *I Am Legend*" in *Science Fiction Film and Television.* She is currently the public programs manager at the Hammer Museum, UCLA.

INDEX

CPSIA information can be obtained at www.ICGtesting.com
Printed in the USA
BVOW08*1843050416

443069BV00002B/3/P